ALL OR NOTHING

By: Corey Thomas

All or Nothing is a work of fiction. The names, characters, places, and incidents portrayed in this story are the product of the author's imagination and are fictitious. Any resemblance to actual persons living or dead, business companies, events are entirely coincidental.

All or Nothing Copyright ©2018 by BestRead Productionsllc, all rights reserved. Printed in the United States of America. No part of this book may be used or reproduced in any manner whatsoever without written permission, except in the case of brief quotations embodied in critical articles or reviews.

For Information on sales, promotion, or events,

Please contact

bestreadproductionsllc2016@gmail.com
Po box 22885
Beachwood, Ohio 44122

Graphic Designer Contact Info
JiffYgraphics@gmail.com

Editor Contact Info
bestreadproductionsllc2016@gmail.com

Library of Congress Cataloging in publication will be available upon request.

Follow us on Facebook: BestRead Productionsllc
Instagram: bestreadproductionsllc

"If you live by the sword, you die by the sword." (author unknown)

I Dedicate this Novel to my Best Friend Jarvis Williams R.I.P.

PROLOGUE

After the upheaval settled there was an eerie silence in the room with a distant sound of footsteps fading further away.

He knew she was dead, and it hurt him more than the pain he was physically enduring. As weakness began to settle in, his soul cried inside.

Only thing he wanted to do in that moment was save her life.........but he couldn't.

Death was imposing upon him, but his resistance was powerful.

He touched the bullet wound on his chest.

"How could this happen," he thought to himself as a tear trickled down the corner of his eye. In that moment, he felt what it was like to cherish life. Although he'd been through so much, he knew that he hadn't even began to live.

After endless minutes passed he understood that there would be no help and eventually he would die too.

While living an extreme life of sin, he didn't know where his soul would go, but hoped it would be peaceful.

As he awaited death, he began to ruminate upon his life thinking back in time as far as he could remember.................

1

It was a boring and starving day for thirteen-year old Jarvis Cooper who sat on the porch listening to his stomach make crazy noises. The time read eight o'clock p.m. and the only meal he'd eaten throughout the day was breakfast. All he could think about was where his next meal would come from. His mother Crystal was in the house smoking crack with associates who would normally drop by when they needed a place to entertain their drug habits. It was Friday, and a lot of traffic was coming, going, and walking pass Jarvis as if he didn't exist. Crystal had been on drugs for the last three years and the hunger pangs became a normality that Jarvis somehow managed to adjust to.

Crystal was still what some men considered fine, despite the blotches that were starting to appear. Even with her addiction, she had a nice figure, however she was slowly but surely losing touch of her femininity.

Jarvis father left her and married another woman five years ago which created her and her son's turmoil. After a year of getting over their separation, she dated a guy name Ale who introduced her to crack cocaine. Shortly after they connected he went down for fifteen years for attempted murder. Things had gotten worse after her introduction of the drug and today was just another one of those days.

Omirah Henderson who stayed across the street, came on the porch carrying a plate of barbeque. She sat in the rocking chair eating while watching the football game that was being played in the street by a group of young boys.

Omirah was mature for her age. She was fourteen years old, half Black, half Puerto Rican, and very cute for an adolescent. Her sister Yasha was two years older than her and responsible for watching the house while their parents were at work. Their mother (who was Puerto Rican) was a nurse at Mt. Sinai Hospital, and worked the 3-11 shift while their father (who was Black) was a police officer for the suburb of Shaker Heights. They had recently moved into a one family house three months ago and hadn't met any friends in the area.

Yasha's boyfriend Rick pulled up in front of the house, driving a raggedy green Regal that he'd bought for 500 dollars.

"YASHAA!" Omirah called out. A few seconds later Yasha emerged from the house wearing a black off the shoulder body Romper, and black and beige open toe high heels.

"I'll be back okay."

"Where yall about to go?" Omirah asked as she placed a fry in her mouth.

"To the lake but if mommy calls you know what to tell her right?"

"I got you girl go ahead."

"Adios!"

"Nos Vemos," replied Omirah.

Jarvis watched the pretty girl fill her stomach up and it added to the pain he was feeling physically.

"YOU WANT WINNERS?" Tommy yelled to him, a guy who stayed a couple doors down.

"Naw I'm cool yall go ahead!"

Jarvis yelled back wanting to play so he could show off for the girl across the street but didn't have enough energy and strength to do it. Jarvis was tall for his age and very thin. His handsome features took after both of his parents, and a lot of women couldn't keep themselves from pinching his dimpled cheeks.

When he saw Omirah look his way, he waved at her, and she spontaneously wiggled her fingers back at him, which gave Jarvis the courage to get up and make his way across the street.

"Can you have company?" asked Jarvis before walking in her yard.

"You mean do I want company...... sure!"

Jarvis sat on the porch steps feeling kind of nervous but very confident that he could win her friendship. At first the moment was awkward for the two, but then their conversation found rhythm and both of their sense of humors flared and clashed together. Before they knew it, the street lights began to glare and most of the neighborhood kids had gone in the house. Jarvis smiled inside as he realized he wasn't hungry anymore.

Rick and Yasha pulled into the driveway at around ten pm.

"Come here Meme," Yasha yelled through the window. Meme was Omirah's household nickname.

"Hold on for a second," she told Jarvis and walked to the car.

"Que?" (What)

"Que tu esta haciendo aqui?" (What is he doing over here)

"Este es mi Amigo" (That is my friend)

"Well tell your friend that it's time to go because Ma is gonna be home in another hour and if dad pull up and see him sitting his ass on this porch with you, he will literally have a nervous breakdown!"

"Okay Yasha daaang," said Omirah and walked away.

Jarvis stood up signifying his departure while staring at Omirah as she slowly made her way to the porch.

"You're about to go?" She asked as if she wasn't about to tell him he had to. At that moment, his stomach screamed in pain and he wondered if she heard it.

"Yeah I gotta go. Aye you got a phone number?"

"I'll be right back." She blurted and hurried in the house. She returned a minute later.

"Give me your number because my father is kind of strict on letting boys call the house."

"Oh okay. You ready?"

"Uhm hmm."

"216-241-2603. You gone call me tonight?" He asked

"You want me to?"

"Of course!"

"Okay but you gotta stay up, it'll be late. Probably around one. Is that cool?"

"That's cool. Aight Omirah well I'll see you later then."

"Adios," she replied as Jarvis reluctantly headed across the street to a place he was forced to call home.

2

Jarvis lived in a two-family home, but nobody lived in the upstairs landing. The previous tenants had moved out last year, due to the drug trafficking activity downstairs. When Jarvis walked pass his mother's room, he heard mumbling voices and the sound of lighters flickering. When he made it to the living room, he propped himself down on the couch, reached over and grabbed his mother's cell phone off the charger. After dialing the number, he put the phone to his ear. After three rings, the party answered.

"Hello!"

"Ada where's Anton?"

"Who is this?" Ada asked irritably.

"Jarvis."

"Jarvis call him back I'm on the phone."

"Tell him I'm about to come around there aight," said Jarvis

"Aight bye."

After he hung up he sat there for a minute, feeling weak in his bones. While he was trying to find the strength to walk around the corner, his mother emerged into the room.

"Where have you been? I've been looking for you! Here's a couple dollars, go and buy you something to eat and hurry up and get back here!"

While going into her pocket to give him whatever money she was about to give him, Jarvis stared in his mother's face. He was very mature for his age and he knew that she was going through a life-threatening change which troubled him deeply, because he was hopeless of the situation. After retrieving the wrinkled five-dollar bill inside her tight fitted jeans, she handed it to him.

"Hurry up boy and be careful," she said as she headed back to her room. Jarvis hurried out the house and jogged to the twenty-four-hour deli store a few blocks over. Once there he ordered a polish boy, covered with a special kind of light barbeque sauce, some fries, and a soda. A dollar thirty was his change he received back, which gave him a slight feeling of relief for tomorrow. While waiting for his food he stood by the window and watched the scenery outside. A circle of older guys and a few girls stood around kicking it as if they didn't have a care in the world. While Jarvis blankly stared through the window, he was wondering how he was going to get school clothes. School was starting back next month, and he was starting his first year at East Tech High School. Omirah told him that her parents had just enrolled her there, and now that he'd become friends with her, he was worried that his tacky appearance would soon run her away. He began to feel as though he was in love with the girl across the street, and all it took was for them to have one encounter for him to realize. While his heart continued to flutter inside his chest, he noticed three unmarked cars pull up on the circle of youngsters standing on the corner. He watched as they searched the youngsters down.

"Oh, they must be drug dealers, but if they were selling drugs why would they do that on an open corner............that don't make sense," he thought to himself.

The woman behind the glass waved at him letting him know his food was ready.

"Here you go sweetie," she said, placing the food in the slot box. He walked to the junior high school he previously graduated from, sat on a bench in the park and devoured his meal while watching the cars pass by. After he finished eating he sighed in relief as energy quickly restored in his body. He got up and headed to the projects to see what was up with his two friends Anton and Damon. He knew his mother wouldn't miss him for the next two hours.

Anton and Damon stayed in the same building next door from each other, but the three of them had been friends for a few years now. Well actually Anton and Damon been friends ever since they could remember, and Jarvis joined their two-man circle. Anton and Damon were both fourteen. Jarvis fourteenth birthday was in a few weeks and he planned to celebrate it with his cousin D-Bear who birthday was on the same day. His Auntie (D-Bears mother) Carol always held their birthday parties at her house and Jarvis loved auntie Carol as much as he loved his very own mother. As he walked through the projects of King Kennedy, he spotted his two boys. They were mingling with a few young and upcoming project chicks who were both a year older than them. Deedra and Shonte were their names, and at the age of fifteen, it would take them both a minute to remember exactly when and where they lost their virginities.

"What's up nigga where you been all day?" Damon asked smiling. "You been posted up on the porch admiring that girl all day. Haven't you?"

"Say it aint so," Anton blurted.

"You in love boy?" Deedra asked.

"With you," he said, reaching out to grab her.

"You still a baby Jarvis I'll drown you," she said moving out of his reach.

His boys started laughing.

"Yeah right! Damn I can't have a hug?" Deedra hugged him and the five fell into association.

Anton and Damon had already had sex with these two girls before, but Jarvis was a virgin and waiting for the chance to pull his nuts out the sand. Day and night the projects were crowded. Drug dealers and friends infested the area as kids still ran around lost in their own fun.

Shonte and Deedra were both cute and thickly built for their age. A lot of the drug dealers who ran these projects took advantage of them sexually and they were now considered hood rats. A line of Cadillacs, Ferrari's, and a few candy-painted old school vehicles pulled into the projects back to back. The five watched in admiration as the posse of youngsters who went by the title, "KKK," (King Kennedy Killaz) hopped out and started kicking it with each other, while drug deals went down and weed smoke went up.

J.d, a twenty-five-year-old member of the click had taken a liking to Jarvis. Every time he saw Jarvis in the projects he would show him some love by kicking it with him as if Jarvis was his little brother. Jarvis watched him while he sat in his platinum colored Ashton Martin, wondering why he didn't get out with the rest of his homies.

"Come on girl let's go see what's up with Angelica and nem," said Shonte.

"Bye babies," she said to the three homies.

Their eyes went straight to their asses as they walked away.

"Babies huh. Aint no got damn babies over here. What's up. Yall comin back though?" asked Damon. "Aye Shonte I'm tryanna see you tonight!"

"Bigger plans boo, not today," she replied while looking over her shoulder.

Damon waved her off and sat down feeling frustrated.

"So, what's going down. We gone lay some niggas down tonight or what?" asked Anton.

"Hell yeah what's up!" Jarvis blurted out. Jarvis was willing to do just about anything for cash to buy some food.

"Anton, go get the gun nigga," said Damon.

When Anton walked in the small apartment, his cousin Ada and King Kennedy Juvis were sitting on the couch. Anton lived with Ada and her mother Elaine, (His aunt)) ever since his mother went to prison five years ago for stabbing a woman to death. Although things were tight financially, Elaine took him in as a responsibility raising him like her very own son. Elaine left the house with Ada every Friday and Saturday while she spent time with her man who stayed in Warrensville Heights, Ohio.

Ada and Juvis had been together for three years and now that she'd finally turned of age to move out on her own, he wanted to place her in her own apartment far away from the projects where he did his hustling. Juvis was twenty-four years old and had a shitload of paper. Although he was a player at heart, Ada managed to hold the key to it.

Anton raised up his mattress, and grabbed a 44 revolver, quickly tucking it in his waist. On his way out the door Ada said, "You know it's almost eleven o'clock."

"Soooo! What does that mean?"

"You're not about to be out all night is what that means!" Ada stood there with her hands on her hips.

"Girl leave that young man alone. Go on ahead and kick it shorty," said Juvis before him and Anton walked out the door. The revolver was Juvis gun. After watching him lay it in the cut, he managed to steal it without him knowing. The three homies walked out of the projects and down the street looking for their first victim.

An hour and a half later they decided to call it quits after robbing a total of 7 crack heads, that were looking to purchase crack from them. They came up with a total of one hundred and eighty dollars. They were happy as hell because the previous nights they had returned with hardly nothing. It was 12:24am, as they stood outside the 24-hour Arab store. A crack head had finally walked by.

"I'll give you a few dollars if you buy us a six pack of St. Ides?" Damon asked.

"Aight cool, give me the money."

Damon handed him the money and he went inside the store.

"We gotta hurry up and drink this shit cause the girl across the street supposed to call me at one o'clock."

"Oh, you must have smashed that already huh?" asked Anton while smiling from ear to ear. "Well calm down its only gone take us a minute to drink two cans a piece. Then after we done we gone find Deedra and Shonte," said Anton speaking for Damon as well who was game for all of that.

"You might as well spend the night at one of our cribs and fuck one of the girls over here tonight. You know they're all over Angelica's house," said Damon.

"Man dis nigga aint had no pussy yet. He aint on it so don't even waste"...............

"Nigga what makes you think I'm a virgin. I get pussy nigga!"

Anton and Damon burst out laughing because they knew he was lying and the look on his face was a dead giveaway.

"Aight whatever man, you still my nigga," said Anton still laughing.

The fiend came out of the store and handed Damon the bag, thanked them for their courtesy, and walked away. Once they made it back to the projects, like always, it was a lot of traffic pulling in and action going on. They posted up on some stairs along the dark piss smelling corridor that was aligned with apartments.

"Damn I should've had him buy us some milds," said Damon while he cracked open his first can.

Neither homie replied as they silently distastefully swigged from the cans. While Jarvis was drinking, happy chills ran through his body because not only did he have sixty dollars in his pocket, he knew that as long as they had that gun he had a way to get some school clothes.

"So, what's up. You staying over here tonight?" asked Damon.

"I guess," said Jarvis.

"After you holla at ole girl, all you gotta do is sneak out yo bedroom window and come back through," said Damon.

"Yeah cause we gone stay out here till the sun come up," Anton added.

"Yeah that's exactly what Imma do. So, check this out, after I hang up with ole girl, Imma slide back through here. Yall niggas bet not go in the house either," said Jarvis then cracked his second can open.

"We chillin, but check Angelica's house first because you know that's where all the hoes gone be posted at," said Damon.

Jarvis quickly gulped down his second can and threw it on the ground.

"I'm out," he blurted.

"While walking to his house, he noticed that he was staggering heavily, and his vision was blurred. When he made it home the door was unlocked, and his mother was still in the room with her company. He knocked on her door checking to see if she had been looking for him and was possibly upset.

"Ma! Have anybody called for me?"

The room was silent.

"No, and don't leave back out this house," she stated with very little authority. He noticed that his mother tends to become passive whenever she hit the pipe, which made him accustomed to taking advantage of the situation.

Basically, he did whatever he wanted to do during those moments. He sat down on the couch embracing his buzz and noticed it was far pass the time Omirah was supposed to call. While waiting for the phone to ring, he began to reflect over the years when his mother's love for him was affectionate. He still loved her the same, but he didn't quite know if she loved him as much as she used to. In his heart, he felt like half of her love for him was gone, and as the thought formed into reality, he began to weep.

The phone started ringing next to him. He immediately brought his crying to a halt, wiped his face with his shirt, and answered the phone.

"Hello," he answered trying to sound strong.

"What's up Jarvis," the pretty voice replied.

"You're twelve minutes late," smiled Jarvis.

She softly giggled.

"I know. I'm sorry. I had to wait until my parents went to sleep. What was you doing?"

"Thinking about you," Jarvis said letting the beer talk for him.

"No mientas!"

"What?" said Jarvis confused by her Spanish tongue.

"No mientas!"

"That's cute coming from you but you lost me shorty."

"I said don't lie to me."

"So, if I told you that I fell in love with you since the first time I laid eyes on you, would you believe me? Make sure you answer me with your American tongue." He decided to pour it on her thick with nothing to lose and everything to gain. She was shocked and surprised by his free will to express himself and unaware it was the beer talking.

"No way. I just met you today."

"Well I think about you every day. I'm just scared of your big ole father. That's why it took me so long to approach you."

She started laughing and the two went back and forth for the next two hours. After they hung up Jarvis was smiling from ear to ear. She told him that she had to think about whether she would be his girlfriend and for now he was satisfied with that.

Crystal's company had finally left, and traffic had seized. She came into the living room and saw her son on the couch.

"Why aren't you sleeping and it's a little after three?"

"I'm about to go to sleep now Ma," he replied as she embraced him with a kiss on his forehead. He held on to her hug for as long as the moment allowed him to, then went to his room. Ten minutes after sitting on the edge of his bed, he quietly climbed out of his window and made his way back around the corner to the projects.

3

"I didn't think you were coming back. Here you go." Anton handed Jarvis a beer from out the bag. Anton and Damon were chilling on Angelica's porch with Deedra and Shonte. Angelica was 19 years old and all the project chicks hung out at her house and most of the girls followed in Angelica's footsteps. Which was the case for Deedra and Shonte who considered Angelica to be a goddess. The door to the apartment was wide open. Angelica and a few project chicks sat at a glass table focusing heavy on their spade game while a blunt continued to rotate. After the hand was over with Angelica looked out on the porch and saw Jarvis, her little young sweetheart.

"There goes my baby right there. Come give me a hug little sexy," said Angelica. Jarvis blushed while walking into the house.

"Why yall got my lil boyfriend drinking? Don't let them turn you out baby," she said in a sweet voice while reaching up to hug him.

The other girls really didn't pay him any attention.

"Yall say what's up to my lil husband," she told the girls as she refocused her attention back to the game.

Angelica was a high yellow broad with hazel eyes. Her 5'8" frame was petite. Her chest wasn't flat, but her breast were what guys considered to be tiny. It was her ass, pretty face and good hair (which stayed in a ponytail) that gave her an appreciable attraction.

Jarvis walked back onto the porch. Anton was freaking a black and mild with Deedra sitting between his legs. Both of his homies were drunk, and his buzz started rising again.

"I see yall niggas done went back to the store, but I'm cool after this one," said Jarvis.

"Here blaze this," said Anton giving Jarvis the mild.

He went inside, got a light and came back out. Damon was standing in front of Shonte who was leaning against the banister and kissing her in the mouth. J.d. pulled up in front of the apartment. Without having to say a word, Deedra called out Angelica's name. She looked and saw his car in the front.

"Hold on yall, I'll be right back. Make sure you watch the game Tracy, don't let em cheat," said Angelica.

"Yall love birds move out the way," she said while making her way to the car.

"What's up my nigga!"

"Here put this up for me and I'll come back and grab it tomorrow," he said handing her a brown paper bag full of Yayo.

"You want this? It's shredded though? He pulled out an ounce of broken down weed from his console. Her eyes got big.

"Hell yeah! Shit me and my girls are down to our last blunt."

He handed her the weed.

"Who in there?" J.d. asked.

"Tracy, Tasha, and Renee."

J.d. had fucked all of them and most of his homies did too.

"Is that my lil man up there smoking?" asked J.d. while squinting his eyes. Angelica looked back and saw Jarvis with the cigar.

"Leave my lil boyfriend alone."

"Tell that lil nigga to come here."

"Jarvis, J.d. want you," Angelica yelled out. "I'll see you tomorrow J.d. with your sexy ass."

"It's on," he replied as she walked away from the car.

Anton and Damon were always jealous of the attention J.d. showed Jarvis. They wondered why he didn't show them the same considering they was born and raised in the projects and Jarvis wasn't. They never exploited their jealous thoughts. Jarvis handed Anton the mild and walked to the car.

"Young nigga what are you doing out here this late?"

"Spending the night over Anton house."

"Why you wanna defile ya temple lil youngin. You a young and upcoming. Meaning, one day you gone be a made nigga, but in order to become that, you gotta be a thinker. Gotta have the ability to out think what's coming at you."

Jarvis stood in front of him trying to comprehend his message.

"You feel me shorty?" asked J.d.

Jarvis nodded his head slowly.

"Now turn around and look at ya homies."

Jarvis turned around and saw Anton turning up a can.

"Yall three gone remain friends for a long time. I can see it but, it's gone come a time when you gone have to think for them too. Hop in shorty let me rap with you."

Jarvis walked around to the passenger side and climbed in the Ashton Martin. Anton and Damon were jealous as hell.

"I got him yall he good," said J.d. and rolled up his back window.

"Youngin you smell like a beer factory. Do you think getting high and drunk is cool? Do you think that is what will impress the women?" Jarvis didn't answer while looking him in the eyes.

"A slick nigga with style is what attract broads. That getting high and drunk shit, kills ya style. So, in other words, don't kill ya style before you're able to perfect it. You feel me little homie?"

"Yeah, I feel you," Jarvis sincerely replied.

"Are you gone leave that kind of shit alone or what? Don't lie to me shorty!"

Jarvis nodded his head.

"Aight shorty Imma let you get back to ya peoples."

"Aye J.d. I need your advice about something but if you're in a rush to leave." -----

"Holla at me shorty what's up?"

Jarvis was looking straight ahead through the windshield.

"It's this girl that just moved across the street from me and I can tell she's lightweight feeling me and I'm feeling her a whole lot. I mean she fine as hell J.d."

J.d. listened nodding his head interested to see where he was going with this.

"It's just, well, shit is kind of crazy at the crib and I know she gone peep what I'm going through in a minute, and it might run her away," Jarvis confessed.

"First of all, what kind of crazy shit is going on at the crib?"

Jarvis dropped his chin a few inches.

"My mother! She's smoking heavy and traffic be running in and out the house constantly. That shit is so embarrassing. Then school start back at the end of next month and I know she aint gone buy me no school clothes. So, I've been tryanna come up with a way to grab em myself because I can't let this girl see me raggedy J.d. you feel me?" he asked with tears in his eyes. His cry for help touched J.d.'s soul.

"Of course, I feel you, but listen to me. Since it's out of your power to control what goes on at the crib, don't let it stress you. You can't let that effect ya self-esteem and when the moment present itself, just be straight up with ole girl. Make her feel ya pain and she will respect you for it. See a good girl gone cherish and respect ya honesty. About your appearance, I will make sho that you're good. You like Fresh?"

"Jarvis nodded vigorously.

"Well you gone be fresh up in that piece. Matter of fact, from this day forward this gone be the little brother I never had. I'm about to breed this nigga," J.d. thought to himself.

"You wanna spend the night over here or do you wanna roll with me?"

"I wanna roll with you," Jarvis eagerly replied.

J.d. rolled down the window and yelled out, "Aye I got him with me all night. He gone get up with yall tomorrow."

J.d. made a U-turn in front of Angelica's spot and headed towards the outlet of the projects.

It was a little after four o'clock in the morning when J.d. had the Ashton Martin on cruise control down the freeway. Jarvis was listening to J.d.'s conversation he was having with one of his hoes on the cell phone.

"LISTEN UP BITCH! What did I tell you to do? See Imma stop fucking with yo hard headed ass because you don't listen. Andrea, shut up you aint making sense right now. Look, just talk to me about it when I get there."

Jarvis was looking at him from the corner of his eye while they drove in silence.

4

J.d. was five feet ten and slender with broad shoulders. He had a dark chocolate skin complexion and due to his Indian blood line, he had a head full of long curly hair that he kept braided in two fat corn rolls. J.d. stopped at a twenty-four hour eat spot, copped them both some grub and then drove a few blocks over to Andrea's house. Before they stepped out of the car, J.d. reached underneath his seat and grabbed his gun, tucking it inside the anterior part of his waistline.

"What kind of gun is that?" Jarvis asked curiously.

"It's called a 357 SID automatic, the best handgun to tote."

"Can I hold it real quick J.d.?" he eagerly asked.

J.d. stared at him for a second then reached on the front of his waistline and handed him the gun. Jarvis turned it side to side, and then aimed it at the windshield.

"J.d. I wanna be a gangsta!"

"You are a gangsta," said J.d grabbing his gun back. "Right now, is not the time for your gangsta to show. It's still trapped in the cage. All in due time but always remember this, it's a big difference between a gangsta and a made nigga. You wanna know the difference?"

Jarvis nodded his head.

"A gangsta is what the majority of these niggas run around calling themselves after they done shot a nigga, been shot, or done did some shooting out here. They drug sale and hang around a bunch of niggas all day. That's what most niggas think the definition of gangsta is. Only a few can even consider themselves to be made niggas."

"Well what's a made nigga?" Jarvis anxiously asked.

"A made nigga is a smart hood nigga that got rich. In order to become that nigga, your every step must be calculated to serve a purpose, and your only purpose is to get rich and get the fuck out the way. It's as simple as that. You stay in the game any longer than you have to, it'll flip on you and leave you stranded. Once that happens, there will be nobody to rescue you, and it won't be no bouncing back. Let's go in here and eat youngsta our food is getting cold."

Before J.d. managed to insert his key in the lock, Andrea opened the door, observed Jarvis with him, and smiled weakly as she stepped to the side.

"Sit down and eat ya food," said J.d.

He grabbed the remote off the table, cut the tv on, and handed it to Jarvis.

"Come here Andrea!"

She followed him into the bedroom. J.d. met Andrea at a block party in Columbus Ohio, (where she's originally from) a few years back. Once a year young ballers, hustlers, and freaks from all over went to Columbus like it was a tradition. Basically, another form of Freak Nik. Everyone was flashy and stunting and the hoes walked around half naked. While Andrea was half nakedly walking pass his car, she started dancing to the Yo Gotti record that was thumping from inside the drop top now later orange candy painted 64 Impala. He knew how much attention she would attract on the hood of his car, so he yelled and told her to get up there.

She had on a soft material skirt and a white lace crop top. Not to mention her body was built like she went to a surgeon in Atlanta, but she was all natural. She took her high heels off, climbed on top of the hood and started twerking her ass up and down to the rhythm of the music. A small crowd gathered and started throwing money on the hood. By her not having anything on under the skirt, every time she turned to face J.d. she gave him a clear view of her fat ass pussy. After she was done dancing, he told her to grab her shoes and hop in.

At first, she was reluctant because so much was going on around her but decided to give the baller a piece of her time. After choppin it up with her for a while, she told him to let the top up on the car.

"Give me 200 dollars and you can have your way," said Andrea. Saying that to J.d. was like asking for 2 dollars. By the windows being tinted, nobody saw what was going on inside the car. At first, she sucked him and then he fucked her brains out. After they were done they exchanged numbers and she went on about her business. A few days later she called him to let him know that her and her partna was about to drive up to Cleveland. They had a hotel room booked and Andrea wanted to know if him and one of his friends could show them a good time. J.d told them to come on and he and his friend Dre kicked it with them the entire weekend and she's been his bitch ever since.

Two months after that Andrea moved up to Cleveland to be closer to him. She knew his baby mother Mahogany was number one, but she didn't care. Hell, she didn't know if she was number 2, 3 or 4, she was just content with being his bitch.

"You mad at me?" asked Andrea as they entered the room.

"Don't ask me no stupid ass questions. Look, when I tell you to do some'em or how to do some'em, just do it. Do it the way I told you to do it!"

"Baby, it wasn't like I wasn't doing what you told me to do. Honestly J.d. I don't have to fuck him to find out the things you need to know."

"But I told you to give him some pussy tonight. Aint that what I told you to do?" He asked angrily.

"I just don't wanna have to fuck this gay ass nigga if I don't have to," she complained.

"Since when did you start second guessing the way I put shit down?"

"I don't second guess you baby— "

"Bitch is you my mistress or my enemy?" J.d. blurted while pointing the gun in her face. She walked up on the gun barrel and seductively wrapped her lips around it and started gently stroking.

"This Bitch is crazy," thought J.d.

"You know it's all about you baby," she assured him.

J.d. had a lot of love for her crazy sexy ass. He tucked his gun back in his waist, opened his arms, and embraced her.

"The quicker you open him up, the sooner he gone put himself in a position for us to snatch up what belongs to me. You feel me?

She reluctantly nodded.

Gianni's dope controlled the 30th projects and it was considered one of the heaviest drug trafficking areas in the city. J.d. knew that once he allied the King Kennedy and 30th street projects together, he would have the key to the city. J.d. could've made his death a reality a long time ago, but since he was a seven-figure nigga, his intention was to empty his treasure first.

J.d.'s dope controlled all the other projects except 30th. He obtained power by discreetly killing every HNIC (Head Nigga In Charge) of every project. He would infiltrate each project after the loss of their leader and bring order to the disarray by supplying the soldiers with limitlessly amounts of top quality cocaine. Since 1996 he managed to take over all of the projects except Gianni's. He knew that after he conquered 30th projects, he would have the city on lock.

On the other hand, Gianni had longevity in the game. He was a very intelligent boss nigga and kept a circle of killers around him at all times. A few weeks ago, Andrea who is unknown in the city, seduced him in a classy way at a club he owned called 'Affinity.' Within the last week it seemed as though her alluring attraction overruled his better judgment and they were waiting for him to place himself in a situation that he wouldn't be able to walk away from.

J.d and Andrea broke away from each other's embrace. He looked at the time on his Gucci watch. She knew what that meant.

"So, I guess you're not coming to spend the night huh?" She asked, folding her arms over her chest.

"Naw I gotta take Mahogany to her doctor's appointment in a few hours but check this out. What I want you to do is fall back from Gianni since he's wide open now."

"What you mean," said Andrea with a confused look on her face.

"I'm saying that once he sees that you fell back, it's gonna make him want to get at you even more. So let that nigga come to you. Listen, my lil homie out there, I'm breeding him Drea and I need your help!"

"What you mean you breeding him? She asked curiously.

"Well I see that he possess some special qualities that can take him far in life. Truthfully, I'm not even sure If I'll be alive to see it, but I feel like as long as I nourish those qualities early, his name gone go up under the made nigga hall of fame." J.d. chuckled.

"You are crazy," she sighed.

He pulled out a bankroll, peeled off twenty-five hundred dollars and handed it to her. She quickly grabbed the cash.

"So, what is it that you said you needed me to do?" She giggled.

"I need you to make him feel like a man tonight. Jack him off kiss his little man and let him put it in you. Give him his man tonight."

Andrea put her hands on her hips while standing double jointed.

"Now come on J.d! I'm twenty-eight years old and he is just a baby. How old is he?"

"He's old enough to be taught and I want ya freaky ass to give him his man while he's still innocent."

"How do you know if he's innocent or not?"

"Come on now just let the nigga enjoy himself. Hell, you know what to do you ole veteran. Let him wake up next to you. Take a shower wit em, take em shopping and just show him a good time. Spend fifteen hundred on him and keep the thousand for yourself. A thousand should be enough. Right?"

"I just don't know what to say about you. I guess that's why I love your ass so much."

He walked up to her and they began to kiss. After a minute, they pulled away.

"Imma go chat with him before I go so don't come in the living room till you hear me leave aight?"

"Whatever you say mister," said Andrea sitting down smiling and shaking her head.

Jarvis was still eating his food while watching a movie on Netflix when J.d. came into the room and sat next to him.

"You aint done eating that food yet? It's gone get cold," said Jarvis.

"Naw I'm taking it with me shorty, but I'm gone leave you here with Drea tonight." Jarvis looked at him in the face.

"Why you leaving me here? I wanna go with you."

"Here me out shorty. I told you I had a surprise for you right?"

"Yeah," said Jarvis with a sad look on his face.

"Well I want you to embrace this situation. Don't be scared or shy. Just be willing to learn. I'll see you later shorty."

Jarvis was lost and confused as he watched J.d. leave out the door. He didn't know how to read his feelings, so he decided to be mad at J.d. for leaving him alone. He lost his appetite for the rest of his food as he sat on the couch trying not to show his frustration.

5

Andrea came into the living room and locked the front door. Jarvis eyes got big when he saw she had nothing on but a black thong covering her butt that was shaped like a heart. She sat on the couch across from him and noticed his cute face and nervous demeanor. Jarvis on the other hand thought she was fine as hell. At that moment, he realized what the surprise was, but his nerves were getting the best of him. He didn't think he had the heart to fuck an older woman.

"What's up cutie. You done eating?"

"Yeah, I'm through," he nervously replied.

She stared at him for a long second causing him to look away.

"So, what's your name?"

"Jarvis."

"Why are you nervous Jarvis and what about this situation that makes you nervous?" said Andrea while realizing that this is going to be interesting.

"I... I aint nervous," he stammered, trying to keep his voice steady.

"Well come over here and sit next to me."

He complied with her request.

"A woman likes a man whose capable of being a man. Are you capable of being a man?"

"I am a man," he answered with authority.

"Ok then daddy I believe you. Are you a virgin?"

Jarvis appeared shocked as he hesitated to answer.

"You don't have to lie and word of advice, a man should never have to lie to a woman. Besides, it's okay if you are honey. Are you scared of me Jarvis?"

He shook his head no. She removed her thong and dropped it on the floor and reached over and grabbed his hand.

"Make a middle finger," she told him.

She guided it inside her pussy and allowed him to explore on his own. His dick stood up rock hard. After he explored for a minute she directed his finger to her clitoris.

"You feel that? Now look at it baby. This is called a clit. When you play with a girl's pussy you rub this in motion with one finger while you stick the other one gently in her pussy. But listen, don't be too aggressive on the clitoris, press firm enough to feel the tissue behind the skin baby."

He pulled his fingers away and watched her finger herself.

"Ahhhhh, she moaned to entice him. Jarvis was watching and listening to the sound of her pussy.

"Okay now you do it."

He was doing it correctly causing her to grind her hips and bite her lower lip. Then she grabbed his hand.

"Step one is completed and baby you did a good job. Are you ready for step two?"

He nodded his head.

"Let's go to my room."

She grabbed his hand and led the way as she sat on the edge of the bed with him in front of her.

"Okay take ya clothes off."

He reluctantly started to undress himself. Once he pulled down his brief she could tell he was uncomfortable but, he took everything off anyway. Her eyes went straight to his member which was already at its fullest erection.

"Damn he got a fat dick and he isn't even done growing," she thought to herself while getting prepared to suck his dick.

Jarvis mind still couldn't believe that this was happening as he watched her head bob back and forth. He couldn't wait to tell his homies about this. He knew they were going to think he was bullshitting. A special sensation started rising and he started pumping his dick in her face.

"Oh, baby yeah," he whispered. Only took a second before all that shy and nervousness was thrown out the window.

"Can I fuck you?" he asked.

"You sure can, what position would you like to try first?

"I wanna lay on top of you."

She gently rolled a condom on him and crawled to the center of the bed.

"Now let me coach you," she whispered as he laid between her legs. She guided him inside.

"Now take your time and concentrate on what you're doing. Don't rush it baby. Fuck this pussy like its meant to be fucked."

He started stroking.

For a beginner and just thirteen years old, he did damn good. He fucked her in doggy style and even made her moan. When he reached his peak, the explosion made him scream and they both came at the same time.

After they took a shower together, she talked to him as a teacher would've talked to a student and before long they were both snoring.

At ten thirty-five in the morning, she woke up with him trying to get in between her legs.

"This little horny motherfucka," she thought to herself. For the next twenty minutes he went to work, concentrating on how to fuck her the right way. She couldn't deny the sensation she was feeling and knew he would be a winner in due time. After session number two they both showered together and got dressed.

"You finna take me home already? He wasn't ready to leave her.

"Nah boo we're going shopping first."

"Did J.d. arrange all this for me?" He curiously asked.

"All this is for you and that's all that matters," she replied grabbing the keys to her Dodge Charger.

He started to realize that everything from this morning until now was J.d.'s work. Jarvis felt a joy that he had never experienced before, and he felt like he owed it all to J.d.

They drove to the mall in silence while listening to Bryson Tiller's c.d. Jarvis sat in the passenger seat with the happiest feeling he'd ever felt before and he felt he owed it all to J.d.

He turned to look at Andrea's pretty face and thought, "I actually fucked her twice." She saw him checking her out from the corner of her eye.

"Are you shocked that I was the first woman you've had or what?" She asked with a smirk on her face.

"Who said I was a virgin, did I seem like one?"

"Men don't beat around the bush Jarvis so why are you beating around the bush. Of course! I could tell you were a virgin and why would you want me to think you wasn't. Honestly it doesn't make a difference at this point."

"Well naw I didn't want you to think I was a virgin," he admitted.

Once they arrived at the Beachwood mall she told him his spending limit was fifteen hundred dollars. Jarvis almost fainted. He browsed the aisles slowly. He retrieved a variety of Levi's, polo t-shirts, a few pair of sneakers. He couldn't believe he was about to be rocking the new Jordan's that were recently released a few days ago. Andrea contributed her input reminding him to grab undergarments. After his clothes were rung up, he had one hundred and fifty dollars left. He walked past a jewelry store and observed seventy five percent off diamond studs. They pierced his ear and placed the diamonds in for ninety dollars and inside he felt like a million bucks.

<u>6</u>

It was 1:22pm when they pulled up to his house. When he got out to open the back door he saw Omirah and her sister Yasha sitting on the porch. He grabbed all his bags but had to come back out to grab his shoes. He didn't acknowledge Omirah as he walked up the steps and into the house. His mother was in the living room drinking a beer with her friend girl from down the street.

"BRING YOUR ASS IN HERE!" She yelled.

He entered the room.

"Where in the hell have you been, and you better not lie! You aint too old for a good old-fashioned ass whooping!"

"Ma, my friend took me shopping and here this is for you," he said as he went into his back pocket and pulled out a twenty-dollar bill that he had there just for her. He knew that would pacify her and it did. She grabbed it anxiously.

"Who is this friend that took you shopping?"

Jarvis was quiet.

"Jarvis all Imma say is that you better not being doing no dumb shit. I don't have time to be in and out of juvenile court because yo black ass wanna be grown!"

"I aint ma I promise," he said as he quickly dropped the bags off to his room. While he was walking back to the car Omirah waved at him and he threw her a kiss. She blushed at his bluntness.

"Before you grab your shoes let me talk to you for a second," said Andrea.

Jarvis got in the passenger seat and shut the door.

"I don't know if I'll ever see you again, but you take care of yourself okay. J.d. really likes you and it's apparent that part of his focus is set on grooming you. Make sure you let him because he's the right man for it. Now give me a hug and it was nice meeting you."

He hugged Andrea tightly and at that moment he understood how a split second could change an entire life.

After Jarvis took his shoes in the house, he came out with the cordless phone and sat on the porch. Signaling for Omirah to call him she got up and went in the house and called.

"What's up beautiful," said Jarvis

"Oh, nothing just sitting on the porch bored to death," she softly replied.

"I take it your parents didn't go to work today."

"My father did but my mother didn't. Me and Yasha are about to walk to the park so she can spend time with her lil boyfriend."

"Is that right. Do you want yo boyfriend to come and kick it with you? He asked.

She chuckled.

"Oh, so you're my boyfriend?"

"I wanna be."

"Well I don't know."

"Okay well let me know real soon because I'm very impatient," he told her.

"Hmm I see, well come up to the park Jarvis so we can talk."

"When yall going?" He asked while noticing his two boys walking his way.

"In about a half hour."

"Okay I'll be right behind you."

"Adios."

****

"What's up nigga!" Anton and Damon greeted in unison. Jarvis noticed Omirah was back on her porch. Damon turned, looked, and then waved at the pretty girl. She waved back.

"Damn nigga she does look good as hell. I might be stalking her ass too if I were you," said Anton.

"Why you let J.d. take you home? What was that shit about?" asked Damon.

"Man, yall wouldn't believe what went down last night. Jarvis spent the next thirty minutes reliving this morning's precious memories. After he was finished telling the story, they were loud in their excitement. Anton and Damon knew that everything he told them was true. Once Jarvis saw Omirah and Yasha leaving out their yard, he cut the conversation short.

"I'm about to change my clothes and shoot over to the park with her for a while. What yall finna do?" asked Jarvis.

"Okay nigga I see you done turned into a playa overnight, but I feel you. Just come through the jets when you're done," said Damon.

Jarvis took another shower and threw on his dark blue denim Levi's, a navy-blue v neck tee, and his all white Nike Huarache's. He felt fresh as he walked to the park.

He spotted Omirah and Yasha sitting on the bench talking to Rick and another dude. The other guy was Rick's cousin Marco who was 15 years old. Marco had a mean crush on Omirah, but he kept it discreet. Marco was oversized for his age. He was six feet two, thickly built, and very handsome. Basketball was his joy and he was very talented on the court.

He walked up to the four and Omirah stood up. Everyone's eyes ran over the apparel he was wearing.

"So Jarvis, you like my sister huh?" asked Yasha.

"Can't you tell," smiled Jarvis as he and Omirah started to walk away.

They silently walked to an unoccupied bench and had a seat.

"I didn't interrupt nothing, did I?" Jarvis asked.

"No, I was waiting for you."

"Oh, okay because dude looking down here like I stole his company or some'em. So Omirah, what's up with you?"

"Just ready to eat some barbeque tomorrow."

"I feel you, but what's up with us?" Jarvis asked.

"Don't you want some barbeque tomorrow?" she asked attempting to let his question linger.

"Aint no barbeque going down at my house."

The way he said it made her curious about what he meant by it.

"What you mean? Why yall not barbequing for the holidays?"

"Naw aint nothing happening over there but I might go by my aunties house or celebrate with a few of the homies but that's about it.

Omirah noticed him looking down at his hands and realized that something was wrong with Jarvis. Something she didn't recognize before. His eyes revealed a deep sadness and up until now his beautiful smile did a great job disguising what was apparent all along.

"You still haven't answered my question lil mama!"

"Before I answer your question, I need you to tell me what's going on with you. I've got to get to the bottom of why you look so sad today?" She sincerely asked.

"You sound like that one lady that be on the Oprah channel. Iyanla," he said jokingly.

She continued to stare at him deep in the eyes.

"Naw I'm good boo! It's just my mom is going through her own situation and by her going through it, I guess I am to."

"Is she okay?"

"Yeah I think so. To keep it all the way one hundred Omirah, she's on drugs real heavy so I really can't say, you feel me. Overall she's a good mother she just gotta bounce back that's all."

"I'll go with you Jarvis," she said developing a fondness for him.

"Why because you think I need a hug or something?"

"No because I want to be your girlfriend," she replied as she leaned over and kissed him on the cheek.

Listening to J.d.'s advice paid off. He made her feel his pain and he realized there was nothing to be ashamed of and nothing to hide.

7

July fourth was a beautiful day in the sky as the fireworks exploded. A few of Omirah's relatives spent the holiday with them. However, she spent most of her day wondering what Jarvis was doing. Auntie Carroll picked up Jarvis and they celebrated their holiday with the rest of the family. Jarvis found out that D-Bear (Auntie Carroll's Son) (Auntie Carroll was his father's sister) his favorite cousin was moving to Baltimore in a few weeks to live with his father. Jarvis was in his feelings about that since D-bear was his closest cousin. They were like best friends and sometimes spending the weekend over aunt Carrol's house was a relief from the drama at home.

Auntie Carroll dropped Jarvis off around ten thirty. When he went into the house he noticed that his mother wasn't home. He immediately left back out and shot to the projects. King Kennedy projects seemed as if they were a having a block party. Drug dealers were shooting fireworks to the sky and a long line of kids were in line to receive a five-dollar bill from the KKK member J-Roc. J-Roc was J.d.'s right hand man. Anton, Damon, and a bunch of other project boys their age was in the cut drinking. Jarvis walked up and mingled but refused to drink or smoke as he held J.d.'s words in his heart. Jarvis usually would act shy around Angelica especially when she playfully made her boyfriend remarks toward him, but since his homies was drinking, he decided to go see what she was up to. The door was wide open like always. He entered the house and saw a house full of females as he began to fan away the weed smoke.

"Hey Jarvis," said Deedra while sitting on the couch. Seem like ever since Deedra and Shonte saw him leave with J.d. a few nights ago, their new aim was to give him some pussy. Jarvis had a star over his head now on the strength of how J.d. treated him. He felt a spark inside of him that made him anxious to learn and embrace the game.

"Where's my wife? asked Jarvis not seeing Angelica. Some of the girls started laughing.

"She's in the bathroom," said Shonte.

Jarvis never played the game with her because of his shyness, but he was done being timid. Tonight, he wanted to see if Angelica serious. She came out of the bathroom and at first, she didn't see him.

"Ya little boyfriend want you," said Deedra.

"Hey Jarvis boo! Where da weed at? One of yaw need to roll up something."

Jarvis figured she wasn't in that playful girlfriend and boyfriend mood, but he wasn't either.

"Aye Angelica, let me holla at you on the porch right quick. Shit I can hardly breathe in this joint!"

The way he came at her caught her by surprise. They walked out onto the porch.

"What's up cutie," she uttered.

"You! Give me a hug girl."

She opened her arms but stood still in shock because she noticed a change in his behavior. He walked into her arms and cuffed her ass cheeks.

"Damn lil boyfriend! You drunk or something," she said while allowing him to continue on holding her ass in his hands. He released her.

"You know I laugh when you call me little right? You must think I'm still a baby or some'em don't you?"

She blurted out a breathless chuckle.

"Let me feel ya forehead to make show you aight," said Angelica.

He caught her wrist in midair and quickly pulled her into his kiss. The kiss lasted only 3 seconds.

"Jarvis! Boy what is wrong with you?"

"Girl you made me this way."

"Aww, I did this to my baby. Well you still got a couple years to go but I'm waiting for you boo!"

"Don't call me that shit and you aint gotta wait."

Jarvis took a few steps back and looked her up and down.

"Keep on discriminating then. You gone be anticipating in a few years," said Jarvis while walking down the stairs.

"My lil boyfriend just broke up with me yall," he heard her tell her girls.

"This bitch think it's a game," he thought out loud as he headed to the house anxious to hear from Omirah.

Jarvis sat in his room thinking about how to get some money. He knew J.d would disapprove of him embracing the game before his time, but it was something he wanted to do. He wanted to have things and didn't want to rely on J.d. to give them to him. He now had a hell of a girlfriend, and he wanted to show her that she had a hell of a nigga. While he was deep in thought, the phone started to ring. He quickly answered it hoping it was her.

"Hey boo what are you doing? asked Omirah.

"Just sitting here thinking about a whole lot of shit."

"Aw okay, well come over to my side door right quick. You gotta hurry up while my dad is still in the shower."

"Aight here I come."

Her sneakiness turned him on and he wondered what she was up to. He quietly ran out of the house and made his way to her side door. Omirah was poking her face out the door and handed him a plate of food wrapped up in foil.

"Here boo this is for you. I'm going to call you shortly okay?

He took the plate out of her hands while smiling.

"Thank you baby! Can I have a kiss?"

For the first time, their lips touched and before you knew it, they were french kissing like grown adults. They finally broke apart after she heard the water stop from the bathroom. "Go go go go, she whispered but Jarvis made her give him another kiss first.

****

Summer time was coming to an end and the first day of school had finally arrived. Jarvis walked his sweetheart to school, anticipating his 9th grade year. This wasn't something new for Omirah, just a new school and she was entering the 10th grade. This was Anton's and Damon's 10th grade year as well and their second year at this school. When they reached the school, a huge crowd of students surrounded the front entrance waiting for the doors to open.

"So are you going to be good around all these other females today," asked Omirah with an innocent smirk on her face.

"Most definitely baby! You just better not make me use these boxing skills," said Jarvis throwing a playful one-two.

She giggled.

"I won't make you have to do that."

He saw Anton, Damon and a few other project boys walking his way.

"J-one what's up," said Damon. They had just recently nicknamed Jarvis that.

"How are you doing," he then said to Omirah.

"Hello," she replied.

Jarvis and his homies fell into association while Omirah stood by his side until the doors opened. After looking over their schedules, Damon realized he had three of the same classes with Omirah. Anton had one with her as well.

The doors opened to the school and everybody formed a straight line. Omirah stood in front of Jarvis while the line moved at a slow pace. Jarvis pulled out a five-dollar bill and stuck it in her back pocket.

"You be cool and make sure you wait for me over by the school mascot. I put a little change in yo back pocket just in case you wanna go across the street to the store on your lunch break. She tilted her head back for a kiss and Jarvis didn't hesitate.

8

The first day of school was cool for Jarvis. Eye candy was everywhere, and everyone was dressed to impress. Jarvis told himself he would drop out before he would fall up in there looking tacky. He didn't run across Omirah in the halls at all that day, but she was posted up right where she agreed to wait.

"How was your first day?" She asked as they began to walk.

"It was cool," he replied.

"Aye lil Jarvis," a familiar voice yelled.

Jarvis looked around and spotted J.d. standing up from the moon roof of his Lexus Lx 570.

"Come on lil homie," J.d. yelled to him.

J.d. had secretly made it his business to pick him and his girl up from school on their first day.

"Who is that?" asked Omirah observing the ocean blue colored truck with the 24-inch blue and chrome wheels.

"He's like a big brother to me babe come on!"

J.d. and the truck had everyone's attention and now the star over Jarvis head was starting to shine even brighter.

J.d. had a fine ass woman in the passenger seat.

Jarvis and Omirah slid in the back seat and at that point Jarvis didn't know what he would do without J.d. in his life. He appreciated being a part of his life and felt that J.d. was a blessing.

"What's up lil homie how was school?"

"It was aight. Aye J.d, this my girl Omirah who I was telling you about!"

"Is that right! Okay then. Now I see why you talk about her so much. What's up Omirah."

"Hey," she replied unable to stop blushing.

He then whipped out of the schools parking lot, leaving onlookers staring in awe.

Before he dropped them off at home, he gave them an option of where they wanted to eat. They chose to order a large pizza from Angela Mia's. All four of them sat in the truck while waiting for the pizza.

"Aye J.d. I need to talk to you about something whenever you have a free moment," said Jarvis.

"Come around to the jets and it don't matter if I'm busy or not we gone holla."

After J.d. dropped them off, they went straight to Omirah's house. Yasha made it home before them since her school let out earlier than theirs.

"Meme is that you?" Yasha yelled from upstairs.

"Yeah it's me."

Jarvis and Omirah sat and ate together. Yasha came and grabbed a few slices and went back upstairs. Yasha agreed to stay out of the way while she spent a little time with Jarvis, considering she would always look out for her.

"You was looking good in that jean skirt today. How many compliments did you get?"

"Was looking good," she replied charmingly.

"Well you look even better now with a full stomach," he persiflage and got swatted with a few love taps.

Omirah had long black hair and her facial features carried a fine sensuousness. At fourteen years old, her five-six frame was already put together nicely. She had caramel thick thighs that were breathtaking.

A horn blared from outside. It was Rick coming to pick up Yasha. She came downstairs.

"I'll be back Meme."
"Okay I'll see ya later," said Omirah.

"You know what? Meme fits you beautifully! I like that name."

"You do?" She asked while leaning in for a kiss.

One thing led to another and before she realized it, Jarvis had freed her breasts out of her halter top. This was the farthest they had gotten but she caught herself.

"Wait Jarvis."

Jarvis caught his composure.

"Yeah you right, we trippin babe," said Jarvis while breathing heavily.

"Let me get up out of here. Call me later aight," said Jarvis while standing up to make his departure.

She stood up too.

"Are you upset with me?" She asked.

"Hell naw Meme. I understand that situations like this take time. Give me a kiss and don't worry. We don't need to rush nothing."

****

J.d. was getting his hair braided by a project chick name Samar, while the other KKK members worked the line of traffic that constantly flowed in nonstop.

J.d. saw Jarvis mingling with his homies.

"Call lil Jarvis for me Samar." She yelled his name and beckoned him with her finger.

"J.d. wants you!"

Jarvis made his way up to J.d.

"What's up boy? What's good with you?" asked J.d.

J.d noticed he was reluctant to talk in front of Samar.

"Wait until she finished then. How many braids do you have left Samar?" asked J.d.

"After this one, two more."

After she twisted up the final braid she kissed the top of J.d's head and walked away.

"All them girls that saw you hop in the Lexus truck, gone chase you until you outta breath now," chuckled J.d.

Jarvis laughed.

"That was gangsta J.d. Good looking for swooping me up like that!"

They both stood over the railing looking down at the projects.

"You asked me what's good, and right now everything is great because you made it that way. You bought me school clothes, put some money in my pocket, not to mention what you made happen with ole girl that one night.

J.d. laughed. "Did you do ya thang boy?"

"I did my thang big homie," Jarvis smirked. J.d. it's time for me to get out here and make something happen for myself. I can't continue to take handouts from you."

J.d. smiled because he understood what he was feeling but he already knew that in time he was going to feel this way. This signified that he was reading Jarvis correctly. J.d. knew this moment would come because he purposely pushed this moment into existence by making him feel what it would be like to have all eyes on him.

"Jarvis man you gotta be a little more specific."

"J.d. it aint Jarvis no more, its J-one. I'm ready to embrace the game for whatever its worth. If it brings me pain then so be it, but the way I'm looking at it. It's either All or Nothing!"

J.d. nodded his head in agreement.

"Okay so umm, at fourteen years old, you think you're ready for this game?"

"J.d. I can handle it, but I just wanted to let you know my decision... I'm not looking forward to another handout. Thanks for everything you did for me. I appreciate it including the knowledge and advice you fed me. I love you for that big homie."

"So, if you're not looking for another handout then how you gone move?"

"I've been saving all the money you gave me."

At that moment, J.d realized it was time to take the chain off the pit bull to see what it could do.

"Now listen to me J-one. I don't wanna tell you how to move with ya hustle and I'm not going to. With the qualities you possess, you gone have to allow yourself to grow into what I know you're going to become......A made nigga. Nobody can teach you how to become that nigga because its already in you. You will become that nigga in time. Now you say it's All or Nothing, right? Define that!"

Jarvis didn't answer him.

"First let's dissect the word "all" in a made nigga way. To get it all and stay the fuck out the way, you can't love no nigga around you. Not even me! You wanna know why?" asked J.d.

"Why?"

"Love gets in the way of a lot of shit and it's hard to kill a nigga you love... Love no one that's a part of this game with you cause aint no telling who you may have to kill, you feel me.

Jarvis didn't know what to feel.

"Every time you kill a man it should be for one purpose and one purpose only. To reach a higher level. Don't worry about ya pride cause yo power will protect it. To have it all, you must constantly think and stay focused and never let a bitch or a situation get in the way of that. Always know what's in front of you and coming at you. Now remember when I told you that you was gone have to think for your patnas? Well at some point you will have to use them to your advantage as well. You gotta use everything around you to your advantage."

They stared at one another through a moment in silence.

"Being soft equals nothing. Not being able to think equals nothing. Letting a bitch cloud your judgment equals nothing and staying in this cutthroat ass game longer than you have to....... equals nothing. All or Nothing? Then It's all or nothing J-one!"

"You said I'm not supposed to love you J.d. but I do," Jarvis said ruefully.

"Look shorty, at the end of the day, I placed a star over ya head. ... Now either you gone make it shine or let it disappear. I've played my part and now it's time for you to live out yours. You are above average so understand and embrace who you are. Trust your mind to guide you into fruitful opportunities, and through situations that's going to test who you really are."

Jarvis understood his words. "These niggas out here are creatures.... They Monsters! This game is deadly, and I don't wanna see you die in it.

Jarvis was overwhelmed by the fact that J.d. really seemed to care about him.

"Don't look down, like I said, I can't hold your hand, but I'll always be here for you shorty and you can trust that."

Jarvis was overwhelmed by his realness.

"Don't look down, hold ya head up. Check this out. I got a welcome to the game package for you. What I'm gone do is have my guy sit down with you and give the game on how to cut it up and price it. After school come holla at me aight!"

"You gone pick me up from school again?"

"Naw young nigga the trend it set."

9

Over the next three months Jarvis put a lot of time and energy into perfecting his hustle. Solo taught him how to cook cocaine and it didn't take long for him to catch on. The hustlers of King Kennedy projects welcomed J.d.'s protégé with open arms, allowing him to build his clientele. He didn't agree with outside hustling, so he posted up in crackhead Deedee apartment and had her bring the fiends to him. He also had a newfound crack spot down the street from his house and by him whipping up 90% pure crack, his traffic picked up at a fast pace.

When Jarvis set the trend on getting money, it didn't take long for Anton and Damon to beg Juvis to put them on. Juvis, Ada's boyfriend fronted them both an ounce a piece and they started from there. Although they were his men, Jarvis didn't share his space with them as far as his hustle environments was concerned. Each spot he created, he ran by himself. When J.d. gave him his welcome to the game package which consisted of 2 ounces and a quarter he also added a 13 shot 380 and 5 boxes of bullets. Omirah wasn't aware that Jarvis sold drugs but he had to tell her, so he could safely stash his drugs and money at her crib. At first, she was shocked, but he poured it on her thick by letting her know that he had no choice but to take care of himself due to his situation at home. Omirah shed a few tears because she felt like he was forced to sell, and she agreed. There was an unused attic that no one bothered up on the third floor and Omirah decided that a small area inside the chipped wall would be a great hiding place.

Jarvis had a locked safe box that he discreetly took over there filled with utilized accessories he managed to accumulate over the last three months. Lately he'd been renting and riding around in dope fiends' cars trying to get his driving skills tight and working off throw way phones delivering his product on call. The hood rats in the projects saw Jarvis being about his business and started throwing themselves at him whenever they saw the opportunity, but the only thing he focused on was establishing his business and the hustle. In other words, he was putting the longevity stamp down on his presence.

One day he sat his mother down while she was high and had a serious talk with her. He noticed when he came home from school that his room was disheveled. It was apparent to her that Jarvis was selling drugs and the disarray of his room today proved it. He decided it was time to put the cards on the table with her.

"Mama, you been doing what you been doing for a long time and now it's to the point where I gotta stand up and take care of myself and you. I'll tell you what Ma, the only way I'll change directions is if you let go of your habit and go back to being the mother I used to know."

"Jarvis, you been selling drugs?" she asked. "I know you have just tell me the truth."

Jarvis ignored her question.

"Look Ma, the choice is yours!"

Later, in the wee hours of the morning, he caught his mother trying to discreetly ramble through his room. He woke up and watched her. Disgusted by the moment, a tear fell from the corner of his eye.

"Ma! What are you doing?'

"Give me something Jarvis I need it," she demanded.

Jarvis stared at her with his head lifted from the bed and could tell that she didn't give a damn about nothing but getting high. That moment caused his heart to reverse sides in his chest and he decided not to worry about nothing other than managing for himself.

✯✯✯✯✯✯✯✯✯✯✯✯✯✯✯✯✯✯✯✯

The school year came and went, but it was exciting for Jarvis who had a hard time keeping girls out of his face. He had a nice stash of money and along with his dope spot, he organized a weed spot out of Angelica's apartment. Angelica ran the spot from 1pm-10pm Monday -Saturday and he paid her five hundred dollars a week. Of course, he knew that his age didn't mean nothing to her anymore and he was sure he could fuck if he wanted to, but he purposely kept it strictly business with her.

Over the last six months him and Omirah had been screwing like grown folks. Their first sexual encounter was at the beginning of the year in her bedroom. Her parents were at work and Yasha was out with Rick. She decided it was time to give Jarvis her virginity. He guided her through it as if he was a veteran and from that day forward, she couldn't get enough of him.

Jarvis, Damon, and Anton's friendship grew even tighter. Everything seemed to be tied into one solid knot while each man perfected his hustle. Deedra was now Anton's main girl and Shonte was Damon's girl which forced their little hood rat personas to go out the window.

Ada moved into her own house across town that Juvis bought for her. Anton was trying to be discreet under his aunties roof, but he knew it was only a matter of time before she realized what he was into.

Anton sat at the living room table weighing up crack on a digital scale while Deedra sat on the couch talking to one of her girls from the projects. Her mother Sonya was outside running sells for Anton.

Deedra had long gotten over the embarrassment of her mother's drug addiction and presented the idea of hustling out of her mother's apartment to Anton.

****

"Girl we definitely got to get at them bitches. We can't let that shit ride," said Deedra talking into the phone.

"HELL NO......ITS WAR!" Freeda retorted. "They scratched up my face and pulled out the gang of tracks all over a piece of dick that wasn't even on shit. This hair aint cheap they got me fucked up sis. Them bitches already know we gone get they asses together."

"These ghetto star struck hoes been jealous of KKS. (King Kennedy Starlets) They just been waiting for a reason," Deedra chimed.

Freeda and Rere had beef because Freeda had messed around with her man. Rere (A 30th Chick) got her revenge earlier that day after catching Freeda and another KKS girl (Tasia) in the malls parking lot. The KKS girls were outnumbered but, Rere wouldn't let Freeda back down. She savagely attacked Freeda leaving Tasia no other choice but to try to help. That's when things became ugly. The four other 30th chicks with Rere got involved as well. By the time security arrived on the scene, both girls had been mauled.

"Hang up that phone, you don't need to be doing no fighting!" Anton told her.

At that moment Deedra's mother Sonya walked in with three different sells. As Anton was serving the customers, Sonya told him that J-one was on his way up.

While she was letting the customers out, she let Jarvis in.

"What's up nigga roll with me right quick. I'm finna cop me a slide shit I'm tired of renting fiend cars every day," said Jarvis.

"Who name you putting it in?"

"Imma put it in Deedee name. She got license and insurance on that little smug she's driving."

"Here boo hold this until I get back." Anton gave her the drugs and left with Jarvis.

Linda drove them to an old-school car lot in Maple Heights. The three of them looked over a variety of whips but Jarvis keyed in on a 1978 steel gray Malibu with a quarter vinyl black top.

"That's me right there, I gotta have that!" Jarvis blurted.

"Damn nigga you make me wanna go hit up the stash and cop me some'em too shit," said Anton.

"So, this is what you want?" asked Linda.

"Yep, this me all day long."

While Jarvis and Anton were driving back to the jets, Jarvis was really starting to feel himself. The respect he was getting made him want to hustle harder. Anton and Damon fed off his ambition and two weeks later they bought them a pair of old school matching Monte Carlos. Anton's was white, and Damon's was baby blue with a quarter white vinyl top.

Other youngsters from the projects who were younger than them wanted to try their hand and before you knew it, they formed a click called the KKBG's, King Kennedy Baby Gangstas. They chose their own habitat in another part of the projects that was located around the corner from the original KKK members spot.

Most of their parents were crack heads and no longer had the power to care about what their children was involved in. Even the parents who were drug free tried the disciplinary route, but eventually gave up. Within time, most parents were accolading their sons progress.

10

Andrea had fallen back from Gianni as instructed, but he never stepped out of his square. He would send his chauffeur to pick her up in his Rolls Royce and they would drive to different hotels where he would already be there waiting. This routine went on for about ten months and his meticulous approach made Andrea frustrated. She was pissed that he was now fucking her more than J.d.

"Just have him killed or let me kill his ass the next time we're together! This shit is starting to really take a toll on my mental J.d. Why are we wasting all this energy trying to kidnap him, so you can take what he got? You're already rich?" Andrea cried.

"Listen up bitch before you make me mad. I didn't put this plan together with the intention to half step. I want everything that I got coming. Everything!"

"Well I want you. You're my everything and it's not my mind that's confused, it's my body. My body craves for you day and night not Gianni."

A tear trickled down her face.

"Come here," said J.d. He held her shoulders.

"Let's give dis nigga another month to see what he gone do aight. If nothing happens then imma just return the nigga to his maker and we can settle with that," he assured her.

She was satisfied with that right along with some good hard fucking he gave her right afterwards.

A few months after Gianni met Andrea last year he had an investigator who's been on his payroll, check into her background to see if her identity was real. He was a little shocked by her deception. He learned that her real name wasn't Janelle but Andrea. He also had factual pictures of her between the sheets with a familiar rivalry……J.d.

He reckoned that she lied about her name to keep her infidelity concealed, but as long as she wasn't an official or someone sent by the officials, he wasn't going to cut her off. He actually liked her more than he would like to admit. Andrea appealed to him in ways that made her seem different from his other women.

✯✯✯✯✯✯✯✯✯✯✯✯✯✯✯✯✯✯✯✯

Today was Jarvis birthday and the Jazz fest in downtown Cincinnati was two days away.

"Aye come pick me up from this spot and shoot me up to creative touch car shop. It's time to bring em out today," said Jarvis.

"Oh yeah. Nigga you know we got some em sweet planned for you. A few KKS hoes is out shopping for you right now so I guess by the time we pick up ya ride and get back, the food should be on the grill."

"Well come on nigga I'm waiting on you."

"Aight give me a minute," said Anton and they both hung up.

Jarvis looked at his watch and it read 1:57 pm. He called Meme and told her he would be picking her up around three.

"You know I don't want to be down the way in them damn projects all day J-one. How about we go to the movies or something, just the two of us?" asked Meme.

"Babe these are my peoples, and this is their way of showing me love, but listen... we still got a movie on the agenda. Don't trip, and Imma still have you home by ten boo aight."

"You better!"

"You just better wear that black fitted dress you had me buy you last week."

"Which one?.......Remember you bought me two of em" said Omirah.

"The one that made this thang stand so tall I had to leave the store," Jarvis smiled.

"Oh, yeah that one." she giggled. "That's the dress you picked out at that store called 'Posh Collection' over in Mayfield. Okay honey I'll wear it for you."

Anton blew the horn.

"Can you tell him to drop me off at the deli?"

"Come on," said Jarvis.

Omirah got in the back and Jarvis climbed in the passenger as Anton pulled off.

"Drop her off at the Arab deli."

"Aight. What's up with you Omirah?"

"Hey Anton, nothing much."

They drove in silence until they reached the store. Before she climbed out they kissed. "Be careful out here okay!"

"I will," he assured her.

****

"Aye J-one, I gotta holla at you about some em," said Anton as he pulled away.

"First of all, would I seem shady to you.......wait, let me rephrase that! Would you look at me in a cut-throat type of way if I told you I had a lick on somebody that's kind of close to me?"

"Nigga you is cut throat. Save the dramatics. Where the lick and who is it?"

"The jackpot is at my cousin Ada house. The lick is Juvis."

Jarvis pondered for a silent moment enticed by the opportunity to advance in the game. He knew that robbing Juvis would be a game changer.

"You my man, right?" asked Jarvis.

"No doubt fam," said Anton.

"Ok, but I trust you like a brother. I don't worry about you crossing me because I know that you won't."

"Likewise," Anton replied.

"So how you wanna play this?" asked Jarvis.

"You know they been lightweight beefing ever since she found out Juvis got a seed by another bitch, right?"

"Naw nigga I aint hip but go ahead," Jarvis urged.

"Well I went over there and she let some shit come out of her mouth that let me know she holds his work there. I bet she got some cash too."

"Have you told anybody else about this?" Jarvis asked abruptly.

"Naw, shit Damon don't even know."

"Well what's up what you wanna do?"

"I can't go in there because I feel like she gone know who I am regardless. So, if we gone do it then you and Damon gotta go in there but I don't wanna make it look like she set him up though cause then imma have to kill that nigga for putting his hands on her."

✷✷✷✷✷✷✷✷✷✷✷✷✷✷✷✷✷✷✷✷

It was 3:19 pm when Jarvis pulled in front of Omirah's house. Yasha and Rick was sitting on the porch. Yasha mouth dropped when Jarvis got out of the car.

"Jarvis, is that your car? Yasha shockingly asked.

Rick showed an expression of pure hatred as he thought about Jarvis being a young dusty bum one year ago.

"Yeah this me. Where Meme?"

"She's in there," said Yasha unable to take her eyes off his car.

The Malibu was now a wet candy apple cranberry color with a quarter white vinyl top. The soft white leather seats were Gucci material and four tv's were adorned for entertainment. He wanted to ride high, so he slapped some 28-inch Lexani rims on it the same color as the car. Rick couldn't believe that Jarvis was doing as good as he appeared to be doing in the streets.

Jarvis found her in the bathroom, in the mirror applying lip gloss across her lips.

"So, did you get your car?"

"Yeah it's out front," said Jarvis as he raised up the front of her skirt to rub the inner part of her thighs. She turned to face him.

"Tiamo," she admitted.

"Babe you know I don't have a got damn clue what you just said," smiled Jarvis.

"I love you Jarvis."

They kissed with heated passion.

The Barbeque cookout was an essential moment for the KKBG members. Each member grew up in a broken home and as they kicked it, each one realized that a family was being created. The KKS girls quickly took Omirah away from Jarvis and into Freda's apartment where all the female action was. Some of the KKS faces were familiar from school and as time went on, Omirah relaxed and noticed she was really enjoying herself. While the young homies were outside bunched in one crowded area, Jarvis had something to say to his newly formed crew.

"Aye, let me grab yall niggas attention right quick before everybody get all drunk and shit."

"What you want nigga," said Marlo and passed the blunt to his twin sister Wanisha. Jarvis waited until everyone became silent and then he began.

"Out of the blue, somehow this crew came together, and I feel like it's a reason for everything. Yall think yall can rep KKBG like the big homies rep KKK?" Jarvis asked the crowd of up and coming youngsters.

"Shit it's already in the making nigga!" M-2 shouted.

"Well then let's turn all the way up! Jarvis sullenly replied. "Since this part of the jets is us, day and night we gotta work this spot until its functioning like it's supposed to," stated Jarvis.

"Man, you trippin J-one dis bitch already jumpin!" Trey blurted.

"Naw this bitch aint nowhere near jumping," Jarvis retorted.

"What the big homies got going on over there is what you call jumpin and guess what? We can have this shit over here like that too. We must supply that A-1 Yola at all times. So, for the ones that don't know how to whip coke, yall better learn cause buying ya shit already hard is gone fuck up the blocks rhythm. We all need to be on the same page if we gone make this side of the jets a gold mine."

At fifteen years of age, Jarvis was ahead of his time. His acumen was sharp, and his leadership was effective.

"Well since I'm the only Starlet that's gone be getting this money with yall then Imma need a gun too," said Wanisha.

"What you tellin us for shit you better go buy you one then," said Lil Tae.

As the crew went back and forth, some of them started lighting up blunts.

"Look I can't tell nobody what to do. Most of yall either my age or a year or two older, but how do yall expect to see what's coming at you or what's in front of you through a thick ass cloud. Yall need ask yourselves this question. Do I wanna get money or get high?" Said Jarvis as he started walking towards Omirah who was sitting on Freda's porch.

Anton and Damon pulled into the Jets at the same time and walked up to Jarvis while he was sitting with Omirah eating his plate of barbeque.

"Aye let me holla at you right quick J-one," said Anton.

Jarvis got up and the three of them walked off.

"Ada is around the corner at my house right now," said Anton.

"What that mean?" asked Jarvis.

"She gone be there for a while. So we need to suit up and lay low at her house. As soon as she gets out the car yall rush her and run up in there," Anton suggested.

"Yall niggas ready for this shit? asked Jarvis. They assured him in unison. "Follow me to the crib so I can suit up and grab my strap."

11

Jarvis pulled into Omirah's driveway while Damon and Anton parked in front of the house. Omirah was upset because their plans were cut short without being told the reason why. Whatever the reason, she let Jarvis slide since she figured it was something important to him.

"Will I be able to see you before my parents get home from work?" Omirah asked.

Without him saying a word, she could tell he was unsure.

"Yeah I ---"

"Just be careful okay," said Omirah. She cut him off and leaned in for a kiss.

Jarvis pulled his car into his driveway and quickly ran into the house. He heard his mother in the kitchen and he tried to hurry up to avoid seeing her, however she caught him before he made it out of the house.

"Let me get a twenty Jarvis!"

"Ma, you gotta wait! I aint got nothing on me right now."

The respect level between a mother and son was slowly starting to fade and Jarvis was becoming numb to it in the process.

He hopped in the backseat and they pulled away. The accessories they needed such as scarves, leather gloves, and skullies, were in Anton's glove compartment. They drove across town to an abandoned house next door to Ada's.

The backyard was spacious and had a fence around it, but the view was close enough to keep a bird's eye on Ada's driveway.

After Anton dropped his two homies off, he parked on the side street three blocks over. He cut the ignition all the way back, so his music could still play and rolled up a blunt. It was 7:47 pm and he knew that it was probably going to be a few hours before Ada came home so he prepared for the long wait. At 8:39pm, two girls slowly rolled pass his car on mountain bikes. Anton quickly noticed them since they both had on tight fitted apparel.

"Aye yo! Wassup shorty. The girls looked back and saw Anton sticking his head out the window. One of the girls slowly kept riding on, but the other one seemed interested as she pointed to herself.

"Yeah you," said Anton even though he really wanted the tall thick one. She rolled back to his car.

"Wassup shorty what's your name?"

"Tracy......What's yours? She quickly answered.

"Anton... You live around here?"

"Umm hmm around the corner," said Tracy.

Anton ran his eyes up and down her body and was pleased with his catch. Tracy appeared to be around 5'6" in height and about 125 pounds. She was a slim thick chic and was rocking some box braids which gave her facial features a flawless sex appeal. To Anton she was just the right size.

"How old are you?" asked Anton

"Seventeen! How old are you?" she asked.

"I'll be sixteen in a few months."

"Daaang you young," she smiled.

"See you got thangs' twisted already. Don't let my age fool you shorty. I'm young but I'm a grown ass man," Anton smiled.

After they talked a little longer she handed him her number and caught up with her sister who was still waiting on her.

✯✯✯✯✯✯✯✯✯✯✯✯✯✯✯✯✯✯✯✯

At eleven thirty-two Ada's truck pulled into the driveway. She was upset because she had just had a heated argument with Juvis in the projects. She demanded that he come and get all his shit by tomorrow and go ahead and be with the broad who claims to have his baby. She didn't get out of the car until she finished listening to Keshia Cole's song 'I should've cheated.'

She finally stepped out of the truck teary eyed and unaware of the two figures that hopped over the fence and were running towards her. As she was fumbling through her keys the sound of footsteps caused her to become fearful. She nearly had a panic attack while trying to open the door without looking back. They ran up on her porch and she screamed out in terror. They both had their guns aimed at her face.

"Scream again bitch and I'm gone shoot you dead in your teeth. Now open up the muthafucking door!" Jarvis hissed.

"Please don't hurt me," she implored and managed to open the door. Damon shut the door behind them.

"All we want is the money and dope. Don't make us have to kill you to find it," Jarvis threatened.

"The d-drugs is-is upstairs," she stammered.

"Aight stop all that crying and shit and show us. I told you we aint gone hurt you as long as you cooperate," Jarvis assured.

They followed her to a closet where two and a half kilos of cocaine awaited them on the shelf.

Ada pointed to the foot locker bag. "That's its right there," she told them.

Jarvis grabbed it and quickly looked inside.

"Where's the rest of the shit at?" asked Jarvis.

"There's nothing else in here. All the money I have is the money in my purse."

She handed her purse over to Damon.

"Keep ya money just give us ya truck keys, "said Damon.

She reluctantly handed them over.

"Take it off the key ring," Jarvis told her, and she complied. She didn't understand the reason behind it. He wanted her to keep her keys to her home.

After she handed over the truck keys, they quickly made their exit from the house. A few minutes later they pulled in behind Anton's car, abandoning her truck.

"Did we pull it off? Anton asked excitedly as they drove away.

"We did good my nigga! It's time to eat," replied Jarvis.

At their age, they didn't realize more money more problems was a true cliché. Tomorrow would be the beginning of a new chapter for the three homies.

Jarvis, Damon, and Anton went straight to Jarvis crack spot on his mother's block. After he grabbed the cooking utensils he hit the stove and went to work. He showed them how to turn cocaine into crack. Out of two and a half kilos of powder, Jarvis produced three and a half kilos of crack. Damon and Anton were amazed that they were an extra kilo richer from Jarvis whip game. It was a little after three in the morning when he finished and realized that he was still alert but paranoid. He reckoned that the drug must have gotten in his pores from breathing in the potent smell.

"Next time imma put som'em over my nose because I think I'm high right now," said Jarvis.

"Ay Linda, do me favor and grab that scale upstairs. Linda was the dope fiend who allowed Jarvis to set up shop for crack.

"Now that I done showed yall the whip game, utilize the knowledge because that's the only way to get rich in this game. Why give another nigga yo extras when you can whip ya own shit up and get everything you got coming to you. I just showed yaw the significance of the whip game. We got an extra brick out this shit."

Both homies nodded in agreement. Jarvis looked at them closely. "Why yall so quiet? Yall understand how to do this shit?"

They nodded simultaneously.

"Yall feel high off this shit too huh? Yeah let's hurry up and split this shit and get the fuck outta here."

After Linda returned with the scale, she grabbed the pot off the stove that was aligned with crack and went to enjoy herself.

As they were breaking the dope down to ounces, Jarvis started laughing.

"We all quiet and shit! Wassup! Yall niggas aight?" asked Jarvis.

"Truthfully even though I do feel that shit, I'm just analyzing where we been as far as young niggas, what we been through, but most of all where the fuck we are going," Damon admitted.

"Sky is the limit as long as we stay focused out here, and loyal to each other. We got a crew of creatures...MONSTERS, that's gone follow us to the death! We gotta feed them niggas. Guide them and watch over each other and we got some work to do. Can I consider you two niggas to be my brothers' keeper?"

"On my grandma grave, both of yall can trust me with yall lives," Damon replied sincerely."

"Same here," Anton stated.

"Yall back is my back, now let's get this money," Jarvis finalized.

Solidarity was set between the three friends, but as everything in life is tested, their unity will be tested as well..........

The next day Jarvis fronted his sixteen-man crew an ounce a piece and demanded that going forward, nobody was allowed to purchase their packages from the outside. Anton and Damon took their cars to Creative Touch paint shop. Anxious to follow Jarvis trend, the three homies were now looking like progressing dope boys, and the rest of the crew was motivated to follow their lead.

12

Juvis and his three cousins rolled around the city, each one strapped nasty while analyzing the situation. He knew it had to be somebody inside his click and as soon as he heard any word of who he thought may have done it, he was prepared to bring it one way without a word to be said. His cousins weren't from the projects, but they were some ruthless individuals with body counts. They were ready to ride at the drop of a dime. Juvis had over 100-grand tucked away so he wasn't hurting financially, but his pride was injured. Nevertheless, somebody was going to pay one way or another.

When Juvis pulled into the King Kennedy jets, J.d. was pulling out. Juvis blew his horn and both cars stopped at the outlet.

"What's up," said J.d.

"Let me holla at you before you pull out big homie."

J.d. reversed the Aston Martin and parked on the side of Juvis and Juvis climbed in with J.d.

"What up?"

"It's what's about to go down. One of these nigga's around here done ran up in my girl spot last night. They took two and a half of the five bricks I got from you last week. I can't believe one of these niggas around here had the audacity, but you know I aint going for dat."

"Shit you done went for it, it happened."

J.d.'s direct statement hit Juvis in the gut.

"Naw I aint going for shit homie and my reason behind hollerin at you about this is because I respect you enough to let you know why I'm finna nut up around this bitch," said Juvis.

"Okay and I respect that but don't bring no unnecessary heat around here. What's in the dark gone come to light and when it do, handle ya business!"

"It's on!" Juvis blurted and opened the door.

"Big homie don't sink ya own ship by not being able to think," J.d warned him. Juvis got out and stuck his head back in the window.

"Nigga whoever was bold enough to run up in my girl spot wasn't thinking and they gotta answer to that my nigga. If I bring heat around this bitch, then it's whatever!" Juvis retorted and climbed back into his car where his cousins awaited, then sharply pulled off. J.d. rolled up to the side of his car at the red light.

"Nigga yo mistake wasn't mine so don't make it mine and as a matter of fact nigga, don't talk to me with yo emotions."

Juvis pulled off and ran the light because he knew J.d. was in danger of being slumped right there on the spot by his cousins from the aggressiveness of his words.

For the rest of that day, thoughts ran through Juvis mind of not only finding out who the robbers were, but also becoming the man who he was hustling to become. Over the last two years he analyzed his situation and what it would take to reach the highest level. He frequently thought about taking the ultimate shortcut but never went through with it. However, after last night, Juvis felt like his pride was being tested and had concluded that it was him against the world. He was now ready to take the shortcut not thinking that this decision could be fatal to his life.

****

The Jazz Fest in Cincinnati, Ohio was lit like it was New Year's Eve. It was more like a negro holiday for the natives of Ohio who were amongst the young and restless. It was a two-day event. Everybody who attended this event came to freak, stunt and splurge as if they didn't have a care in the world. Juvis and his three cousins Snatch out, Dink, and Killa was at a hotel party at one of the busiest strips in downtown Cincinnati. While many enjoyed the outdoor festivities, there were plenty enjoying the indoor Jazz fest hotel parties that took place simultaneously. However, these parties were far from normal. They were saturated with sex, money, and drugs.

"Yes baby, fuck this pussy poppy. Fuck it!" (Clap...clap..clap)

Juvis had a fine ass Dominican chick bent over the toilet pounding her pussy from the back. He grabbed a handful of her long hair and roughly pulled her head back.

"Harder poppy harder!" She begged breathlessly and in total ecstasy. Juvis stabbed inside of her aggressively while holding onto her hips, pumping her hard and fast.

"Oh my God oh my God fuck me nigga got dammit fuck this pussy!" She screamed as she began to cum all over his dick which made her juices flow down her leg uncontrollably. After Juvis got his off they both were breathless and at a loss for words. Juvis took the condom off and dropped it in the commode. She put the toilet seat down and sat on top of it.

"Come here poppy," she softly uttered.

She put his dick in her mouth and sucked out the rest of his jism as if she didn't want it to go to waste.

"This bitch aint playing," Juvis thought. Her services outweighed the two hundred dollars he gave her by a long shot.

He didn't recognize any faces in the hotel room when they stepped out of the bathroom.

"Damn bitch was it that good?" One of the girls asked her while looking Juvis up and down.

The nigga who lap she was sitting on said, "Shit you finna find out what's good right here!"

"Like I told you before, it cost three hundred for this pussy with yo cheap ass."

"You got some weed for sale?" The Dominican chick asked Juvis who was headed for the door.

"Naw I aint got none," said Juvis as he stumbled his way out of the room.

✱✱✱✱✱✱✱✱✱✱✱✱✱✱✱✱✱✱✱✱

As the sky was transforming into night, the downtown streets of Cincinnati were congested with people partying having the time of their lives. Juvis and his cousins were on the walkway mingling in the crowd when a line of cars slowly rolled by tailing one another. Gianni was in the middle of the line standing out of the roof of a champagne colored S-class Jag throwing money into the wind as if it was useless scrap paper.

"YALL HOES EAT YA CAKE, IT'S YA BIRTHDAY! Gianni yelled as he watched the women go crazy as they ran in the street snatching money off the ground. After Gianni emptied his hand he ducked back inside the car as the 30th Posse slowly continued driving down the street.

"Look at this stuntin ass nigga here," Juvis heard someone say but Juvis was focused on the Jag wondering where it was headed. He kept looking and saw they turned into a parking lot up the street.

"Aye, I'm finna walk down here for a minute yall niggas chill."

"Aight we'll be right here," Killa replied and turned his attention back to the broad he was probably going to leave with tonight.

It took Juvis almost 20 minutes to make it through the crowd just to get down the street. He spotted Gianni leaned up against the passenger door of the Jag. Two dime pieces were in his face. Juvis walked straight up to him and interrupted his conversation with the two broads.

"Excuse me for interrupting but Gianni can I holla at you for a minute?"

At first Gianni looked at him as if he were crazy for interrupting him, but he told the girls to hold tight.

They walked a few feet away from the girls.

"What up Juvis?" Gianni skeptically asked.

"I know you engulfed in all this good action, as I am too, but I need to enlighten you to something that I think you should know."

"Talk," Gianni insisted.

Juvis knew this wasn't the right time and needed his undivided attention.

"Wednesday night is old school night at the Affinity, right?" (Gianni's Club)

"Yep!" Gianni confirmed.

"Well I'll just slide up there and holla at you then cause right now is not the time," said Juvis.

Gianni read the look in his eyes which told him that Juvis knew something that he needed to know. He didn't display his anticipation to find out.

"I'll be there. Just let one of my security officers know you're there to see me. As a matter of fact, just tell' em ya name and they will VIP you right up."

13

It was 11:42pm and the 30th street projects were empty on this Friday night. All the D.T.W (Down the Way) members had left early in the day and wouldn't be back from the Jazz fest until Sunday. Not even the young and upcoming were out that night who consisted of about 20 adolescents ranging from the age 13-17. They called themselves the YG Posse (Young Guerillaz). Not to mention every member had a girlfriend from their projects who endured the same struggles as them. Needless to say, they were a ghetto tied project click. Only five members of the YG click was out. Juju, Lavar, Foo, Ubie, and Mouse. They were posted up in the cut, going over their plans for the umpteenth time. The next day the mission was going down against all odds.

"Yall think we can get away with this?" Asked Mouse who was 16 years old and the youngest of the crew.

If yall move quick with securing the place while I take the bank teller in the back, then everything should be a clean getaway. I mean shit we should be in and out if we stick to the script. By the time police get there we should be ducked off already, counting up the money," said Foo.

A silence occurred while they sat in deep thought.

"Fuck it, either we gone make it out or lay down some years for trying got dammit," said Juju.

"If I lay it down, I aint getting back up so we gotta make it out. Aint no question about that. I feel like we're the elite of Yg. We need to pull this off, so we can help some of our homies that are in some fucked up situations that have it bad around this muthafucka. Not to mention, it's time to eat good out here. Are we living or just existing? I'm ready to live and become somebody that this city gone remember even after I'm long gone," said Foo.

"Foo was another youngsta before his time and that trait alone is what gave him mind control over the majority of the Yg crew. He was tired of struggling and seeing his friends struggle because of what their parents were going through. Jealousy also played its role in his motivation. Whenever he saw the KKBG members they were shining. Driving fly cars, flossing, and dressing fly. Not only were the Yg boys envying them, but their girls were too and that didn't sit well with Foo. So he decided it was time to round up the elite for one reason and one reason only. To pull off a heist at the National City Bank.

****

It was a grey day in the sky as it continuously drizzled. The elite team was seated in Foo's living room dressed in disguises. Juju and Ubie had on women's attire wearing a pants suit with bra cups to modify their feminine look. They even had on lipstick topping it off with wigs and sunglasses to cover their eyes.

Lavar and Foo were dressed in male attire. Lavar wore fake dreadlocks that hung shoulder length, fake sideburns that were connected into a fake mustache and a goatee. Foo had on a fisherman hat along with the fake facial hair hookup as well. Although they could tell who each other were, they knew they could easily deceive the naked eye.

As they sat in the living room making sure they had their plans in order, Foo's mother called out his name from her bedroom which made the conversations come to a halt.

"Yeah Ma? Aye yall get ready cuz we finna dip out," he whispered to his crew as he went to see what his mother wanted.

"What did I tell you about having company in my house this early?" She bickered.

"Take em outside."

"Aight Ma."

"Bring me a glass of ice water so I can wash this Tylenol down."

Foo's mother was born blind at birth. When she was 20 years old, she was raped, beaten and left for dead after her house was burglarized by a wanted rapist. Unfortunately, it left her pregnant, but she refused to kill her innocent unborn child who she named Terry Waters, Aka Foo.

They drove the two stolen cars to the designated location which was a one-way street, and only a few blocks away from the bank. Once they parked Foo and Juju abandoned their car and climbed inside the getaway car with the rest of the team. Mouse, whose job was to be the driver, nervously puffed on a Newport.

"Yall niggas ready or what?" Foo asked excitedly while cocking back his nine-millimeter Beretta.

The rest of them followed suit while Mouse started up the car and pulled away. At Eleven fifty-two the bank had several people waiting in the lines. The Yg members came inside one at a time. Before you knew it, they were patiently observing the place waiting on Ubie to make his move. Ubie keyed in on the toy cop and saw that he had the drop on him. He pulled out his gun and rushed the toy cop impetuously.

"GET ON THE FLOOR BITCH BEFORE I KILL YOU!"

At that moment, all hell broke loose. Within seconds Juju and Foo were standing on the counters hovering over the bank tellers.

"GET DA FUCK ON THE GROUND OR DIE!" Foo shouted, and the workers frantically complied. Lavar and Ubie had the patrons and the toy cop faced down on the floor. Foo took a bank teller in the back at gunpoint. He spotted the manager hiding behind the desk.

"STAND DA FUCK UP AND KEEP YA HANDS UP!" Foo sneered to the manager and then turned to the female bank teller. "Imma test it for dye packs and if you give me dye Imma blow ya got damn head off!"

"Give him clean money Cheryl," the manager quickly insisted. She quickly swept the shelves of money into the garbage bag, leaving behind the money that was camouflaged with dye.

He returned to the front two minutes later with the two hostages in front of him and noticed his homies had everything under control. He looked through the glass doors and saw Mouse parked out front and the scenery appeared normal. Foo's adrenaline was surging from knowing he was seconds away from a clean getaway.

"You'll never get away with this boy!" The white cop told Ubie. At that moment, Ubie wanted to see what it would feel like to kill someone.

"Boy?....... You ole white son of a bitch. Let's see if I can get away with this." ----------Pop Pop!

Everybody went into a frenzy.

"COME ON YALL LET'S GO, COME ON!" Foo shouted. They ran out the glass doors towards the stolen car. Mouse was nervously smoking a square, looking in all directions for police. Before they could shut the doors, he was sharply pulling away from the curb.

"WHY IN THE FUCK DID YOU SHOOT EM UBIE?" Yelled Foo.

"Right now, we gotta get away," said Ubie.

Three minutes later they had switched cars and was safely headed back to the projects.

<u>14</u>

Mouse apartment was the go to spot because his mother was at work. After they closed the front door they all started talking at once.

"Why did you shoot that muthafucka? Nigga you just made shit hot for............

"Get the fuck off me nigga!" Ubie broke away from Juju's tight grip and quickly snatched the thirty-eight off his hip.

"Grab me like that again," Ubie sneered, aiming the gun in Juju's face.

Everyone froze in panic. After witnessing him kill that toy cop, he had everybody shook up. Well, everyone except Foo.

Foo walked up on Ubie with the money bag held high.

"Look fuck the pig. It's over with, you killed em. That nigga dead, we got the money and plenty of it."

Ubie still had the gun pointed at Juju. Foo reached out and lowered the barrel with his hand.

"Imma act like you never pointed that burner in my face Ubie, but don't ever do that shit again nigga or I swear," -----

"Aight yall just leave it right there," said Lavar. "Yall wanna beef with each other or count this money up?" The tension quickly settled.

"We better put this money under some water first, it may have some dye packs inside this shit. This old head told me that's how you beat it," said Foo.

Mouse went straight to the bathroom and cut the water on in the tub. All the homies posted up in the bathroom while Foo held the garbage bag under the water.

"What happened today stays between us, but I aint gotta tell yall that right?" Foo asked while looking up at the homies.

They assured him that they were on the same page.

"What gun did you shoot em with?" Foo asked Ubie.

"His gun."

"Give it to me so I can have my uncle break it down and dispose it. It's on now yall," Foo said grinning ear to ear.

The other four youngsters started violently hugging each other as reality had set in, that they got away with robbing a bank.

"You know I wasn't gone shoot you right?" Ubie admitted to Juju.

"Yeah, I know nigga but like I said, don't do that shit again."

After they burned all the accessories that was used in the robbery, Foo sat back and analyzed his next move. He wanted his team to eat but since the older homies had the crack on lock, he knew it was time to bring a new kind of clientele to the projects. That's when he thought about his cousin Chris who was full blood Jamaican and lived in New York. Chris sold every kind of exotic weed you could think of. The kind of weed that was rarely found in Cleveland. Since loud was the majorities choice, Foo planned to bring an exotic strand to the city. Foo had a plan to introduce something new to the game.

Old school night at the Affinity was doing what it does regularly on Wednesday nights. A couple of bouncers governed the behemoth line of partiers, anxious to pay to get inside. Juvis was glad he didn't have to participate in such misery. He walked directly up to the bouncer, "I'm Juvis. I have an appointment with Gianni."

"Follow me," the bouncer replied on que and led Juvis to the V.I.P. section.

When Juvis entered he saw a few of Gianni's D.T.W. homies being entertained by some half naked stallions. Gianni was sitting on a leather made luv seat with his arm around a sexy woman that appeared familiar, but he never gave it much thought. Gianni stood up and held out his hand.

"Juvis, I've been waiting for you."

Juvis met his handshake.

"I hope I didn't hold you up," said Juvis.

"Not at all... Drinking tonight?" said Gianni.

"A simple Heineken will be cool."

"Come on, said Gianni as they walked to the other side of the room. He motioned for Juvis to have a seat on the couch while he retrieved two bottles of Heineken's from the ice box. After handing one to Juvis, he pulled up a chair whereas though he was sitting directly in front of Juvis.

"What brings a fella from your neck of the woods to my establishment," Gianni curiously asked before turning up his bottle.

"Listen. I know it may seem strange considering my hood and yours have no relations, but I'm looking to build a relationship with you."

"I'm listening," said Gianni.

"Well in order to have a relationship we have to trust one another," said Juvis.

"Before we even discuss trust, enlighten me," said Gianni.

"Somebody that's close to me wants you out the way, he's ready to move on you."

"Who?" Gianni blurted with a blank expression.

Juvis quickly turned up his bottle and lowered it back down to his thigh.

"J.d.'s aim is at you Gianni. He wanna control yo jets like he controls all the other ones."

Gianni turned his head and rested his eyes on Andrea who seemed to be patiently waiting for his return. He chuckled and turned up his bottle.

"Aight, so what's your reason for telling me this. That's supposed to be your guy, right?"

"Like I said man, I'm just trying to build a business relation with you that's why I came to you and told you all of this. On top of that, I also wanna make a proposition."

Gianni didn't respond but his stare penetrated Juvis soul.

"First of all, we don't' need a war to arise. That won't be good for either or our environment. Definitely don't need the law turning up on us," said Juvis.

"I agree," Gianni replied.

"I'll get rid of him for you, that's no problem, but after I'm done I'm hoping you and I can establish a business relation that's beneficial to the both of us."

"How much are you paying for a kilo?" Gianni inquired.

"J.d. sell them to me for twenty a piece for five or better. Four or less I pay twenty-five thousand."

"My price to you will be fifteen thousand a kilo, but the minimum you can purchase is five at a time."

"Now that's what I'm talking about," Juvis replied.

"So how long is it gone take you to put him under the earth?"

"Within forty-eight hours. Ya Facebook timeline gone be full of condolences. Facebook gone let you know."

"Well after you get him out the way then our business liaison will begin. If he's not dead by Sunday, I will take matters into my own hands. Not only will he be in my sights to kill.... You will be as well."

"Don't worry," Juvis assured and stood up."

Gianni followed suit.

"I'm not worried, just handle the business."

After Juvis left, Gianni sat back down next to Andrea and fired up his blunt. She sat with her arms folded over her chest looking passively into Gianni's face while he inhaled the good smoke. He was no longer a naked eye to her deceit but at the same time, it enticed him that she had that kind of courage to go on the front line for her nigga. He debated on killing her but realized wasn't no thrill in that. Andrea was a thrill to him and a challenge that he wanted to keep around for reasons of his own.

15

"Pull in the drive thru J-one so I can grab me some mild's and a swisher," said Anton.

Jarvis pulled in.

"You aint finna smoke that shit in here playboy!"

"Aight J-one damn! Imma see if Tracy wanna blow with me."

"What's her sister name again?"

"Roxanne, and she look good too dog so don't be acting all shy and shit."

Jarvis laughed at his remark.

"Boy, you know you be saying some of the silliest shit sometimes," said Jarvis. "Why would I act shy? The only thing a hoe can give me is a sexual healing nigga!"

Anton started laughing.

"Nigga yo ass don't know nothing about Marvin Gaye!"

"Shiiiit!" Jarvis blurted and started singing the chorus. Anton started laughing harder and Jarvis followed suit after hearing his broken vocals. After they bought a few items from the drive thru, Jarvis cut the music up.

Anton hadn't saw Tracy since the first time he met her which was almost a week ago, but they talked on the phone frequently. Tracy's parents were out of town so her and her eighteen-year-old sister had the house to themselves.

When Jarvis turned down their street, they noticed it was a lot of action going on. Typical block action such as loitering and drug dealing.

"Damn I didn't know this strip was hot like this," said Jarvis. As they waited for the traffic to move, Jarvis car was being scrutinized by the youngsters. While Anton was busy looking for Tracy's address, Jarvis locked eyes with a dude who saluted him, respecting the cars gangsta.

"Yea, there she go right there on the porch," Anton uttered. Jarvis pulled in front of her house.

"Nigga pull in the driveway before we have to kill a couple niggas today."

Tracy stood up as they pulled into the driveway. They got out and walked to her porch.

"Wassup Tracy," said Anton as he walked up and hugged her.

"Hey Anton," she replied in his arms.

"Tracy, this my guy J-one." They greeted and went inside her house. Jarvis immediately keyed in on Roxanne who was sitting on the couch face timing on her phone. Her golden-brown skin was perfectly tanned, and her hair was in a wrap like hairstyle. Although she was nice looking, it was something about her eyes that intrigued Jarvis the most. Even though she was sitting down he could tell she was curvy below the waist and estimated her to be about 5'7" 130 pounds.

"I didn't know yo street was a hot ass strip."

"When I told you I lived on Ohlman, I thought you knew," replied Tracy. Anyway, what difference does it make. Aint nobody gone mess with your friend's car if that's what you on."

"Trust me we aint worried about none of that," Anton countered.

"Tracy beckoned Anton with her finger, he followed her onto the sun porch.

Jarvis had a seat across from Roxanne.

"Aight girl Imma call you back later.... bye." After Roxanne hung up she spoke to Jarvis and got up from the couch.

"Got damn," Jarvis soliloquized.

"Aye so is you gone keep me company while I'm over here with my guy or what?"

"What's your name?"

"J-one."

"Yeah, I got you J-one, hold on for a minute," she told him and went out on the front porch.

Her ass was immensely fat and appeared to be suffocating in her dark denim destroyed Levi's. Jarvis admired the cut in her arms and the way the wife beater accentuated her figure.

Jarvis smelled a strong aroma of marijuana and went out on the porch.

"What's up my nigga she aint showing you no love or what?" Tracy was sitting next to him with a blunt in her fingertips.

"Her ass is probably out there looking for L.k's ass," said Tracy.

"Who is L.k?" asked Jarvis.

She passed the blunt back to Anton.

"Her friend but they don't go together. Talk to her, she'll talk back."

Jarvis went out on the porch and sat down on the stairs next to Roxanne, who appeared to be looking down the street for somebody.

"Who car is this in my driveway?"

"Why you ask that?"

"Because the color of it is sexy and I wanna know."

"Well it aint as sexy as you but that's my car."

"Yo car? And boy are you flirting with me?"

"You know it's disrespectful to call a man a boy right?"

"I'm sorry," she apologized. "So is this your car for real?"

"You gone just ask me that same question again huh? Yeah this my car girl."

"Well can you give me a ride to Mr. Hero's?"

"Yeah I can go for a roman burger myself. Yo treat?" He asked.

"I got you," she replied.

Jarvis didn't talk much while they rolled with the music loudly thumping. Roxanne put her fingers to her ears signifying the music was too loud, but Jarvis didn't pay her any attention. She reached over and grabbed the remote out of his hands and cut it down herself.

"Daanng....talk to a Sista."

Jarvis fell in a conversation with her that lasted until they made it to Mr. Hero's. Once the meals were ordered, Jarvis told her to put her money back in her pocket and pulled out a thick wad of bills. Roxanne was enticed to say the least. When they made it back, Anton and Tracy were nowhere to be found. Jarvis and Roxanne sat on the sun porch and ate their food.

Then out of the blue Jarvis said, "Yo, I'm feeling ya vibe where ya dude at?"

She sucked her straw.

"I don't have a dude, I just have friends."

"Well can I kick with you on a higher level?" asked Jarvis.

"What do you mean a higher level? You just met me," she chuckled while sipping her lemonade.

"Well give me a chance and let's see what tomorrow will bring."

Roxanne was feeling Jarvis no doubt.

"Aight well let's see what it do.

"Man, that girl got some good ass pussy J-one, bullshit aint nothing!"

"No shit, damn she look like it too," Jarvis admitted.

It was 9:45 pm and they had just left the girls house headed back to the hood. Some girls pulled up on them at the light and started looking in the car.

"What in the fuck is these ugly ass hoes lookin at," Jarvis said looking back at them.

Anton started laughing when Jarvis acted like he was cutting his throat.

When the light turned green, they noticed a police car coming their way.

"You see 'em?"

"Yeah, I see em," said Jarvis.

When they pulled into the Jets, a five-car lane of KKBG members were pulling out. Jarvis rolled his window down to talk to M-2 who pulled up in his two-toned gray 81 Bonneville.

"Where yall finna-----------"M-2 cut him off.

"Aye dawg follow us down here on 30th, the KKS hoes down there fighting!

Jarvis made a boomerang turn and fell in line as they quickly made their way down to the 30th projects.

16

"BEAT DAT BITCH ASS KIKI!" Foo Yelled.

Kiki a (30th chick) and Gina (KKS chick) were in the park across the street from the projects fighting like cats and dogs. Wouldn't none of the Yg members let any of the KKS girls break it up and Gina was losing the fight by a margin.

"Yall hoes get back! Yall bet not touch em. That's what the fuck yall get for coming down here on some bullshit," Juju shouted.

Kiki had now managed to climb on top of Gina and was pounding her out. Ubie came running through the cut with a bat in his hand, but when he saw Kiki handling her business, he instigated her to pound harder.

"FUCK DIS SHIT BITCH GET OFF MY GIRL!" Deedra yelled and rushed Kiki landing some tough blows on the side of her head.

At that moment, all the KKS girls rushed the 30th girls and it was a fist fighting war zone. Ubie handed Karmen the bat and she swung and hit Beatrice on her back side. The KKBG members began pulling up and hopping out of their cars.

"HOLD ON HOLD ON HOLD ON! Jarvis yelled as he rushed the girl swinging the bat while aiming his gun at her face.

"Bitch drop the motherfucking bat!"

She did, and Beatrice picked it up and started attacking her with it. The Yg members backed up because the majority of the KKBG's hopped out aiming guns and within the blink of an eye, the KKS girls was kicking ass. Foo was laughing the entire time.

"Get in the car and hurry da fuck up before the police come," Damon yelled to his girl Shonte.

They had to forcefully put the KKS girls in their cars. Foo was staring at Jarvis as he was climbing in his car to pull off. Foo opened his arms and yelled, "So what is this gone turn into?"

"Whatever you want it to turn into nigga, I aint ducking nothing," barked Jarvis as he pulled away from the curb.

※※※※※※※※※※※※※※※※※※※※

After letting the money sit for almost a week, the elite team had finally counted it all and split it up in five ways. Totaling $126,780, each member received approximately $25,000 apiece. Foo's cousin Chris will be in Cleveland in a few days and they would talk business then. The Elite team was planning on purchasing a plentiful amount of exotic weed so that everybody in the Yg click can get money.

Now after what happened tonight, Foo knew he had to buy a lot of guns. The guns they used for the bank robbery were borrowed and neither Yg member had a gun of their own. Well, that was about to change because Foo was refusing to ever get caught strapless again.

All the KKBG members and KKS girls were packed inside Angelica's apartment hyper, especially the girls. Angelica didn't know they had went down there because she was busy running the weed business as usual, so she was in shock!

As Jarvis was looking at everybody in the room (Which was damn near 30 people) he saw a vision that he wanted to form into a reality.

"Aye yall AYE!!!! AYE yall hear me out for a minute!" He waited for all the noise to settle. Once things settled, he continued.

"After what happened tonight this is how I'm suggesting it be. And the reason why I'm suggesting this is because......If we gone put our necks on the line for yall hoes, then yall gotta be ours, and all the way ours. The shit yall beefing with them 30th hoes about, shouldn't even be a beef, because if you was ours then you would've never been fucking another nigga from another projects in the first motherfucking place."

Freeda felt qualm by his words because she knew this mess was behind a sexual relation she had with Foo.

"Now look, I'm not saying that every KKS girl should grab a homie to be their man but every KKS should become an assistant to a homie starting tonight."

"What do you mean by assistant?" asked Dasha.

"Everybody in this click stacking bread right?" asked Jarvis while scanning his eyes around the room at his homies. A bunch of yeah's and hell yeah's answered his question.

"Well don't yall think it would be easier if everybody had a partner that is willing to stand out there and run a dope spot with yall? Shit hold the work and the hammer when necessary and be the eyes that's always watching ya back!! That's gangsta and what a gangsta need."

Everyone became aroused by his idea.

"Hold on now hear me out," said Jarvis as he chimed into the instant chatter. "You gotta take care of ya partner and hold her down for better or for worse. She shouldn't have to need or want for anything, she's your responsibility just like you are hers. Now if we can operate this thing like that then we will all be ghetto tied and sticking together as a family."

Silence followed Jarvis words. Then Lil Bit walked over and sat on M-2's lap and stated, "Imma hold you down baby."

Before you knew it, every KKBG member had them a partner including Jarvis who now had Angelica sitting on his lap. There were now 13 couples. 26 people in all who were two-man teams. Only two KKBG members were shy of a partner because it wasn't enough KKS girls and that was Wanisha and Rio. Wanisha (who was the only KKBG female) didn't want no partner no way, and Rio was cool with being solo. They told the girls to leave that beef shit alone and focus on the money to be made, and they agreed. But Jarvis knew that Foo was going to be a problem, possibly his problem.

17

J.d. pulled up in the KKBG side of the projects and drove up to the circle of youngsters.

"J-one, what it do shorty! Holla at me!"

Jarvis quickly climbed off the Dayton bike and hopped in the LX Lexus land Cruiser. J.d. circled around and pulled out of the jets.

"What's good young homie I'm seeing the progress."

"Ah I'm just doing what it takes to get this side of the projects on a level close to yall."

"Well everything comes with time but take ya time so you can be out here to make that happen," J.d. advised." "Now listen, I heard about them crazy ass hoes going down there fighting a few nights ago and how you and ya patnas came through like yall was their shining armors or some'em."

"Look, I know what you finna say J.d. but I saw a vision within that move and brought it to reality," said Jarvis. "And I believe that move will prove to be beneficial down the line."

"I recognize the order of ya organization you have set into motion. As long as you keep that leadership, then they will follow you to your grave, and wouldn't have a problem with going to theirs for you."

Byron, a KKK member rolled up on the truck at the light and exchanged words with him until the light changed green, before giving his attention back to Jarvis.

"Listen lil homie, I came to yo side to holla at you tonight for a reason.... I'm not asking you nothing, just listen."

J.d. cleared his throat.

"Ya man's cousin Ada got her house ran up in, and Juvis from my side of the jets is on a prowl. Never leak ya business to the streets J-one and you make sho you establish that with ya patnas.

J.d. knew without searching for the truth who robbed Juvis. Jarvis eyes told it all, but he didn't care about Juvis getting robbed, he was simply advising Jarvis to be smart about it.

"Don't look like that, you aint done nothing wrong, just be smart ya hear me," J.d. warned. He observed the skittish body language. "In this game, you can't afford to slip and fall because you may not get back up."

When J.d dropped Jarvis back off, he pulled off in admiration of his protégé for having such strong ambition. He praised himself for having the acumen to see what was inside the boy from day one.

"Got damn the boy is a genius," J.d thought silently to himself. He looked at his watch it read, 10:35 pm. His thoughts drifted back to Andrea, wondering where she's been for the last couple of days.

Ever since Gianni had his people pick her up Wednesday night she hadn't returned home. It bothered J.d because obviously she hasn't been able to make a way to call him which caused a precarious feeling to invade his chest.

"What happen Drea......shit!! Been damn near 48 hours. This shit doesn't add up," J.d. thought as he headed to the Maple Tree with a lot on his mind.

The Maple tree was a famous strip club in the city. Every other Friday was exotic night where beautiful dancers, danced, freaked and tricked inside the spot. Only certified ballers had VIP's to enter exotic night because it was strictly for the chosen.

J.d. did his regular at the Maple Tree. First, he ordered a batch of barbeque hot wings and posted up on a lounge seat in a darkened corner. As he ate, he observed some nude women shaking and twerking on by. After he bashed the wings, he washed them down with a Corona, sat back and burped. As always, he started looking for the one who appeared to have extraordinary head game. A brick thick chocolate chick walked by his table sucking on a lollipop seductively.

"Wassup shorty!! Come over and show ya boy what it do," said J.d.

She stopped and J.d. patted the lounge seat beside him. Five minutes later, and for the next twenty minutes that followed, she was bent low giving J.d. a good and sloppy fifty-dollar head job.

Juvis was in a darkened corner on the opposite end of the room, closely watching J.d. as the girl worked on him. By it being only a dim light in the club he only saw a shadowy figure. He called one of his hoes on his cell phone to kill time. When the girl left, Juvis ended the call, anticipating J.d.'s next move. A half an hour after that, J.d. stood up, stretched, and walked from around the table. After conversing with a few people, his body language told Juvis that he was about to leave. Juvis quickly made the awaited call. The voice answered on the first ring.

"He's on his way out," said Juvis and both lines went dead.

"So this is what it comes down to," Juvis uttered. He leaned back in his seat and smiled at the idea of a new tomorrow.

On J.d. way out the door he stopped and hollered at Joe, the door man. They went back and forth for a couple of minutes before J.d. finally stepped out into the fresh air. He naturally scanned the scenery as he headed towards the parking lot.

Andrea jumped in his mind and he hoped she was alright. At that moment, he concluded, if she didn't call by tomorrow, verifying she was safe then he promised himself that Gianni would be dead within a week. Before he turned into the parking lot he crossed paths with a guy who was wearing dark sunglasses and a baseball cap pressed down tightly on his head. At first J.d. didn't think nothing of it, then suddenly he had an uncanny feeling about the stranger because he seemed out of place. Before J.d. could react off his feelings, the stranger whirled around and let off two booming shots from a 357-snub nose into the back of J.d.'s head. The pedestrians on the sidewalk ran, tucked, and took cover as a car made a screeching stop in front of the scene. Snatch-out fired off two more shots into J.d.'s lifeless body, then ran and hopped in the car as it sped away.

While Jarvis and his homies were out working, Angelica and Dale (Another KKS girl) pulled up and got out of the car teary faced. They delivered the news about J.d.'s death. Jarvis world came to a standstill as he stared blankly in Angelica's eyes.

"What......Who.... Where?" Jarvis inquired.

"Don't nobody know who did it, but it happened at the Mapletree," said Angelica.

Everyone out there knew how much J.d. meant to Jarvis, and they couldn't relate to the pain of loss that had just invaded his heart.

"So it may just be a rumor. Maybe he's not dead. As a matter of fact, let me call him." He whipped out his phone and nervously dialed J.d.'s number. It went to voicemail. Angelica wrapped her arms around him.

"Jarvis....... he gone."

Jarvis pulled away and exploded into an angry wrath. Consolation at the moment was impossible. He jumped in his car and violently pulled out of the jets.

Jarvis drove to the park around the corner from his house. At 12:52 am, the park was pitch black. He got out and made his way to a bench, where he grieved heavily. His cell phone started ringing. At first, he had no desire to answer it, until he shuddered with hope that it was somebody calling to tell him that the information was false. It was Omirah.

"What's wrong baby?"

He tried to gather himself between sniffles.

"Somebody just killed my man J.d."

Omirah was taken aback.

"Oh, baby I'm so sorry. Where are you?" she asked sounding very much concerned for him.

"I'm around the corner at the park."

"Don't go anywhere Jarvis I'm on my way."

Without waiting on a reply, she hung up.

Ten minutes later she was walking through pitch blackness up to Jarvis. He was in a trance like state when she sat next to him

"Jarvis are you okay! Please talk to me."

He turned and looked her in the face and realized that he needed her at that moment.

"O... Omirah, this shit really hurt," he confessed as she wrapped her arms around him holding him tight. She was shedding silent tears from seeing Jarvis so distraught. After a while in her embrace, he broke away and stood up. She remained seated while he hovered over her.

"Omirah, you just don't know the things that nigga has done for me! He looked out for me when I aint have nobody. When I aint have nothing he gave me the world. He showed me who I was before I even knew...... And just like that Meme, he aint even here no more."

He caught his breath, letting his tears run freely. Omirah chose to remain quiet because she could tell he wasn't through.

"I swear Meme, imma make him proud from the sky. Imma become that nigga he pushed me to become. I aint gone let him down I swear!"

"What about me Jarvis? Are you going to let me down? I don't want you making this way of living into a career. It's only two ways out of this baby."

"Omirah it's a lot of things we don't like but have to accept. You accept me for who I am right?" He asked wiping the tears off his face.

She sincerely nodded her head yes.

"Because Meme that's the only person I can be."

18

The unfortunate demise of J.d. shook the streets, and the KKK members were conducting their own investigation. Since J.d. was the only one with the Miami connection, the areas that his dope controlled was in a disarray to say the least. But J-Roc, (J.d.'s right hand man) had a second-string connection, and his goal was to take over all his trap spots and get things back in order. What he didn't realize is that J.d's death had given birth to a new era.

Jarvis couldn't stand to look down upon J.d.'s lifeless body in a casket so he sat in his car, repeatedly listening to Tupac's song 'Tear drops and closed caskets'. He took swigs from the Hennessy bottle as the lyrics touched his soul. When everybody exited the funeral to make their way to the grave site, Angelica, Anton, and Damon walked up to his car. They could tell he was wasted.

"Damn homie, you want me to give my keys to one of the homies and drive you to the grave site?" asked Damon.

"Naw I got him," Angelica insisted. She gave her keys to Tasia. "Girl drive my car. I gotta take care of my nigga." Jarvis reluctantly slid over allowing her to take over the wheel. Lil Tae, and Marlo climbed in the back.

"We'll meet up with yall at the site," Anton uttered as they retreated to their cars.

Right before she put the gear in reverse, Jarvis tapped her thigh, held up his index finger, opened the door and called a two-minute earl. While he was throwing up Angelica took the bottle and closed it up. When he sounded like he was through, Lil Tae passed him some spring water.

"Here J-one gargle this."

"Rest in peace J.d.," Jarvis mumbled as he laid his head back against the seat.

Jarvis, Angelica, and the two homies with them, were the last ones standing at the grave site, along with a few relatives. The older woman who Jarvis figured was J.d.'s mother kept her head down as she painfully turned away to leave. An attractive younger woman was holding the hand of a little boy who looked like a spitting image of J.d, followed J.d.'s mother. This woman gave them a respectful yet weak smile as she passed them. Now they were the only ones left among the dead.

After a long silence, Jarvis turned to Angelica and said,

"You're my partner, right?"

"Of course," Angelica assured.

"What's gone happen when you get you a nigga?"

"I don't need no nigga as long as I got you for my partner.......besides, I'd rather get money."

"Do you need me to be ya partner in more ways than one cause if so, I can hold you down like that too. Reason I'm saying this is, I don't want you to get sidetracked by nothing outside of what we have going on. You feel what I'm saying?"

"I definitely feel you, we'll consider this a thug love."

Andrea didn't have any idea where she was at and didn't really care. It's been this way for ten days now, but she would continuously cry herself to sleep unable to cope with the knowledge of J. d's death. She was being held at Gianni's country house on the outskirts of Cleveland, where there weren't any neighbors close by, only acres of land. Gianni had the house under twenty-four-hour security and the farthest she could go was to the bathroom and she had to knock on the door from the inside of the bedroom just to go there because it was dead bolt locked. Gianni's men watched her around the clock and a female maid servant served her three-square meals a day, that she picked through. After being there without Gianni for the first two days, she was confused as to what was going on. Then on the third day (the day after J.d. was killed) the unbolting of the door aroused her out of her sleep and Gianni entered with a newspaper tucked between his arm and a cup of coffee.

She propped herself up on her elbow, giving him a fake, wanting smile as if she was happy to see him. He sat on the bed next to her.

"Where have you been and why have I been here without you?"

He didn't answer her as he sipped from his mug. She stared at the back of his head, trying to read his silence. He opened the newspaper and handed it to her. He heard her gasp and turned back to face her." She was shaking uncontrollably in a state of shock.

"You killed him," she said blankly. Her eyes met his and suddenly anger engulfed her. She lunged at him violently, but he caught her by the wrist.

"YOU BASTARD IMMA FUCKIN KILL.........."

He pinned her to the mattress as a couple of his men came rushing through the door with their guns drawn.

"It's cool it's cool, lock the door back," said Gianni. They complied leaving him to tussle with Andrea.

"You want me dead bitch? HUH!" He sneered while managing to get her silk, Gucci brand gown up over her waist. She vigorously jerked, cursed, and cried. He yanked her panties off.

"YOU KILLED MY MAN YOU BITCH ASS NIGGA. IMMA KILL YOU!"

He slapped her viciously. She didn't even feel it as she continued to make threats. Gianni unzipped his fly and his largely erected penis busted through looking for its prey. She tried to bite his hands to free her wrist and this time he punched her in the jaw, causing stars and circles to appear before her eyes. She was dizzy and unable to stop the forced entry. He rammed his dick into her dry tunnel and she gnashed out at him, still pinned to the bed. His vicious strokes made her submit under his power, but if the look in her eyes could kill, he would be a dead motherfucker. Gianni never felt this kind of thrill before. The thrill to make a woman's' hatred for him turn into love. To Gianni that was a challenge that was well worth it.

❋❋❋❋❋❋❋❋❋❋❋❋❋❋❋❋❋❋❋❋

The Affinity was high in action the night of J.d.'s funeral. The same bouncer as before immediately recognized Juvis as he passed everybody up to get to the front entrance.

"I'm Juvis and here to," -------------- the bouncer cut him off.

"I know who you are. Hold tight."

The bouncer pulled out his phone and called up to his boss.

"You have a visitor....... Okay, will do."

He quickly patted Juvis down.

"You can go on up," said the bouncer.

As he passed through the crowd he was forced to stop a few times to acknowledge condolences being displayed for his supposedly friend J.d. While he was walking up the swirling stairs, the D.J. announced into the microphone," Let's take a moment in silence to honor a fallen soldier. A special fallen soldier. Let's give J.d. a moment in silence. Salute J.d. R.I.P."

"Damn!" Juvis thought to himself, "I did enough acting at the funeral and now this shit."

His ascension up the stairs came to a halt as he pretended to salute J.d., disrespecting him even further.

"You will always be remembered J.d. Rest in peace." The D.J spoke and broke the silence with a Tupac classic, 'How Long will they mourn me.'

When Juvis entered, only a few people were in the room. Gianni was sitting on the same couch as before with another beautiful chic under his wing. This time he didn't stand up to acknowledge Juvis, he just open handedly pointed to the couch across from him. After Juvis was seated, Gianni took his arm from around the girl and scooted up to the edge of the couch.

"Juvis....Juvis......Juvis... talk to me Juvis!" Juvis didn't like the vibe he was receiving from the few DTW members who was posted up watching him, but he wrote it off as them being some straight fuck boys.

"A sad day for some, and a beautiful day for others, but now that the opposing situation is dead, I'm ready to move forward," said Juvis.

Gianni got up from the couch and walked over to the glass windows staring down at the club action and giving Juvis his back to look at.

"Can I trust you Juvis?" Gianni asked while never taking his eyes off the dance floor.

"Time will show you that you can because my actions will prove it to you time and time again," Juvis replied sullenly. Gianni turned to face him.

"Did J.d. trust you?" Gianni's question startled him, leaving him in search for the right answer. Juvis knew that the whole city of underground hustlers believed him and J.d. to be ace boon coons.

"Well did he?" Gianni reiterated.

"I can't answer a question that only a dead man has the answer to."

"Well answer this, how can I trust a snake who had the heart to snake his own man."

"That nigga didn't love nothing, that wasn't my nigga for real. Damn Gianni Wassup man?" Juvis voice pleaded. "I enlightened you of the situation and handled it for you and you call me a snake!"

"If I can't trust you ten years down the line, it aint no use in me trusting you now. You can let yourself out," Gianni said firmly and turned back to the dance floor.

Juvis sheepishly looked at the broad on the couch then to his boys who stood with their arms folded, adamantly grilling him.

"Imma fade this bitch ass nigga, he got me fucked up!" Juvis voiced in his mind as he stood up.

"I can't change the way you feel Gianni but it aint no hard feelings. The nigga tried to get at you and I faded him for you, everything else is water under the bridge," said Juvis as he made his way to the door. Once he closed the door behind him, Gianni nodded his head at a pair of eyes that was watching from the dance floor....

Juvis left the club in his feelings.

"I know this faggot ass nigga don't think Imma let this shit ride!" Juvis hissed making his way to the parking lot. He kept a keen eye on his surroundings, figuring Gianni had to have an after-effect plan to his disrespect. Once inside his BMW, he anxiously opened his ashtray and grabbed the half of black and mild cigar and blazed it. Then reached underneath his seat and grabbed his ten-millimeter placing it on his lap. He sat the mild between his lips, started up the car and sharply pulled out of the parking lot.

"Fuck!" Juvis blurted, recognizing a Dodge Charger following him.

"Why in the fuck is these pigs fuckin with me?" He asked himself. A split second later, a small single-handed siren was flashing from the roof. Juvis didn't obey, he had to separate the gun and clip before he could pull over. He turned down a narrow one-way street to buy him enough time to transfer the weapon to the glove department. By this time, the unmarked Charger was on his bumper. Finally, Juvis pulled over and looked in the rearview mirror.

"Is there a problem officer sir?" Juvis asked through the cracked window.

"Can you hand over your license and registration please." Juvis complied. After the officer perused over his info he stated, "The reason why I pulled you over is because you have a warrant in Euclid Ohio."
"Hell naw that can't be true sir. I know I don't have any warrants."

"I'm only doing my job so can you please step out of the car."

"Fuck it, I aint dirty and have a license to carry a gun so this shit aint about nothin," he thought to himself.

"Put your hands on the hood," the officer ordered.

After giving Juvis a quick frisk down, he slapped the cuffs on his wrist and walked him to the car. Juvis was ranting about it being a mistake in the computer.

"Well if the computer is wrong then everything should get cleared."

After he put Juvis in the backseat, he climbed in the driver seat and pulled off.

"Wait a minute dawg, so you just gone leave my car like that?" Juvis blurted out. "Man, what the fuck is going on?"

The officer didn't reply or look back, that's when Juvis realized that he was caught up in a trick bag. His heart started racing and his eyes went straight to the door handle, there wasn't any.

"Relax, relax," said the so-called officer. "If there's a mistake then we will take care of it." An evil burst of laughter followed.

19

This so-called officer was really Perry Shaw, a retired narcotic detective, who's been on Gianni's payroll for a little over four years now and still had strong inside connections. Not to mention he also had a nephew who was an active detective, that kept him updated on sting operations, raids, giving him the heads up to certain information that was useful to Gianni.

After a long drive, Perry turned off a dark road, onto a small passage way surrounded by endless woods. He pulled to the end of the passage and cut the car off. He knew he had to move quick. Without wasting another second, he got out, opened Juvis door, and forcefully yanked him out. Juvis wasn't about to beg or make a plea for his life. He felt like since he was born a gangsta, it was only right that he died one. He thought about the ones that he put under the dirt, and now as he observed his final moments of life, he was finally convinced that what goes around was guaranteed to come back, as he witnessed his actions hunt him down. Faced down in the woods, eyes shut tight, he awaited the death blow that he knew would surely come. Suddenly he yearned for Ada, for love, to live, but life was no longer an option. Death was prepared to swallow his existence.........

****

The elite Yg members had put up ten thousand dollars apiece towards their new investment. Fifty thousand dollars was spent with Foo's cousin Chris, for 25 pounds of purple Haze marijuana, which was smuggled from New York to Cleveland by one of Chris female smugglers. A week prior to the transaction, Chris had come down to discuss business with Foo. He told Foo that the perfect weed of choice would be purple haze since the niggas in Cleveland were foreign to it.

"Since I'm selling you pounds of this bomba at $2000 you set your original price at $3,500. Your half pounds at $2000 and quarter pounds at $1000. Now you say you wanna get rich bombaclot boi," said Chris in his thick Jamaican accent. With a connect like me you should have no problem getting there."

Each Elite member (Foo, Levar, Ubie, Juju, and Mouse) all received five pounds apiece for their ten stacks. Before they gave front packages to their 15 other crew members, the Elite team set the trend. They were selling grams for 30 dollars at the huge park across the street from the projects. Within a months' time the YG members was known as the purple haze boys and the park was on fire.

People from all over the city was pulling up day and night and all throughout wee hours of the morning, looking for the special plant. The elite team soon fell back and fronted each member a quarter pound a piece. That was enough to put each member on their feet.

Before they fronted out the packages, they gathered all the Yg members up in the park which was now a gold mine. After running everything down to them, Foo said, "Now the trend is set and the way is paved. This is a gold mine strictly for Yg. Now today I'm fronting three niggas each a quarter pound. Lavar fronting 3 and Mouse, Juju and Ubie is doing the same thing. Whoever front you today, that's who you're assigned to cop from. That's ya re-up man. Each one of yall got a strap comin with yall package. That's why it's a thousand back off the quarter pound instead of eight hundred but yall still gone profit tremendously. Just keep yall hustle alive and we gone eat until we get full. FLAT OUT!"

The youngsters got emotionally excited. Even their girlfriends from the projects who were out there felt a special kind of way and were anxious to shine in their man's glory.

✽✽✽✽✽✽✽✽✽✽✽✽✽✽✽✽✽✽✽✽

It was around two in the afternoon, KKBG side of the jets was littered with drug transactions while some of the KKS girls was posted up on the police watch. Since everybody was starting to go down to the 30th projects to get their weed, Jarvis closed shop on his weed house that Angelica was running. Now he had her riding around delivering off phone sales, while he hustled in the Jets. If she wasn't delivering she was posted up with him. Now they been fucking almost every night and seemed like the perfect Bonnie and Clyde.

"Why he always driving crazy like he got his license or something," Angelica inquired.

Anton was sharply parking his freshly painted candy apple green cutlass.

"Shit that boy is crazy," Jarvis shrugged.

Anton hopped out and asked the homies where he was at. Jarvis gave a whistle and Anton beckoned him over to the car. At that moment Angelica phone vibrated. It was a sale for a c-note.

"I'll be back daddy. Ole crack head Dave just sent me a text message."

"It's on," Jarvis replied and walked over to Anton. As he was walking he was noticing how many of his homies cars were inked up, sitting on shiny rims all old schools. He felt good to see everybody doing good.

What's crackin."

"Yo hoe in the backseat nigga she wanted me to bring her over here so she could see you."

"Oh yeah."

When Jarvis looked through the back window, she was bending her index finger up and down at him. Jarvis made his way to the car. Roxanne got out.

"Wassup stranger," she greeted him with a warm smile.

"What's been up with you?"

The look of her butt in those tight fitted blue jeans was breathtaking, and the glittery gold braw like top revealed her smooth golden-brown skin with perfection. Her hair was different from before, today it was naturally hanging down to her shoulders.

"Shit.... just paper chasin.... What's a pretty face like yours doing down here in these jets?"

"Don't let this face fool you boo, I'm from the hood too you know. Anyway, I came to see you. It's been a few weeks now and I was wondering why I haven't heard from you."

The spark in Jarvis eyes turned dull.

"My big homie got killed a couple days after we met so I guess I've been out of touch lately."

"Damn I'm sorry to hear this......Is that him?" She was referring to the shirt Jarvis was wearing. It was a R.I.P picture of J.d.

"Yeah it's him," he replied as they went back and forth. Deedra (Who now had her own car that Anton bought her) pulled into the huge parking lot and parked. Her, Freeda, Dale, and Shonte went to get something to eat at Hot Sauce Williams barbeque spot for themselves and their partners. Deedra noticed a female in Anton's car, but she kept her composure as they got out with orders of food in their hands.

Ever since Anton been getting money, he been treating Deedra like shit, and the disrespect he displayed in her presence was noticeable. He would acknowledge another girls' beauty in her face, but behind closed doors he took care of her like she meant the world to him. Truthfully, he envied Jarvis and Angelica's gangsta relationship and wanted theirs to be the same way, but Deedra was his woman before the money started rolling in, so he felt obligated to keep her in the number one position. Only stipulation was that she had to accept what came with it..............

"What's up boo! Who is that in your car?" she asked while handing him his food.

"Just somebody I got working for me over her way."

Her look turned into a grimacing stare.

"I'll appreciate it if you keep her over there and not bring her over here again."

"I would appreciate it if you let me do me the way I do me. I aint disrespecting you so fall back. And what did I tell you about all that jealous shit!"

"Anton, you know what- WHATEVER! Just keep ya little bitches from over here that's all I got to say." She walked off and went inside Freeda's place.

"Roxanne what's up for the night then, let's get a room and kick back," said Jarvis.

"You wanna get a room but you aint even gave me a hug yet. Boy stop playing," she countered and adamantly folded her arms over her chest. The way she looked him up and down turned him on.

"Damn Roxanne don't do me like that." He wrapped his arms around her body bear hug style. She wrapped hers around his waist.

"Is tonight a night for us or what?" He asked with her still in his arm.

"Yessss... Just call me when you're on your way."

A few hours later, Jarvis, Damon, M-2, and Wanisha was riding around in Damon's wet canary yellow 4 door cutlass. The power hole was wide open, and the shiny rims sparkled from the reflection of the sun. Wanisha, who had just turned eighteen a few days ago was in the passenger seat, swaying sexily in cadence to Ray Jr's song, 'Nozebleedz.'

Damon's trunk was loudly thumping, and Jarvis had his elbow bent poking out the back window as they cruised pass the Yg boys park. There were so many people in the park copping weed it was ridiculous and were pulling up by the seconds.

Jarvis and Foo locked eyes and stared at each other. Ubie opened his arms wide looking for trouble. Damon and Wanisha both spontaneously stuck their arms out of the power hole, throwing up the 'K'. "What's up with them fools they act like they wanna beef with us or something," said Wanisha who's a five-foot five petite redbone and cute as all hell.

"Yeah homie what's up with that hoe ass nigga Ubie?" M-2 reiterated.

"Fuck them niggas, Damon shoot over Meme house right quick."

Damon pulled into Meme's driveway with his music beating vigorously. Yasha came on the porch as Jarvis was climbing out the car. Damon cut his music down.

"What's up Yasha where's Meme?"

"She's upstairs."

Jarvis got out the car and went into the house. She was lying on her back. One leg bent, and one leg stretched out with her head cocked to the side. To Jarvis she looked beautiful as he stared down on her. He gently climbed on top of her and her eyes blankly opened. Once reality registered to her she weakly smiled.

"How long you been here?"

"Not too long," he said while planting soft kisses on her freshly scented neck. His lips met hers and they instantly locked tongues.

"Did you lock the door?" She quietly whispered.

He nodded.

"Hold on boo, said Meme as she reached over and turned on Drake's song, 'Teenage Fever.'

"Aye, that's what I'm talking about baby, that's my shit," smiled Jarvis before kissing her slowly on her thighs.

After they kissed and made love to each other in cadence with a rhythm that moved to the beat of the song playing, she took him upstairs to the bathroom to freshen up.

They went downstairs and found Damon and Yasha in the living room talking.

"Look at her trying to be a player," said Omirah.

"Yeah yo ass better not be carrying that same trait," said Jarvis.

"I'm good honey, I'm a one-man type of woman," laughed Omirah. "Besides, I love you J-one and when you love someone you don't cheat or play mind games. I just hope you feel the same way."

Before Jarvis could answer, Wanisha popped up from the driver's seat.

"Heyy Omirah girl. Why you don't come around?"

"Hi Wanisha! Girl because Jarvis don't want me over there."

Jarvis wrapped his arms around her from the back side.

"Aint nothin over there for her. Every female aint thugged out like you Wanisha."

"Jarvis gone head on with all that and give my girl some freedom to kick it sometimes. Hell she aint 75 years old," said Wanisha while grabbing the blunt from M-2 fingers.

"Well Wanisha any time after three you can always come over here."

"Okay then girl that's a bet," said Wanisha and stuck her tongue out at Jarvis before she ducked back inside the car. Jarvis mother came out on the porch.

"Come here Jarvis," she yelled.

"Boo bring one of my straps down and two ounces."

"Does it matter which gun?" She asked.

"The foe five," he said and made his way across the street.

Jarvis and his mother got into an argument inside the house because he told her that he didn't have anything on him. She started cursing at him demanding him to give her something or move out.

"Ma! What do you mean If I don't wanna give I gotta go? I take care of all these bills. If it wasn't for me, we wouldn't even have a place to stay!"

"Well you heard what I said Jarvis Lance Cooper. Since you wanna be grown before your time, go ahead on and stay out there." Then you can see how it really feels to be grown!" Jarvis walked out the house while she was still yelling.

"Have something for me when you come back in the house and I mean it!"

Damon, Yasha, and Meme were on the porch when he walked up. He knew they heard everything but truthfully, he didn't even give a fuck anymore. Omirah stood up.

"You ready to bounce homie?" Damon asked.

M-two and Wanisha was in their own world listening to the music.

"Yeah here I come," he replied as he followed Omirah in the house.

****

Later on that night he took Roxanne to a hotel and they fucked good. They didn't get to know each other better until after they had sex. Jarvis liked Roxanne a lot. He didn't have intentions on brushing her off, but he knew that he should've been told her that he had a main chic and let their relationship go from there, but for some reason, he kept that a secret from her.

While he drove, she fingered through his blue ray disc.

"Let's watch this." She put in the movie 'Shottas'.

"Are you tryanna tell me you got some gangsta in you?" asked Jarvis.

"That would be a no, but yes I do like it gangsta though."

"Well that's the only way you gone get it from me," smiled Jarvis.

"Why did you tell me not to worry about your age when I asked you how old you are?"

"Because, age don't make a difference. Unless you think it do."

"It doesn't make a difference, but I'd still like to know."

"I'm fifteen. Matter of fact I just turned fifteen."

She stared at the side of his face. She didn't believe that for a second because his character didn't reveal immaturity. His puppy dog eyes revealed a sadness that made him look years ahead of his time. Then his thugged out lifestyle made her doubt his age.

"Whatever J-one." She concluded he was playing about his age and left it alone. She quietly watched the movie while he navigated though traffic.

While they were at a light, a Poppa smurph blue 76 Fleetwood Cadillac curtly stopped on the side of his car immediately catching Jarvis attention. He saw who it was and quickly freed the forty-five auto from his waist and lowered it to the side of his leg. Her eyes went from the gun to his face. Ubie the driver was mean mugging Jarvis. Foo who was in the passenger was bent forward giving Jarvis a cold stare as well. Jarvis looked over at Roxanne and told her not to panic.

"Baby it's cool. These niggas faking," said Jarvis while rolling down his window.

"What's 'up!"

"Nigga that's what we tryanna find out!" Ubie barked.

"You don't know me dawg, and I don't know you, so let's leave it as that!"

"Nigga fuck you. You stepped in my world when you and ya fake ass homies hopped out pointing guns captain saving them dumb ass hoes!" Foo sneered.

"Yeah aight," Jarvis retorted and pulled away at the change of the light.

****

School had started back for the youngn's around the city. Needless to say, it was tension in the air between the 30th Yg boys and the KKBG homies. KKS girls were following orders and leaving their beef alone, but the 30th chicks were constantly provoking the beef.

After the first week went by, Jarvis pulled Foo over in the hallway. At first Foo looked at him like he was crazy for even trying to talk to him, but Jarvis ignored that and went straight to the point.

"Look homie! We acknowledge what yall got going on in yall neck of the woods and we got a lot going on in ours. It aint no room for unnecessary beef and me personally I would rather get money. So, since it aint nothing big dawg, let's dead this shit."

Foo nodded his head and said, "It's on."

"Big dawg tell ya girls that our girls aint on that beef shit," said Jarvis.

Foo nodded his head in agreement and Jarvis walked away.

20

When Juvis murder was confirmed to the hood a little over a week ago, The King Kennedy hood went into a mournful state. Ada took it bad to say the least. She hated that he passed away while they were on bad terms and wished she could somehow rewind the hands of time. All she wanted to do was tell him how much she loved him, something that she didn't get the chance to tell him at the end of his life. He didn't have a funeral. His mother followed his wishes to have him cremated, and his name was spray painted amongst all the other RIP's on the brick walls of the King Kennedy Projects.

By the middle of the school year, the parking lot, during school hours looked like and old school car show. Cars were gleaming, and rims were blinging and the owner of those vehicles were either a Yg youngster or a KKBG homie. But homies from both clicks were dropping out of school like it was the right thing to do. Their only desire in life at this time was to give the streets a full-time obligation.

It was Omirah's lunch period and she was seated at a table by herself eating a slice of pizza with a HI-C drink. Thoughts of Jarvis was running through her mind. He hadn't been coming to school much lately. He would drop her off in the morning and pick her up after school. She'd been trying to install it in his mind to finish the two years he had left but it was hard to tell an adolescent anything, who had close to one hundred thousand dollars of his own money. She was worried that someone in her house may stumble across his stash, so after bringing her concern to his attention, three days later he removed everything from her house. Some nights he wouldn't come home, but even if he didn't, he still managed to pick her up for school the next morning. She smiled to herself at the thought of successfully learning how to drive thanks to Jarvis. For an entire week, he took her through a beginner's drivers course, not caring if she wrecked his beautiful Malibu. To his surprise she didn't. She thought about the times they had sex at the drive-in, in the backseat of his car. Those memories caused her to wiggle in her seat.

"Damn I love that boy," she whispered to herself.

Wanisha's lunch session was on the first floor with the 12th graders, but she came up to holler at Omirah for a quick minute. Omirah was still daydreaming when Wanisha came into the cafeteria.

"Girl Wassup!" Wanisha greeted her with excitement and propped herself down at the table.

"Hey girl I didn't even see you," said Omirah.

"Girl you always slipping tell me something new." Wanisha always appeared out of nowhere, without Omirah noticing her presence. Omirah liked Wanisha. She was a live wire. She had on a blue loose sweatshirt with KKBG capitalized across the backside. Underneath the letters were rows of airbrushed big faces. ($100 bills) with the matching blue lady Polo sweatpants and some butter Timberlands on her small feet. What was unique about her to Omirah was her attractive face but boyish personality. Omirah led the conversation to Jarvis.

"Girl he got me thinking he about to drop out."

"Shit I know if I don't pass this year I am. It's a wrap," said Wanisha. This was Wanisha's second year in the 12th grade.

"Girl don't drop." -------- They both heard his name at the same time.

"Don't yall bitches see my nigga girl in here," Wanisha growled.

The three girls at the table behind them stared back defiantly but said nothing. The cafeteria lowered its volume tremendously.

"Yeah I'm talking to yall disrespectful ass hoes!"

One of the three decided to be the spokesperson.

"Wasn't nobody talking about her man. My girl was just admiring his car."

"Well whoever like his car need to redirect their attention elsewhere or we gone have some problems," Omirah stated with just enough authority, but the short bodied, petite framed Wanisha wanted one of them to get stupid but the girls didn't bite. Then the bell rung. Omirah and Wanisha stood up.

"Thanks girl for having my back."

"Meme save that. You wanna go shopping with us after school?"

"Who?"

"You!"...... Oh, you're asking me who's all going?"

"Yeah," said Omirah.

"Dasha and Beatrice."

Omirah thought about it heavy before making her decision.

"Girl you know what----maybe next time. I've missed one cheerleading practice to many. If I miss another one the coach gone have a baby."

"Well when we get back from the mall I'll slide through your way."

An hour after school let out, Omirah and her cheerleading squad was practicing their moves, while the basketball team repeatedly went over the same few plays. Marco (Rick's cousin) was considered to be the future face of the N.B.A. Everyone came to see the magic he displayed on the court. This was his first year at the school and the girls loved him because of his six feet three frame, handsome features and his raw talent on the court. The team was 4.0 and it was pretty much evident that without him those numbers would probably be reversed. His crush on Omirah was open and he displayed it by winking at her every time he scored a basket. One game, after about twenty winks, she told him not to do that anymore because her man sometimes come to the games. He complied but his flirtatious ways towards her never stopped. Omirah had a friend who was the head cheerleader, name Maria. They were tight and plenty of days after school, one of their houses would be the kick it spots. After practice was over and everybody was getting ready to leave, Omirah cell phone rung. It was Jarvis. He told her to give him ten minutes. Marco offered to take the girls home, but Omirah and Maria declined, but a few of the other cheerleaders climbed in.

"See you around shorty," Marco said to Omirah and winked at her before pulling away.

The girls talked as they waited for their ride and a few minutes later an emerald green navigator sharply pulled into the parking lot and up to the girls, who was sitting on the parking lot stairwell. Omirah and Maria didn't know who it was until Jarvis rolled the window down and revealed his face.

"Wait, that's my baby.... Come on girl."

After they climbed in, Omirah leaned over for a kiss. It was quick but sensual.

"Whose truck?" She asked as they were pulling away.

"I copped this today. You like it?"

"Hecks yeah baby and the color is pretty."

"This interior is nice too," Maria chimed, rubbing her hands over the leather seat.

"What you gone do with the other car....... Give it to me?" Omirah asked playfully.

"That's a dude car, I wouldn't put you in that."

Omirah leaned back into the seat enjoying the smooth ride.

He pulled up on the side of an ES Lexus 300 that was parked in front of his house. Jarvis was looking down at the car observingly. Then looked over at Omirah.

"Boo that's you right there. You like that?"

She quickly leaned her body over and put her hands on his laps to brace herself, so she could get a good look.

"Oh my goodness babe you bought me a Lexus," she blurted out with excitement, planting a strong kiss on the side of his face, before hopping out to explore her new ride.

Maria was right behind her.

"Here boo, test drive it around the block," he said and gave her the keys.

"Since you already got them license, tomorrow we gone get it put in your name."

"Thank you so much baby. I love you gimme me a kiss."

"I love you too boo, but listen, I'm finna hit the block aight?"

"Okay daddy and be careful."

They kissed passionately before he pulled away.

Since school started, Jarvis now had two houses that he was renting in Angelica's name. One was across town out the way. He was using that house as a stash away spot. The other one was a getaway spot for him and Angelica. He also was paying Roxanne's rent every month and taking care of her faithfully not to mention she was two months pregnant and extremely happy to be having his baby.

She knew about Omirah and their relationship and of course when she found out, they went through their fall out stages. She promised herself that she wasn't going to mess with him anymore for lying to her, but when she found out she was pregnant, she put her guards down and allowed herself to open back up to him. Jarvis had Roxanne under his control, but the baby situation was troubling him daily. He didn't believe in abortions, and even if he told her to get one, he knew Roxanne wasn't having that, and to tell her that would make her hate him. A mistake that was evident as reality itself was staring Jarvis in the face day to day. A mistake that may cost him a valuable piece of his life.

After several months and several forced fucks under Gianni's captivity, Andrea's hatred had turned into a remorseful need for Gianni's sex. When he would stop by the country house, he'd give her a tongue fuck, and fuck her good enough to last until his next visit. She was now allowed to cook her own food and walk outside for fresh air. Every time he'd stop by he had bags of expensive clothing for her. When she would ask him why he would buy expensive clothes for her when she's not allowed to go anywhere, he replied, "Punishments isn't forever."

Gianni was going to put her in her own house in time, therefore he had already installed it in her heart not to cross him, by running down a dozen of her relatives addresses in Columbus Ohio. He warned her that if she ever pulled a disappearing act or an attempt on his life, her action will be the reason for her family members getting killed. She realized that she went up a size in her waist, and asked Gianni to put a treadmill in the basement of the country house. He did, and she spent her mornings running, squatting and doing sit ups. That helped ease the pain towards her deceased lover. Seven months into captivity, she was finally removed from punishment and placed into her new home, in a quiet neighborhood in Cleveland. Gianni now had entrusted her, and her actions had proved to be faithful.

****

It was jammed pack and full of nonstop action inside Club Affinity. Ubie and Maria was on the dance floor grooving while the other Yg members were attracting weed sales like flies on shit. Ubie and Maria never spoke any words to one another in school (before he dropped out) because they hardly saw one another but after he laid eyes on her tonight, he wanted to get to know her. He approached her with his game face on.

"Don't try to do too much boo I got you," said Maria as she noticed how stiff he was dancing. He caught her drift and threw his hands in the air. While he was doing the two-step, she turned around and started grinding her butt against his crotch in slow motion while listening to Tank and Wale song 'You don't know.'

Maria gave him a hard on and he knew she felt it. She was wearing a destroyed wash denim tightly fitted off the shoulder jumper with some red Chuck Taylors. At 5'8" 150 pounds, her frame was stacked. Maria was thicker than a snicker. After the song was over, she walked off the dance floor with Ubie's arm around her.

Gianni, Andrea and a few of Gianni's close ones, including Perry, occupied the VIP section. All eyes were on Andrea who was standing on top of a round table dancing in nothing but a thong and a bra. Of course, she was doing it under Gianni's authority and at first, she was uncomfortable although it didn't show by the movements of her alluring body. Perry had just informed Gianni to shut down a few of his spots, that was less than 24 hours away from being raided by the task force.

Gianni was distracted, calling shots, and not paying attention to Andrea who kept cutting her eyes at Perry and giving him the best views of her voluptuous shaped body. He thought he was tripping until she confirmed her deceit with a quick wink. Andrea had a thing for dark skinned thick built men. To her they were the best lovers in bed and as soon as she laid eyes on Perry, she was instantly attracted to him. A little after two in the morning, Gianni escorted her home. He had some traps to check in the streets, and she was pissed that she wasn't going to get some dick tonight. After she had bathed, and changed into a silk night gown, the doorbell

rang. It was unusual to hear the doorbell ringing because Gianni was her only visitor and he had a key.
"Who is it?" she asked cautiously.
"P," he replied.
"Do I know you?"
"No but we've seen each other. We saw each other tonight."
There was a few seconds of silence followed by a quick rustle of the chain and turn of the lock. She cracked the door and peeked out. At first, they just looked at one another.

"Did I overstep my boundary by coming here tonight?"
"Depends on why you came here. How did you know I live here?"
"I'm his investigator, I know everything."
"What if he comes by here and sees your car?"
"My car is nowhere around here."
"What if he comes over while you're here?"

"Then you gotta hide me!"
"Oh my God I cannot believe I am doing this," she sighed and stepped to the side.
As soon as she shut the door back and turned around, he pinned her up against the wall aggressively shoving his tongue in her mouth. Their lustful moans went into each other's mouth as they kissed in desperation. She unbuckled his belt and unsnapped his pants. He still had his gun in his coat pocket as he lifted her up against the wall. He ingresses inside her wet entry.

"My Lord!!! Mmmmmmm!" She moaned and held on tightly to his neck while he pushed inside her causing her head to hit the wall.

"Yessss, keep it coming baby. Deeper, Deeper DEEPER!"
They managed to get to her bedroom. They fell on the bed glued to one another.

"He quickly put a condom on his penis and began ravaging her pussy with powerful thrust. He dug deeper and deeper and finished in doggy style position. She laid on her stomach with her gown still over her waist, catching her breath.

"My pussy is so sore P."
He smiled while he started to get dressed and wrote down his number and placed it on the dresser.
"When you need me, call me. If I'm available, I'll come. You gone let me out?"

"Yep," she replied still recovering from the brutal dick whipping.

21

The night was young on this gloomy Friday. Omirah and Maria had just smoked a joint and had the munchies and decided to head out to Taco Bell. Omirah recently started smoking marijuana after Maria practically begged her to smoke a few joints with her one night when she spent the night over her house. Maria enjoyed getting high, but Omirah didn't make it an everyday habit.

"Meme, I got one nigga that's pussy whipped and another man that loves me for me. What is a girl to do?"

Omirah smiled and chuckled at Maria's inquiry.
"You got some good advice for me girl?"
"Well how do you feel about the guy who's whipped, and girl don't lie because I can tell you feel some type of way about him. So, tell me the entire truth!"
"Don't get it twisted, the nigga pleases me one hundred percent sexually. Not to mention he got mad paper and spoils me like how J-one spoils you, but he's a street nigga and we all know street niggas don't last long. They either go to jail for a long time or die at a young age. Even though Jermaine aint got a lot of money, he does work every day. He got some bomb sex too, but most of all, he loves me like crazy!"
"Maria girl you've answered your own questions, but if you must hear it from me, Jermaine is definitely the one for you."

"But Meme I've come to realize that I have a thing for bad boys, like I find myself wondering what Ubie is up to. I just hope things are okay for him, you know stuff like that. Omirah pulled into Taco Bell's drive thru.

"Even though I feel it's Jermaine, you should do whatever makes you happy, and if the choice happens to be a bad one, then so be it. Life is about learning and love is love."
They froze their conversation once they pulled to the speaker. While Omirah was ordering, Maria was receiving a text message that read: 'What's up shorty, hit me back, this Ubie.' She dialed his number with alacrity.
"Hello," Ubie answered placidly.

Maria heard a lot of action in the background.
"What's up baby! Where you at?"
"I'm at the park."
"Why is it so loud over there?"
"It's just doing what it do. Where you at though?"
"Me and my girl at Taco Bell."
"Damn drop ya boy off something to eat!"
"What do you want to eat?"

"A number six from McDonalds. Hold on for a second."

She heard him asking some of his friends did they want anything.

"Aye!"

"I'm listening," replied Maria.

"I want a number six, Coupe want a number three and Juju want a number four."

"Okay, so......why didn't anyone drive to grab you guys something to eat?"

"Now you know we can't be missing money out here!"

"Alright well give me about fifteen minutes," said Maria.

The girls stayed in the car, while they came and picked up their orders. Ubie stayed by the car to talk to Maria through the passenger door.

Foo pulled up and parked in front of Omirah.

Omirah watched him as he got out of his car. He had on an Al Wissam Cleveland Browns jacket, a matching Cleveland Browns skully, with a black doo rag showing underneath. His skin complexion was a magnificent brown and although she'd never paid him any attention in school, she had to admit that he was very handsome. He walked up to Ubie and looked in the car.

"Oh okay......These them famous cheerleaders! What's up sexy!"

"My name is Omirah and hello!"

"My name is Foo and I know your name sexy!"

"Damn nigga go over to her side," said Ubie.

"Nigga stop whining," Foo blurted as he made his way around to Omirah's window. She rolled it down halfway.

"Excuse me Foo, but I have a man and I really would hate for him to drive by and see us talking."

"Yeah I know you got a small fry. When you're ready to super-size holla at me."

"He aint hardly a small fry," said Omirah as she rolled her eyes. Maria girl you ready to go?"

Maria caught her drift and cut off her and Ubie's conversation.

Aight shorty," said Foo as he took a step back. "Keep it sexy!"

Around thirty minutes after Omirah and Maria left, three girls who went by the title B.L.P, pulled up to the park in a black Escalade. These girls sold PCP otherwise known as wet on the street. Half of the Yg members smoked wet cigarettes and the B.L.P girls were their suppliers. After they copped what they were buying, they didn't waste any time dipping their cigarettes and before you knew it, half of them were moving in slow motion.

"Juju, roll with me to pick up Re-re from work," said Foo.

"Alright let's go," Juju replied.

"Imma roll with yaw cause this bitch hot," said Lavar. "I aint trying to go to jail." They headed towards the car. Ten minutes later a wet candy paint blood red Impala pulled to the park. It was Eric and Marlo, two KKBG members, looking to buy some weed.

"Fuck them niggas, don't sell them hoe ass niggas shit. As a matter of fact," ......Ubie cut his words short and headed towards the driver's side of the car. He was wetted out.

"Let me grab a quarter ounce of that good shit homie," said Eric with money in hand ready to transact.

Ubie didn't conduct any business because all he could think about was the time they hopped out pointing guns. Before Eric realized that Ubie was on some bullshit, a flurry of punches rained into his face. Other Yg members started running towards the car with their guns out. Eric sharply pulled off but couldn't escape the fusillade as bullets penetrated the car like butter. Unfortunately, everything on Marlo's body from the neck down had went completely numb.

"Aye J-one. I'm at Metro Hospital, Marlo just got shot! Them hoe ass Yg niggas man. Call me asap!"

Wanisha was the first one to come storming through the hospital's front entrance. She was teary eyed and was followed by a handful of people. She went straight to the counter and asked about her twin brothers condition. She was told that he was placed in ICU while doctors awaited the results of the several tests and x-rays they performed. He was shot in his spine and was instantly paralyzed. An evil energy surged through her body as she held her head down at the counter and cried.

Jarvis placed his arms around her as they walked over to where the others awaited. Before you knew it, the lobby was filled with KKS girls and KKBG members and everybody was ready to put in work. Jarvis remained quiet while he strategized. He knew he had to set some order into motion or else everyone would soon be in jail.

"Aye yall let's go outside for a minute," said Jarvis.

They all walked to the hospital's parking lot.

"This is a beautiful sight to see how everybody is ready to go hard for our guy, but all of us don't need to move at the same time. As you can see, this situation is much bigger than fighting. We gone answer their request for war, no question, but we gotta move in a low-key fashion."

Wanisha started venting.

"My brother laid up in that hospital paralyzed and my crack head ass mama aint nowhere to be found, what the fuck type of shit is this!" She tried calling her mother's house again but there was still no answer.

"I hate that bitch I swear!" She sneered and turned from everybody and went back into the hospital.

Jarvis aim was to answer in a quick retaliation, but whoever wasn't going to be a part of the move he felt it was best to keep them in the blind as to who did what. Not that he didn't trust any of his partners, he was just calculating his steps and being safe. After everyone went back inside of the hospital, Jarvis managed to break away to call Damon's cell phone, who was at the hospital as well.

"Hello! Look, don't say my name because I don't want the homies to know it's me on the phone. Tell Anton, Wanisha, M-2, and Eric to meet me at the park around the corner from the Jets at one o'clock which is only two hours from now I need you there too. Do it discreetly so wont nobody else know. Aye yo, them niggas just fucked up. Shit's about to get ugly out here."

Each individual pulled into the pitch-black parking lot in spurts. Jarvis was sitting under the picnic shed and every time one pulled in, he would blink a flash light off and on. Ten minutes after one o'clock am, six emotional KKBG homies gathered underneath the shed. At first everyone talked at once, but Jarvis took over.

"The reason I had Damon discreetly pull each one of yall coattails to meet here is because, don't nobody else need to know what we're about to do. Of course, they gone hear about it but all they will be able to do is speculate. You feel me?"

Everybody acknowledged his words with nods and murmurs of agreement. "What's up! We finna hit these niggas up or what?" asked M-2.

"What the hell you think we here for," said Anton.

"Hell muthafuckin yeah shit they just shot my brother!" Wanisha acrimoniously chimed in. Then Jarvis called the first shot.

"In a few days, we gone catch our targets. After six o'clock Sunday, we can surveillance that park from a distance. We gone rent two fiend cars with three people in each car. Then we can post up on the side of the park, on Wilshire street, and blend in with the other parked cars until the moment presents itself.

"J-one, when I look my brother in the face tomorrow, I want to be able to tell him that we answered that for him."

"But Wanisha, this aint just about you," M-2 confirmed. "What the homie is saying makes hella sense. If we go over there tonight, they may try to ambush us because they're expecting us to come. Tomorrow they gone think we some hoes for not coming. Then the day after, we gone reach out and touch some of them niggas unexpectedly."

"I'm not saying what he said don't make sense but, I'm going over there tomorrow to retaliate for my brother!"

"Damn Wanisha you gone break order like that?" Asked Jarvis, sounding as if he was hurt by her defiance against his motive. Even through her anger, she didn't want Jarvis to feel like she was disrespecting him or betraying his word. She loved Jarvis like he was her own brother and credited him for bringing them as a click to where they were.

"J-one...... J-one...... They paralyzed my brother J-one.... They paralyzed him." She let it all out in J-one's arms.

"Just two nights Wanisha, just two okay?"

She weakly nodded her head in his arms. Those two days felt like an eternity to Wanisha.

The next day Marlo could have visitors. Tubes were in his mouth and nose and he was in an unconscious state. Wanisha and their mother was told that the injury was very serious, and the physicians were almost certain that he may not be able to walk again. In a few days, they were going to do a special surgery to remove the bullet that was resting on his spine. Physicians from Arizona were flying in to perform the surgery and all his people could do was pray.

Saturday dragged by as the hustlers of the KKBG's ran their side of the projects. Sunday, the six chosen ones woke up refreshed and determined to set a mean example. Jarvis woke up on the side of Roxanne. Wanisha did her early morning rituals, then grabbed her baby 9 milli, 14 shot, and headed to the Jets. Anton dropped Tracy off from the hotel at about eleven o'clock and Damon woke up with his dick in Yasha's mouth. She was still Ricks girl, but all Damon had to do was leave Shonte for her and she would leave Rick.

Several homies and their KKS partners were out early. Angelica was busy doing her job for Jarvis. Everybody else was grinding and assisting their partners as well.

By six o'clock, it was snowing heavily, and the wind was blowing fiercely. Fresh snow was building its layers upon the sidewalks and streets.

Wanisha, Eric, and M-2 was parked four cars away from Jarvis, Anton, and Damon, amongst a street full of raggedy parked cars on Wilshire. They watched the Yg members serve the customers with back to back transactions as the snow poured heavily from the darkened sky. At eight thirty-five the police slowly cruised by. They put the spotlight on the youngsters in the park and said into the speaker, "CLEAR THE PARK OR GO TO JAIL!"

As soon as the police turned the corner, four of the Yg homies made an exit from the north side of the park headed towards the projects. Only two stayed.

Both were posted up on the side of a tree. Juju had a huge stack of bills in his hands putting them in order and Coupe was waiting to knock down the next sale. The KKBG members noticed that instead of walking up to their cars, they were making all the customers that pulled up get out.

The plan was for Jarvis to call Wanisha to give them word as soon as the moment presented itself, but when Ubie passed their cars in his old school Cadillac, Wanisha, who was seated in the back, screamed out, "M-2 GET BEHIND HIM!" Without thinking he started the car and pursued Ubie.

Ubie turned off the one-way street, onto the main Avenue (where the 30th projects agglomerated on the left-hand side) and stopped at the first light. His girlfriend Karmen was in the passenger seat rolling up a blunt of marijuana. To the pursuers favor, traffic was extremely light. Each one had a devilish mask over their face as they simply pulled on the side of Karmen. Ubie never saw the move because his attention was toward the projects. Wanisha hung her body out the window and fired shots into Ubie's back window. M-2 let the 40-caliber rip through the passenger window of Ubie's car. Instantly Karmen was slumped over into Ubie's lap while he tried to make a desperate getaway.

"HOW THE FUCK IS HE STILL ALIVE!" Wanisha yelled while leaning out the back continuously busting shots into the rear window. 'Psssshh!' The pulverizing glass of the back window was no longer a shield. Ubie zig zagged in front of them, made a wide left that led to the heart of the projects. M-2 was forced to let him go.

"Damn! You hear that shit! WHO IN THE FUCK WAS THAT!" Juju blurted.
"Come on nigga let's go see what's up," Coupe said excitedly as he ran out the park headed to his car. Juju wasn't behind him, because he was still pissing on the side of a tree.

Then suddenly more gunshots exploded. The closeness of the shots caused Juju to piss on himself. He looked just in time to see the car pulling away, but one of the shooters still had their arm hanging out the window firing rounds into Coupe, who was lying dead still on the side of his car.

22

What started as an immature conflict between the projects girls had turned into something much bigger. Something that neither of the youngsters could walk away from, nor did they wanna face. A retaliatory war. Karmen and Coupe were killed in cold blood, and Ubie was released from the hospital the following evening with a gash on the back of his head from a grazing bullet. He was also grazed on his neck, shot in the shoulder, and in his side. Ubie had to have been touched by an Angel to make it out of that car alive, but he didn't give that any thought as the picture of Karmen's bloody face stayed in his mind's eye. He still felt the warmth of her brains on his skin. The deathly blank stare that he saw in her eyes ignited an eternal vengeance against the KKBG Posse........

After the shootings, everyone from both sides had dropped out of school. Although they all survived, about four KKBG members had been shot at the beginning of the summer. It was a task to retaliate on an Yg member now because they had shut the park down. Neither click was in danger in their own projects because of how the Jets were set up, but if either member was caught slipping out of bounds, death was the encounter. Two days before Jarvis sixteenth birthday, Roxanne had given birth to Jarvis Jr, a spitting image of his father. A handful of Roxanne relatives were present at the hospital but none of Jarvis people were there because he didn't want anyone to find out yet. As he held his newborn son in his arms, he knew that he could no longer hold the truth back from Omirah. A truth that created a day to day fear since the day Roxanne revealed she was pregnant.

Jarvis and Lil Tae were riding with Wanisha in her Lexus. They were headed out to Beatrice and Marlo's crib. Beatrice was more than Marlo's assistant in the streets, she was his girlfriend too, and ever since he left the hospital as a permanent paraplegic, she dedicated herself to take care of him. She had strong faith that her man would one day be able to walk again. Beatrice had switched positions with him. She was now the hustler for the two and he watched over her shoulders keeping two forty-five autos in his chair at all times, he never let her go to the jets without him. Their sex life consisted of him oral sexing her, something he became great at. Although she wanted to feel his hardness inside of her, she was satisfied with their forced situation.

****

"Wanisha, how you think Meme gone react to this?" asked Jarvis while sitting in the passenger seat. Wanisha passed Lil Tae the blunt.
"J-one that's a hard one for me to call boo. Since she loves your ass to death, my assumption is that she'll forgive you, but if not, then you'll be alright! Right?" she asked while taking her eyes off the road to look into his eyes.

"I aint got no choice, but she'll always be my heart though."
"Well then not only do you need to tell her the truth but let her know how much she means to you."---------

Lil Tae cut her off.
"What is this shit and bitch who is you Oprah or somebody?" Jarvis started laughing.
"Nigga make her feel your gangsta and if she decides to let go of that then that's on her!"
"Boy shut yo corny ass up you don't know nothing about

women...... Now pass me that got damn blunt nigga!"

"Let me hit that one time, my nerves are bad," said Jarvis who only hits the blunt every blue moon. He hit it one strong time and passed it to Wanisha. When they pulled up to Marlo's crib, they noticed a few of the homies cars were parked out front. Beatrice let them in.

"Damn I didn't know all yall hoes was over here," said Wanisha as she bent down and hugged her twin, kissing on his cheek.

KKS was doing what they do. Playing spades and smoking weed while the homies gambled on the Ps4 games. Deedra was sitting on Anton's lap with a blunt in her fingertips as if she was happy, but in her heart, she was sad. She was putting up with a lot of bullshit from Anton who was causing her strong grief. A little after they came Beatrice was letting Lil Bit and M-2 in the house. It was starting to get noisy and crowded. Almost two hours later Jarvis drank three Coronas out of a six pack and hit every blunt that was passed his way.

"Here J-one," said Anton. "It's Damon." He passed Jarvis his phone.

"What up fool," Jarvis greeted.

"I aint on shit probably about to shoot that way. I'm at your girl house. She wants to holla at you hold on."

"Damn!" Jarvis blurted. He didn't think Damon was over there and even though he was planning to reveal his secret, he didn't need to hear her voice beforehand.

"Hey baby," said Omirah.

"What's up boo," said Jarvis.

"Nothing...... Just sitting around thinking about you."

"Is everything good?" asked Jarvis.

"Well I had a bad dream last night that something bad happened to you. I don't want to speak about it in words to you, I just wanted to know that you were okay."

He could tell by her voice that whatever she dreamed about had her shook.

"Meme baby I'm good."

"Are you being safe J-one?"

He was taken aback by that question because the true answer was no, which is why he had a son that wasn't by her. He had the urge to tell her everything over the phone but knew that she deserved to hear the truth face to face.

"I always move safe out here Meme, but I need to talk to you later okay."

"Okay... Can you come now?"

"Alright give me about a half an hour," he replied with very little confidence in his voice.

"Let me see your keys Wanisha," said Jarvis.

She slammed the last card on the table.

"Yall hoes set!" She yelled and reached over and high fived Tasia. Freeda and Renae was pissed.

"Here J-one," said Wanisha as she fumbled through her purse for her keys and handed them to Jarvis.

"Are you coming back here, or will I see you in the Jets?"

"I don't know how long I'll be, I'm about to go holla at Meme."

"Oh, you finna............yep I'll see in the Jets."

It was seven twenty-five in the evening when Jarvis pulled into Omirah's driveway. Damon had left and Yasha was using Omirah's car. Omirah came on the porch as he was getting out of his car. He ran his eyes over her curvy body. She was wearing a pair of pink leggings that complimented her thighs and hips with a white tee tied in a knot revealing her belly ring. Her beautiful toes were openly displayed in her Chanel sandals as her jet-black hair hung freely down to the middle of her back.

"Damn girl you look good," said Jarvis as they embraced.

"Are you hungry boo? I can whip you up something really quick!"

"Naw I'm good shorty."

He followed her into the living room and they sat on the loveseat. She grabbed his hand and held it in her lap.

"Boo ever since you got into this project beef thing with them other guys I've been worried about you. Then the dream I had didn't make it any better. Can you call me more throughout the day to let me know that everything is okay?"

Omirah knew about Karmen and Coupe getting killed and the attempt on Ubie's life. Then the following retaliation on some of Jarvis friends, because Ubie believed that they were the ones behind the hit.

Omirah knew they had started a war related to Wanisha's brother but the only thing she cared about was the safety of Jarvis.

"My bad Meme for not calling enough, but you know how it be in the Jets."

"I know baby but regardless of that just call me more ok?" She reiterated as the phone started to ring. She reached on the table and answered it. It was Maria.

"Let me call you back Maria. Okay Bye!"

"You still talk to that damn girl?" Jarvis inquired.

"J-one, she doesn't mess with Ubie anymore, but to answer your question. Yes."

"Meme do you think that you could ever hate me, if I give you a reason to?"

She stared into his eyes questioningly as he stared back with regret.

"What's wrong J-one? Why would you ask me something like that?"

"Because I made a mistake Meme. A mistake you may hate me for."

Her heartbeat quickened as reality set in. Something was terribly wrong.

"What have you done J-one?" Omirah asked in a calm tone.

"Omirah I love you more than anything you know that right?"

"Yes, and I love you the same but dammit tell me what is going on?" Her patience started to run thin.

"I have a son Meme."

Her hand went limp in his hand.

"Love me enough to understand Meme. I've made a huge mistake."

She pulled her hand from his and covered her mouth as she began to cry. He scooted closer to her attempting to place his arm around her. She repelled against his embrace.

"Jarvis don't.... don't touch me!" She angrily spat.

Jarvis stood up.

"Let me let you calm down before we start saying things we don't mean."

"What have I done to you Jarvis?" She asked in between sobs. "For you to do this to me?"

Not knowing how to answer that a lie fell from his tongue.

"I was drunk Meme!"

"Drunk" she breathlessly repeated with a disgusted look on her face.

"I didn't know I was dealing with a weak ass nigga."

"Meme watch ya tongue."

"Fuck you nigga don't tell me to watch my tongue!" She jumped up from the couch.

"How could you do this to me? How could you just throw away our love? I thought you said I made you happy! Didn't I satisfy you enough?" They stood eye to eye.

For some reason Jarvis had a hard time expressing himself.

"Well you know what Mr. Cat got ya tongue, you can take yourself and all of your lies out of my life for good!"

"Damn Meme that's how you feel?" She stood adamantly with her arms folded over her chest. At that moment Yasha walked in the house. She instantly knew something was wrong.

"Hi yall," nobody answered her greeting. Not knowing what else to say, Jarvis said," I love you Meme and I'm sorry. He made his exit from the house leaving Omirah staring at the wall. Yasha walked up to her and put her arms around her.

"Whatever's wrong girl it will definitely work itself out." Omirah busted out in tears in her sister's arms.

Omirah couldn't find it in her heart to forgive Jarvis. She felt deeply betrayed by the man she loved. He tried calling her cell phone, but she would continuously hang up on him without a word. His heartfelt messages did no justice so eventually Jarvis stopped calling.

Omirah continued to hang with Maria and what used to be an occasional get-high session, had turned into a weed habit. To Omirah it was a stress reliever that helped her get over Jarvis. Although she was now smoking weed every day, it didn't affect her ambition to finish her final year at school. Her and Maria revamped the cheerleading squad and Marco tried out for the school's basketball team once again and lead them to back to back championships. Since he brought the last season's trophy, the girls loved him. All of them wanted to be his girl, but he was set on winning the likes of Omirah. She had opened up to him about her and Jarvis break up and he soon became a counselor of her pain. Before you knew it, he went from being her counselor to becoming a part of her decision making. Omirah was confused in whether they were going to be a couple. Her feelings were still strong for Jarvis, so she told him to give her some time. He agreed.

On the other hand, two attempts had been made on Jarvis life by the Yg's. The first time was in Trey's SS Monte Carlo which was bullet riddled but neither was hit. The second time was around the corner from the King Kennedy Projects, at the 24-hour Deli store. Jarvis was missed but his homie Dae-dae was shot in the shoulder and the leg. A few days after Dae dae's injury, Yg member Lavar was caught slipping coming out of a convenience store down the block from the 30th street projects. Before he made it to his car, an all-black escort yanked up on him and two shots were fired into his chest and one into his stomach. Leaving him critically wounded on the ground next to his car.

****

Omirah was hearing through gossip what was going on between the two clicks, and she couldn't deny the fact that she still worried about Jarvis. Every time she would be in the house and hear gunshots, she would say a quick prayer in her mind for him. Then half of her world came crashing down when her father was killed in the line of duty. When Jarvis got word from Damon, he immediately called her to pay his respect. She answered in a rueful voice.

"Hello."

"Meme, I just got the news from Damon. Are you okay?" She was slow to respond.

"I guess...... Jarvis what's happening to my life?" She broke down crying on the phone. Then suddenly a male voice said into Jarvis ear, "Look here no disrespect but your condolences aren't welcomed here!" CLICK.

Jarvis face became contorted. He stared at the phone as if it was something disgusting. He then ran over to his truck, climbed inside, and sharply pulled out of the jets. When he pulled up in front of Omirah's house, he saw Yasha and Rick standing on the porch. Jarvis hopped out and made his way up the landing. He stopped at the foot of the porch. He could tell Yasha was distraught from her father being killed, but at the moment he felt disrespected.

"Aye dawg was that you who just said that bullshit to me on the phone?" Jarvis asked Rick aggressively.

"What!" Rick strongly replied.

"Aye Yasha can you tell Meme to come outside?"

"Hold on," she told him and went inside the house.

Rick and Jarvis stared at each other until Yasha returned with Omirah behind her. As soon as he got ready to talk, Marco walked out, and everything became clear to Jarvis.

"Nigga who is you to tell me the shit you just told me on the phone?" Jarvis sneered while pointing his finger at Marco.

"Jarvis please just" ....Marco's voice drowned out Omirah's.

"Just like I said nigga you have already hurt her enough!"

"Meme come here," Jarvis said curtly. He could tell that she was confused as to what to do. J-one walked up on the porch and grabbed her by the arm.

"Meme you let this nigga,"------------- he never finished because Marco pushed him backwards, causing him to slightly stumble down the stairs.

Jarvis anger engulfed him. He snatched his forty-five automatic off his waistline and pointed into Marco's face.

"BITCH ASS NIGGA I WILL KILL YOU!"

He hissed through his clenched teeth. Rick and Marco froze. Yasha and Omirah both yelled out at the same time.

"JARVIS WHAT THE HELL IS WRONG WITH YOU!" Screamed Omirah. Their voices brought him back to reality and he quickly tucked his gun back on his waist, just in enough time before their mother emerged from the house.

"What's going on out here?"

"Just leave Jarvis. I appreciate your respects regarding my father, but you need to leave."

Jarvis felt mortified as he pulled away. J.d. words of advice echoed in his head. 'Never let a bitch or a situation cloud your judgement.'

He had done just that, and the result was almost killing a man in broad daylight in front of the eyes of several witnesses.

23

Two hours later, Jarvis received a phone call from Omirah. She was calling to apologize for Marco's actions.

"He didn't mean it and he doesn't want any trouble J-one."

"You don't have to apologize for that nigga. That's your man and he took up for you and I respect that." A dragging silence followed.

"You're not holding a grudge against him, are you?"

"Look, as long as he doesn't jump out there again then I'll respect you enough to let that go. So that's who you are worrying about........him?"

"And you J-one.... I don't want you to get in any trouble," she admitted.

"Well once again, I'm sorry about your father and if you ever need anything, don't hesitate to call me. I hope you have found the happiness I failed to give you."

"Whatever J-one, BYE!"

After the funeral, a reception was held at Omirah's house. Marco stopped by and was offered a plate by Mrs. Henderson, Omirah's generous mother. After he received his plate, Omirah took him in the basement so they could be alone. The basement was nicely furnished with a three-piece furniture set, an eighty-four-inch smart television with a Bose surround sound system. While Marco sat down and began eating, she put in Aaliyah's greatest hits c.d. and let it play before sitting next to him. The song 'I'm missing you' pervaded the room.

"He looked peaceful laying in that casket, didn't he?" asked Omirah.

"Yes he did. Now it's people like you who have to keep him smiling from above."

"You're right and I intend to. Have you thought about what college you want to attend yet?" she asked.

He was being offered several athletic scholarships from different colleges, but he hadn't made a choice.

"Well a few of those colleges that are trying to holla at me don't have dominant basketball programs. So basically, it's between UNC, Duke, Wake Forest, Kansas, Kentucky, and Florida."

She nodded her head as if she understood the importance of his decision.

"Reason I'm asking is because with the life insurance money my mother received from my father, my mother and I decided that I enroll into a college that is close to home as possible. And after discussing it with her we decided on OSU. I'm sure you won't be going there considering they don't have a great basketball program."

He didn't respond as he stared into her eyes.

"What?" she asked passively.

"What are you trying to say babe, talk to me," said Marco.

"I was just hoping there was a chance we could attend the same school. I don't think there's anything wrong with Ohio State's program........ Is there?"

"Well not too many people go to the NBA from there, but I'm a diamond that can't be overlooked," said Marco with self-confidence. "Listen Omirah, I would follow you to the moon baby even if that meant going in the opposite direction of my dream. You are more than worth it."

She was stunned by his words. He gently ran the back of his fingers down her neck, cuffed her chin and leaned over and kissed her softly. For the first time, their tongues clashed together as their lips locked as one. Memories of her and Jarvis popped in her mind causing a strong tear to fall from her eye. She knew that their relationship was over, but it was taking all that she had to let go of him. When they broke apart, he noticed the tear and erased it with his finger.

"A painful ending created a beautiful beginning," said Marco as he kissed her gently on her forehead.

****

Wanisha was the first one in the crew to have a bad encounter with the law officials, causing her freedom to be threatened by the face of the system. After taking police on a deadly hi speed chase, eventually she was trapped and besieged. After being apprehended they confiscated 154 grams of hard crack, a 357 S&W revolver, and an ounce of marijuana. After a three-day investigation while in the city jail she was taken to the county where her name would be called any minute since Jarvis took care of her bond. After being finger printed and processed, she was placed in a pod. She just so happened to run across a familiar face she hadn't seen since elementary graduation day. A girl named Rhonda.

Rhonda was playing spades with three other women at a steel table. Everyone's attention went towards the door to see if the new comer's face was familiar. When Rhonda saw Wanisha come in, she squinted her eyes as her face began to register.

"Wanisha?" Rhonda blurted out loud enough to get everyone's attention.

Wanisha dropped her home coming bag to the floor at the wall and grabbed the unused pay phone as if she didn't hear her name being called. Rhonda got up and walked towards her after she realized that this girl was Wanisha Black without question. Even though she was nineteen now, she never forgot about Wanisha and from time to time she wondered what had become of her. Wanisha's eyebrows lowered as her eyes settled on the familiar face that was still vague in her mind.

"You don't remember me?...........Rhonda Shaw!"

Suddenly her name and face registered.

"What's up girl! What's been up with you," said Wanisha.

She dropped the phone and the girls hugged one another.

"Girl where in the hell have you been all of these years? Well I know you're not from my hood but dang, it feels like it's been forever since the last time I've seen you. About what, eight years or so?" said Wanisha. "I be all through the city so I'm hard to miss," Wanisha finished.

"Wanisha girl I don't know why we've never ran across one another in all these years, but I've always wondered about you though. I stay on Harvard and I see you're still looking good honey. Still short as hell though?" smiled Rhonda.

"Yeah girl I didn't do too much growing, but I see you did. You all shaped up. You look good girl!"

Rhonda was 5'10" one hundred and sixty pounds and had beautiful skin with a southern thickness and a smile to die for.

"What they got you here for?" asked Wanisha.

"A felonious assault for shooting my ex-boyfriend twice in the leg."

"How much is your bond girl you need some help paying it or what?"

"The judge just gave me four years yesterday. I should be riding out in a few days."

"Damn girl you gotta do four?... Well look, give me an address or somebody I can get in touch with to get your inmate number, so I can write you. I'll send you some money too and girl we just gone keep in touch like that."

"Rhonda felt it in her heart that Wanisha's words were genuine and the energy she was receiving from her made her wish that they'd never fell out of touch.

"So, are you about to get out tonight?"

"Yeah they should be calling me any minute, but girl go get yo hook up together while I call my people to make sure everything is taken care of."

Wanisha called Freeda spot in the Jets. Freeda instantly accepted the collect call.

"Girl what's up! When is you getting out of there it's almost eight and J-one paid ya bond a while ago," said Freeda.

"Yeah, they should be calling me any minute now, but who's all outside though?"

"Some of everybody but you know Damon got hit in his back today."

"WHAT!"

"Yeah, they say it was Foo, but he alright. The good thing is, it wasn't close to his spine and didn't hit anything vital...... He's still at the hospital though."

"When this shit happen?" asked Wanisha

"It just happened a few hours ago."

A wave of evil energy washed over Wanisha causing her to get dizzy. She was ready to put some work in for her homie.

"Is J-one out there?"

"I think he's at the hospital, but his car is out there."

The county officer yelled her name, then told her to rag and bag.

"Come get me Freeda they just called me!"

"I'm on my way."

"What's wrong?" asked Rhonda.

"My man just got shot."

"Yo boyfriend?"

"Not my man like that but my homie. Girl you got yo hookup?" asked Wanisha.

"Yeah here it go right here but even if I don't hear from you, take care out there and it was damn sure good to see you!"

"It was good to see you too, but I keeps it real and when I say I'm gone do something, then imma do it. As long as I'm on the streets Imma hold you down. Rhonda, you still my girl."

She took the folded-up piece of paper from her and hugged her again.

"You take care of you Rhonda and stay strong girl!"

Before summer arrived, various members from the KKBG posse had cases on their hands. Wanisha, Dae-dae, M-2, Mont, and Lil hurt, were now out on bond with pending drug charges.

Wanisha had got in contact with Rhonda's people and sent her a letter with a two-hundred-dollar money order inside of it.

Damon's back injury had healed into a permanent war wound and he was looking to kill Foo the first chance given. Even though Shonte was still his main girl, he made Yasha leave Rick Alone.

Somehow, he managed to get an understanding between Shonte and Yasha and they all shared a relationship as one. Tracy was two months pregnant by Anton and Deedra knew about the situation.

When she first found out she literally tried to fight Anton, forcing him to put hands on her, but after the bitterness settled and reality set in, her love for Anton kept her by his side.

A few weeks after Jarvis 17th birthday, Maria was throwing Omirah a going away party. In another week, she was going off to college to spend four years of her life majoring in communications. Marco accepted OSU's scholarship, so they could be together. Several family members were disappointed by his decision considering he was passing up some of the best colleges, but he had faith that he was going to the N.B.A. regardless of what college he played for.

It was a little after six when Wanisha pulled her brand-new Pepsi can blue Durango trunk into Omirah's driveway. Omirah had called her and Jarvis over so she could express the love she felt in her heart for them. Wanisha climbed her short petite sexy frame out of the big truck, decked out in a Gucci sweat suit, the same color as her truck, a pair of Louis Vutton sunglasses raised over her head on top of her wrapped like hairstyle, and a pair of all white Gucci sneakers covered her feet.

"What's up girl. So, are you ready for the big step or what?" asked Wanisha as they hugged.

"I guess I'm ready," replied Omirah.

They sat down in the chairs on the porch.

"How's everything coming along with your case?"

"Well, my first court date is in a few days, but my lawyer told me the case won't be wrapped up until about October."

"Damn girl I hope you don't go to jail."

"That's what I hope to but if I do oh well. It aint shit I can't handle."

A silver Porsche truck rolled by slow dumping a 'Yo Gotti' Classic. They gave the truck a second of their attention letting the music fade.

"You know you my heart right?" Omirah inquired.

"Fa-sho and you my dawg too girl. Just don't get there and forget about ya people."

"Wanisha please. If it's up to me, we gone be friends forever girl. I just gotta put these four years in to the good."

"I don't know exactly what all these streets got to offer me, but since this the route I chose, I'm just gone live it to the fullest for better or worse. Girl these streets is my college. From beginning to end this is me, so you can always find me out here!"

Omirah never realized Wanisha's dedication to the streets until now. She wanted to beg Wanisha to do something good with her life, something different than to give it to the streets, but when Jarvis pulled up in his cranberry Malibu, her mind froze. Both girls focus was on him as he walked up the porch stairs.

"What's up J-one. What it's doing over there?" asked Wanisha.

"Vice out tough, but it's going!"

"Girl let me let yall be, I'll call you later Meme."

They hugged and Wanisha made her departure. Jarvis sat down next to Omirah.

"Meme What's up!"

She turned her face around to stare him in the eyes.

"I'm gonna miss you J-one."

Jarvis redirected his attention at his house straight ahead, not wanting her to see the hurt in his eyes. He didn't want her to leave even though he had lost her to Marco.

"Imma miss you too Meme." His words came out flat.

"Look at me J-one." He was forced to look into her eyes.

"What's up Meme?"

"You!... Are you going to be safe while I'm gone?"

"You say that as if you are coming back this way or some'em," Jarvis replied sullenly.

They still loved each other. Even the naked eye could see that.

"Truthfully, I don't know which way I'm going, and I can't say I'm happy either, I guess I'm just riding the wave. How's your son?"

"He good."

"Are you going to bring him over here so I can see him?"

"Why Meme!"

"What do you mean why.... He's a part of you so I wanna see him."

Jarvis didn't wanna subject to her request but gave in.

"Alright meme I'll bring him."

They stared at one another for a moment in silence.

"Jarvis, you've been through a lot. Don't allow what you've been through in life to cause you to hit rock bottom. Your life is worth so much more than living in a cell or an early death.

Can you just please promise me you will be as safe as you can be. I do wanna see you again!"

"Meme, in time I'll only be a dying memory in your mind. Don't worry about me. I'll be fine. You just go down there and do what you gotta do to be successful out here."

"Jarvis you'll never be a dying memory to me. So, are you gonna promise me or what?"

"I promise," Jarvis assured and hugged her tightly in his arms before he turned to leave.

24

Foo and Rere had a spot they were renting on the outskirts of Cleveland. Foo had called each Elite member and told them that a meeting was being held at his spot at 7 o'clock sharp. Earlier today him and Re-re bought up the mall spending close to ten-thousand-dollar's on a shopping spree. They got in around 5 o'clock. She fried him a T-bone steak with two sides, then hung up her brand-new apparel with the rest of her expensive wardrobe while waiting on him to finish eating his meal. She sucked his dick for almost a half an hour, before he fucked her into a couple of orgasms, followed by a deep sleep.

She was still peacefully at rest when the Elite team was coming through the door. Foo gave each member a glass and filled them up with Ace of Spades and Blazed a 12-inch-long house of Windsor cigar filled with loud marijuana. They all puffed it twice and passed it along. There was no tv or music playing, just the sound of socialization from the homies. Lavar who was almost killed earlier in the year started choking off the smoke.

"Somebody pat that nigga on the back before he wake my bitch up!"

After he stopped coughing he said, "Nigga fuck you, what the fuck Re-re ass sleep this early for anyway nigga?"

"Aye yall I called this meeting for a special purpose. An important purpose. A purpose that must be fulfilled in order to reign over the city like I plan on us doing." He scanned his eyes over each member. (Ubie, Mouse, Lavar, and Juju).

"What's up big homie what you got in mind?" Juju asked.

"A whole lot but first let me ask yall.........Did we successfully rob the bank?" They answered concordantly.

"Did we lock the city down with that special plant or what?"

After they answered that he said," Now there's another obstacle in front of us that's no harder than the ones we have already conquered."

Everyone was attentively focused on Foo. He grabbed the blunt from Juju and hit it a few times then passed it to Ubie and wet his mouth with the Ace of Spades.

"We must remove the big homies out of our way and take over the projects."

He studied their reactions which were unreadable.

"Remove em! How the hell we gone do that?" asked Mouse.

"Easy! We pick em off one by one. The hardest person to touch is Gianni, so let's kill off his workers first. I'm talkin all the way down to the niggas that's out there working for themselves. Them Niggas soft...... But the whole purpose is to take over their crack business and tie it in with our weed business. Once we make this happen, we will be the richest and most powerful niggas in the city!"

"Nigga I'm feeling this shit!" Ubie blurted out loud.

"Nigga you's a master minder for real. Let's go get these ole washed up ass niggas out our way," Juju said as he passed the blunt to Foo.

"So how we gone move?" asked Lavar.

"We in August, so by January we should've put a dent in that click. By the middle of next year, the projects should be out of the hands of Gianni and in the hands of ours and that's at the latest!"

He passed the blunt to Ubie.

"Now look as yall can see, our crew is divided into five sections, and each man in here is a leader of a section. We established that in the beginning. I want each circle to be assigned to a D.T.W. member, meaning five of them niggas gone be under surveillance simultaneously. Each five-man circle is gone do their homework and monitor their assigned man until the moment of kill presents itself. After a circle execute their target, I'll assign that circle to their next target. We're the captains of our circles, so we must make sure our surveillance is discreet, and our kills are not done sloppy. Now yall will enlighten yall circle to what's going on, and I'll enlighten mines. Then yall report to me once yall got yall circle on the same page. Once everybody reports to me and tell me they car ready, that's when I'll round up the whole click and put words in their heart. And from that point on the killing spree will start and won't end until the mission is accomplished."

SIX MONTHS LATER

Jarvis, Damon, Anton, and Marlo were headed to Marysville prison to visit Wanisha, who was four months in on her two-year bid.

The day before she was sentenced, she handed over seventy thousand dollars of her money to Jarvis leaving it in his care. Of course, she knew it was a chance that bad luck could befall on Jarvis and in the process, she could lose her savings, but she didn't care.

She told him to put her money with his and continue to hustle, and if his luck was still up when she got back then she knew that she'll be 70 thousand to the good.

Either way it went, she let it be known that she was going to love him regardless. He also had her truck in the garage of he and Angelica's lay low spot. It was clear to see that she trusted and loved her some Jarvis.

****

It was freezing on this February morning as the four homies rolled down the highway in Damon's new truck.

"Man, this bitch better be the shit, whoever she got me coming to see. I already feel like I'm getting pimped........Smuggling some got damn dope to a bitch I don't even know!"

"Stop whining Damon you're doing it for Wanisha," said Anton. "And how you think I feel. I gotta tongue kiss Wanisha ass twice. At the beginning and at the end of the visit."

"Nigga stop faking," said Marlo. "She told me you tried to fuck before and she told you that she aint see you in that light because you her dawg."

"Oh yeahhh," Jarvis and Damon harmonized in unison.

"Man your sister was lying, I aint never tried to fuck her."

Jarvis and Damon started laughing at him.

"Thirsty ass nigga you tried to fuck the homegirl," Jarvis said through his laughter.

Anton started laughing his damn self.

"Yeah I once had a thang for her sexy gangsta ass I'll admit it. But I aint on that shit no more that's my homegirl."

"Fire up that burner," said Marlo.

Anton did. Jarvis who was in the back cracked his window.

Anton inhaled, blew the smoke out and said, "What's up with ole girl Meme, you still aint heard from her since she been in college nigga?"

"Naw she's doing her like I'm doing me. She aint my woman homie. She's not obligated to me."

Neither one of them replied because they knew he felt some type of way about her not calling since she's been gone.

"I know she always tell Yasha to tell me to tell you that she said hi though! Shit I'm not the 'messenger boy' she need to call your motherfucking ass her damn self," said Damon.

"Damn Marlo can I hit some'em," Damon whined.

Marlo hit the blunt and passed it to him.

An hour and a half later they were pulling into the parking lot of the women's prison.

"Damn I hate how they got my twin locked up in this bitch!"

This was their first time coming to see her and they each could feel her pain through those penitentiary bricks. After they put Marlo in his wheelchair, they headed to the prison's entrance.

Anton, Marlo, and Jarvis were on the opposite side of the visiting room from Damon, waiting for their visitors to come out. Wanisha came out first, dressed in a beige khaki suit with a fresh pair of all white Nikes on her feet. Her hair hung down to her shoulders and her frame had picked up some weight. The homies stood as she walked up smiling from ear to ear.

"What's up my niggas!" She greeted happily and bent down and hugged her brother tightly. Then she hugged and tongue kissed Anton with fake passion as she easily swallowed four balloons of ice. Anton was caught up in the moment and squeezed her ass. After the balloons were swallowed, she pulled away.

"Thanks. Now boy get your hands off my ass......Hey J-one! What's up baby!" she hugged J-one tight as she hugged her brother. Damon didn't know if he could interact with another visitor, but he didn't give a fuck, he had to go and hug his homegirl. She hugged Damon with love.

"I miss you girl you looking good. I see you alright in here," said Damon.

"Damon, now you know yo girl gone hold it down and I love you boy now get back over there and wait on Rhonda for these people show they ass. She's on her way out next."

When Rhonda came out, Wanisha nodded for Damon to stand up so she could be sure of who he was.

"Okay then," said Damon with satisfaction written all over his face. Their mouths locked, and the balloons went down her throat.

"Damn Damon you got me all horny bro. You know it's been a long time since I felt a man's touch," said Rhonda.

Damon ran his eyes all over her body.

"Shit I may have to keep my eyes on the prize. When you say your release date was again?"

They both laughed as they sat down and got lost in each other's company.

Although Wanisha and Marlo were twins, their love for one another was clearly observed from others even more than before. They both were shedding tears at the same time from having to be away from one another for so long. She couldn't stop hugging him. Besides the KKBG family, all the two had was each other and in their minds, that was more than enough.

"Girl you bet not be up in here on pussy," said Anton

"Get real! Can't no bitch please me. Nigga you are crazy you know that. Oh Yeah, J-one, guess who wrote me a few days ago?"

"Who?" asked J-one.

"Meme! She looked me up on the internet. It was good to hear from her, but half of the damn letter was talking about your ass. She still loves her some Jarvis baby. She sent me fifty dollars too, but I wrote her back and told her that she didn't have to do that because I'm good up in here."

"What did she say about me?"

"Yeah what did she say about lover boy?" Anton joked.

"She just said that she hasn't been in touch because hearing from you would probably make her want to leave and come running back to you. She talked a little bit about her boyfriend's first year on the basketball team and how everybody loves his game. She said she believes he is definitely going to the N.B.A."

"Yeah I saw him on tv a few weeks ago. The nigga a beast," Anton confirmed.

"O-State gone be in the March Madness Tournament's this year, shit they're 24 and 2. He's definitely the heart of the mob," Damon chimed.

That's good," said Jarvis.

Wanisha changed the subject. "What's up with them bitch ass Yg niggas?" she inquired with hate.

"It aint been nothing for real. Aint nobody been seeing them niggas. A lot of them D.T.W. niggas over there been getting murked though. I'm talking about back to back. Somebody running through them niggas like water," said Jarvis.

"Well shit they can rest in piss too. I still wanna Murk Ubie ass myself," she hissed as her eyes fell on her brother who was buying her some hot wings out of the vending machine.

"What type of drink you want sis?" he yelled.

"Sunkist grape!"

Damon walked up and ordered some hot wings for him and Rhonda.

"Okay then. I see you playing the husband role," Marlo joked as he wheeled himself back to his peoples.

Before the visit was over, they assured her that they were going to keep her with enough drugs to flood the compound so that she could leave the joint hood rich. Anton went to the bathroom and came back out with four more balloons in his mouth. These were filled with weed.

"VISITS ARE NOW OVER!" The c.o. yelled. They all stood up.

"Yall play it safe out there. I'll go crazy in here if something happens to one of yall!" She hugged her brother first not wanting to let go of him.

"I love you boy and be careful out there," she told him and kissed him on his cheek. She hugged J-one next.

"I look at you as our leader you know that? You have showed us all love from day one and I trust your instincts as much as my own, if not more."

She fell into Anton arms and they did the tongue kissing thing again. Everybody heard the deep moan that escaped his throat as she quickly swallowed them and pulled away.

"Boy sometimes I wonder about you," she blurted.

"I gotta fake like it's genuine shit!" Everybody started laughing.

25

"We have a bit of a problem," said Perry's nephew Dominick. Perry heart beat quickened to the notion of trouble.

"Meet me at Gordan Park immediately!"

"I'm on my way now," Perry confirmed and hung up.

Dominick Shaw was a narcotic detective for the same division Perry retired from. Dominick kept Perry informed of all information that was threatening to Gianni, and Perry paid him a healthy fee for his assistance. By Gianni having the heads up on what was coming at him, his dope spots flourished and held longevity.

When Perry pulled up into Gordan Park, he spotted his nephew in a crown Victoria, that had smoke blowing out the tail pipe, dissolving into the night. He parked on the side of him, got out and climbed in the passenger seat.

"Straight to the point," Perry demanded.

"The Feds are in town and been running an investigation for over two years now. It has finally leaked towards our way. The King Kennedy Projects is under investigation along with Kelso Avenue. Now a guy from the Kelso neighborhood was arrested and released by the Federales and has already given Gianni's name up as one of his suppliers."

"GOT DAMMIT!" Perry barked, slamming his fist into his thighs.

"That little fucker is lying. Gianni doesn't supply, his men do."

"Well what's broke can't be fixed on his end, but must be fixed on yours," Dominick affirmed.

"Yea yea, I have no other choice," said Perry.

"As soon as possible Unc! The feds are riding on his trail!"

"If not tonight, best believe by tomorrow. When you get the text 781, which is 187 backwards, you'll know."

Without another word to be said, he got back in his car and sharply bagged back and pulled away with an unwanted mission on his hands.

Perry couldn't chance his name popping up down the line by the mouth of Gianni once he was caught inside the Feds web. A six-year business relation had to be abolished, along with Gianni's life.

Gianni sat naked in his hot tub with his back against the wall resting his elbows against the landings. He had a bottle of Hennessey in his hand staring at the huge HD TV screen in front of him as the news reporter went over yesterday's killings. Each three victims were D.T.W. members.

Within the last six months over a dozen D.T.W. members were killed in cold blood. Some were his right-hand men and others-controlled crack spots of his that raked in no less than an easy fifteen thousand a day.

The latest three victims were killed faced down execution style after the crack house was invaded and robbed. Gianni was forced to shut down all his crack houses in the 30th block vicinity because it was clear to see that his clique of men was the target. Now on top of the regular business that flowed through the projects, it was now a major overflow but many of the project members fell back because they felt they were targets of the unknown. ...

After the reporter finished, Gianni turned up the bottle. He swallowed the strong toxic liquor and vigorously cleared his throat. Then suddenly he threw the bottle against the brick wall as it shattered into pieces. His main woman Reva came rushing in.

"Baby what's wrong?" she asked in a frantic tone.

"Bitch just clean it up!" He hissed and dropped his chin to his chest going into a drunken meditation. He knew that it was somebody inside of his clique that was behind these murders and paranoia had gotten the best of him. He didn't know who to trust.

Not to mention his occasional snort sessions, had turned into an intense habit over the last six months. He was starting to wonder was all this a message for him to get out of the game while he was on top. He realized that his mind was becoming weary from constantly thinking and trying to maneuver ways to stay at the top. A life he's known since the age of fifteen. Now at thirty-six, he reckoned that his time was up and it was time to move on. First, he had to find out who was behind these killings, so he could revenge the death of his close cronies and dedicated workers. Then maybe he could walk away with a smile.

****

As soon as Perry pulled out of Gordan Park, he dialed Andrea's number. Her sweet hello answered after the fourth ring.

"Andrea, I need to see you."

"Okay… Is there something wrong?"

"It's nothing that can't be fixed. Give me ten minutes."

"I'll be here Perry," she softly replied.

He parked around the corner and made his way back around to her house. The door opened without him having to knock. He entered and went straight to the living room. A few seconds later they were adjacent on the cream-colored love seat.

"I'm in a tight situation. A situation that can cost me my freedom."

Her soft facial expression was replaced with a genuine care. She had fell in love with Perry ever since their first encounter, and one day she had begged for him to take her away from Gianni. He knew what she meant and they both knew what had to be done for that to happen. All he would reply to Andrea was 'In time," but he wasn't banking on that time coming so quick.

He understood why she had a personal vendetta against Gianni and knew that with his consent, she would kill him with revenge for the death of J.d. She also was hoping that their relationship would be able to openly blossom.

"What kind of tight situation?" she asked with concern.

"Gianni alive in the near future will be a threat to my freedom. With him dead, everything will be good, and we can do us the way it's supposed to be done."

Her expression turned blank as a moment of silence followed.

"Okay so what do you need for me to do?"

"Kill him and I'll take care of the rest. I'll make it where as though nothing points towards you."
"How are we going to do that?"

"I'm going to explain everything to you but first I need to know if you can get him over here tonight. I need him dead tonight!"

She took a moment to think up a motive.

"Do you think that maybe by me telling him that the drugs he left over here is missing will make him come here tonight?"

"How much is it?" He questioned.

"I don't know, it's in the unplugged deep freezer in the basement."

He stood up abruptly.

"Show me."

She led him into the basement and opened the deep freezer and counted fifteen kilos of cocaine.

"Telling him that these is gone will only hurt his pride not his pockets, but he is definitely going to come."

She shut it back and turned to face him. He grabbed her by the waist and pulled her into him.

"Are you with me baby or what?"

If she would've said no, he was going to kill her and plan a different motive, but he knew she wanted Gianni dead so J.d. could finally rest in peace.

"I'm with you for more reasons than one baby."

"Well look, let me get this plastic out of my trunk and then I'll tell you how we gone move."

He cuffed her face in his hands and passionately kissed her lips.

"I'll be right back," he blurted and headed for the steps with her following behind him.

Gianni sat at the living room glass table snorting lines of grade A cocaine. Reva was seated on the side of him tooting lines of her own, something she had recently started doing with Gianni. His cellular started ringing which was only a reach away. He grabbed his phone and answered it gruffly. Andrea, who was using a throw away phone, cut straight to the point.

"Gianni have you been here today?" She asked with a touch of frantic.

A numb buck-eyed Gianni said, "Drea what in the fuck are you talking about?"

"After I came back from getting my hair done earlier I didn't notice but now I can tell that someone has been in here rambling. I'm figuring maybe it was you considering it wasn't a break and enter and your stuff in the freezer is gone."

Reality of her telling him that he'd been robbed was quickly comprehended.

"This bitch done crossed me," he thought to himself. He didn't want to scare her before he got there.

"It's gone?" he asked calmly.

"So, you didn't come? It wasn't you?" she asked timorously.

"Not over the phone. We'll talk when I get there." Without waiting for a response, he hung up.

"I should've killed this bitch from the jump!" yelled Gianni. Reva looked up at him from the table but remained silent. Ten minutes later he stormed out the house, jumped into his car and pulled out. He had every intention to kill Andrea with his bare hands.

The entire drive there, he didn't fully analyze the situation. In other words, he was moving without thinking, something that he never did in the past. Stress, paranoia, and his toot addiction had become his downfall in so many ways. His third eye was now blind, and he could no longer see what was coming at him. His thinking capabilities had been altered from the day to day numbness of his brain. Gianni was no longer at his best. He was at his worst falling into a trap that only spared one alternative.........Death!!!

Gianni pulled into the drive way sharply and killed the engine. He hopped out and fumbled for the right key until he found it, inserted it into the door, and entered the house.

"I'm in here," said Andrea.

Gianni came around the corner into the living room and quickly froze in his final step. He looked shockingly at the gun she had trained on him to the thick plastic under his feet. Then he looked back to her face with his mouth open.

"Andrea, what the fuck are you doing? Do you want your people to die behind this?" His threat sounded more like a plea.

"Nigga kill the threats. You're the only one that's going to die, and I hope J.d. kills you in the next life."

Gianni knew his life was about to be over.

"Do you really think I had one feeling in my heart for you? You didn't do nothing but beat J.d. to the punch. I wish he would've gave me the okay to kill you like I'd asked him to. Then he would still be here."

She locked her arm out with the gun barrel aimed at the center of his forehead. Gianni tried to make a desperate reach for his waist as the first bullet flew past his head.

He fumbled for his gun and rushed her at the same time as three silent shots penetrated his face. She jumped up from the couch not wanting the body to fall on her. She instantly smelled bodily fluids as his corpse slid off the couch onto the floor. Seeing his body violently jerking caused her to fire two more shots in the side of his head to make sure he was dead. Suddenly he became still. By the shots being muffled from the silencer, they never escaped the walls of the living room. After Perry got the call that the task was finished, he drove from around the corner into the driveway behind Gianni's beamer. Once inside he quickly wrapped Gianni's body up in the plastic, took the murder weapon from her, and told her to be ready by the time he returned.

He took Gianni's keys and opened his truck, entering and exiting the back door. Five minutes later he was pulling out of the driveway. He abandoned the body on a narrow quiet street, then headed to a familiar chill out bar a few blocks over.

Two months after Gianni's death, the Yg members had managed to completely take over the 30th projects. Only a few D.T.W. members tried to resist which resulted to on sight gun clapping and they were forced to let go of the gold mine they once controlled. By the time May rolled around, Clientele from all over the city was pulling through the projects, looking for the special plant. They were no longer in an open park, they now felt safe and secured. They were no longer in the shadows of the D.T.W. Posse, they were now the men themselves, operating both the crack and weed establishments. ………

Perry sent Andrea at Foo, to establish a fake friendly relationship with him so he could sale Foo the fifteen kilos that he took from Gianni. After going to a bar, the Yg members hung at, eventually she met him and seduced him into her web. Numbers was swiped, and the pattern was set. The following days she strung him along, in his anticipation to fuck her before she finally allowed him to take her to a hotel. After they had sex, she told him that they had to be discreet, because of the relationship with her husband. She went on ranting about her husband's lifestyle as a big-time drug dealer and how it brought forth infidelity between them. Then Foo asked questions and she answered them. Her job was done because the seed was planted.

Foo was already looking for a strong cocaine connection. He had one, but he needed a second string to compensate for the first one. So eventually he cut in to Andrea and she arranged for them to meet. Once Foo found out that his Kilo's was going for ten thousand, he put an order in for twenty of them, but Perry told him that he only had fifteen left. Foo took them off his hands. He also told Foo that he was at the end of his career in the dope game. That he was going to dedicate his life to Andrea. Perry did that so Foo wouldn't get comfortable fucking his bitch or having him as a connect. A little after their transaction, Andrea broke it off with Foo, telling him that her and her husband was trying to rebuild their marriage back with honesty. Foo didn't trip or try to hold on, and everybody walked away happy.

26

Jarvis and Angelica were lying in the bed at their lay low spot across town. It was 10:34 in the morning and they'd just finished a session of hard core sex. After they caught their breath, they made it to the shower and took one together. Angelica threw a long white t shirt on over her thong and slid her feet into some pink fluffy made house shoes and went downstairs to cook breakfast for the two. Jarvis was putting on lotion when the telephone rang.

"Hello."

"What's up nigga! Aye get dressed. Me, Damon and M-2 are on the way through. Shit done hit the fan dawg," said Anton.

"What done happened now?"

"Them laws nigga. In a minute!" Click.

Less than ten minutes later, he was letting his homies in through the front door. A fully clothed Angelica was sitting on the living room couch.

"Turn to the twelve o'clock news," said Damon, the first to enter the living room.

"The feds hit the hood today."

"What!" Angelica blurted, while reaching for the remote on the table in front of her. As they waited for the update, they informed Jarvis of everything they knew. Then the news reporter broadcasted the situation in its verity.

"Through the wee hours of the morning, the Federales did a sweep on several KKK members known as the King Kennedy Killers. Over twenty members were arrested and charged under conspiracy and approximately 5.8 million dollars was confiscated in the process of this morning arrests. A handful of unsolved murder cases are also being reopened and eighty five percent factual proof that Andre Wimms, A.K.A. Dre, Johnathan Taylor, A.K.A. J-Roc, Terrence Duncan A.K.A. T-kill and Therman Williams, A.K.A. T-money, were behind the killings of............"

They went from showing the accused mugshots, to showing alive pictures of the victims. Then the news reporter stated, "Each of these KKK members were affiliated with the notoriously known, Jermaine Doss, who was killed almost two years ago while under the same ongoing investigation. His sobriquet to the streets was J.d. and he was the notorious crime boss of the King Kennedy Killers."

Within forty-eight hours Jarvis had sold both of his vehicles, packed up his belongings and caught a Greyhound bus out to Baltimore Maryland.

Prior to the feds invasion, Jarvis Aunty Carol had given him a number to reach D-Bear out in B-More because D-Bear was trying to get in touch with him. When Jarvis called him, they both were happy and excited to hear from one another, considering they hadn't spoken in almost four years. Jarvis could tell that it was a lot D-Bear wanted to say but couldn't over the phone. He could tell in D-Bear's voice that he was doing good. After they made plans to hook up soon, they hung up. Then two weeks later he received another call from Jarvis instantly detecting trouble in his cousin's voice. Jarvis was making a desperate getaway from Cleveland and needed to lay low. D-Bear welcomed him with open arms. Before he left, he touched a few of his close ones with money gifts because he didn't know how long he would be gone. He left Angelica with five thousand dollars, gave his baby mama

Roxanne ten thousand dollars and gave his mother who was six months drug free five thousand dollars. He was proud of his mother and felt secure since she had finally met a good man who helped her kick her habit.

He was paranoid as all hell riding the bus with over two hundred thousand dollars in his luggage, but some chances had to be taken. Jarvis didn't know if he was being watched by the Feds or not, but to play it safe, he had to get away for a while.

When Jarvis emerged from the station into daylight, he spotted D-Bear sitting on the hood of a brand-new silver Chevy Malibu. Jarvis dropped his luggage and they hugged violently. Pedestrians walked around them as they cluttered the sidewalk.

"What's crackin nigga this you," said Jarvis while pointing to the car.

"Hell yeah nigga. This my baby. But what's up with you man, I couldn't wait to see you! Is everything good or what?"

"Man I don't know. I'll holla at you about it in the car," said Jarvis.

"Well come on nigga we out!"

After Jarvis threw his luggage in the trunk, they hopped in the car and pulled away from the curb. Jarvis put D-Bear up on what's been going on in Cleveland.

"Yeah you're doing the right thing by getting the fuck from down there. Besides nigga, it's a different type of bread to eat up here. I think you gone like the taste of it," said D-Bear with a huge grin on his face.

"I really just want to stay out the way for a minute. You feel me."

"Oh yeah most definitely. But when the smoke clears, I got a million dollar block you can eat on. Meaning you aint gotta be in no rush to go back home. As a matter of fact, I need you on my time."

Since D-Bear moved to Baltimore with his father, he became a member of the G-Click. The G-click ran a million-dollar establishment in the Gilmore projects. But just because it's a million-dollar establishment doesn't mean the hustlers are millionaires. The ones that made millions left the game alone and the ones that's following in their footsteps is traveling down bumpy roads.

"What kind of bread it is fam?" Jarvis asked.

"First of all, the dope game up here is different from the dope game in Cleveland. What yall call dope is crack. What we call dope is heroin. Statistically, at least a million dollars a day flow through this city getting spent on that mud because mutherfuckers need it fam. They need it so bad they'll kill if they can't have it. That should give you a clear picture of how it's poppin."

His words enticed Jarvis to say the least and he was anxious to hear more.

"Well shit, if it's poppin like that nigga you should be rich," said Jarvis.

D-Bear chuckled.

"Nigga I don't give a fuck if it was a billion-dollar block, there's always obstacles in the game. Obstacles will set niggas back continuously until niggas learn to overcome those obstacles. The niggas who can overcome, get rich and are able to get out the way. The ones who can't overcome their setbacks, might die trying."

"Damn! Is the entire city the projects? I thought Cleveland was raggedy. This city looks beyond repair."

"Eighty five percent of it is, but its real low key and I think you gone like it."

"Good looking though Fam I appreciate you!"

"Nigga this is what family is for. I had one of my broads furnish it out with a brand-new bedroom set and all that. Took care of all that yesterday so you good. So here me out bro, I can guarantee that once I give you the game and you play it, you aint gone think about going back to Cleveland. At all."

****

Jarvis was starting to hang out in the Gilmore projects with D-Bear and his cronies. He wasn't hustling but he was amazed at how much money was being made off heroin. Gilmore projects consisted of ten high rise buildings and all the G-Click members controlled each building. The drug dealers ran a certain floor in each building and the buyers would regularly stand in a twenty to sixty-man line in each building waiting to purchase and go. A few nod heads rotated a two-hour shift police watch, constantly making the police and task force job strenuous. There was only one way in and one way out of the projects. So once the nod heads give word that they're coming, nine times out of ten, their effort to arrest went unsuccessful.

Since Jarvis hustle remained at a standstill, he realized that he'd been doing a whole lot of fucking.

Every day D-Bear had different women over and almost each one had a thing for Jarvis out of town Swagger. Some wanting more than what they were worth, which was only a one-night stand.

Jarvis bought himself a midnight blue S-class Jag for his 18th birthday. Low profiles and Giovanni rims stood the car up. A moon roof was customized at the top, the windows were tinted, and the leather interior was a magnificent cream color. After treating himself with a luxury ride, he became eager to eat some of the bread that constantly flowed through Gilmore.

D-Bear and Jarvis were in D-Bears' lady friend's living room discussing matters of business while she stood over the stove preparing dinner. By heroin being a scarce entity in Cleveland, D-Bear had to school Jarvis from step one. First, he told him the quantity prices from lowest to highest. Then he taught him how to cut pure heroin, what to cut it with, and the benefits from cutting it.

"Aight so if a Kilo of this shit run me sixty-thousand, how much will I get back if I sale it in all fifty-five-dollar vials?"

"If you were to go out there with a brick right now and didn't stop until you were finished, you gone make no less than two hundred thousand dollars!"

Jarvis let out an enticed whistle.

"That's one hell of a profit cuddie," said Jarvis.

"Damn, and by Cleveland only having a few strips that sale heroin, how much do you think a kilo of this would go for up there?"

"It almost double. About seventy-five bands."

"Why you aint never bring the hustle back home. You could've been the man."

"This is my home now Fam, and besides, I aint with transporting over the state line," said D-Bear. "So, don't let that be ya motive yo. I'm telling you right now, that is not a smart idea. You can get rich right here with me. You aint gotta go nowhere. My dad's brother run the Jets and If I buy a half a key or better, I get a five-thousand-dollar discount. Here's my catch 22, that gambling bug been hitting me J-one. The dice killing me. I done dropped down to a quarter key status," he admitted.

"Fuck them dice nigga let's get this money!"

"See that's what I'm talking about. Your presence alone motivates a nigga. I remember when we were little, and you used to come over and spend the weekend at my mama's house, and we used to play two on two crate ball against Fonzo and Tiger! remember them?" asked D-Bear.

Jarvis started laughing.

"Yeah I remember them niggas."

"But it aint all about them niggas," D-Bear confirmed. "It's about the ambition you've always had in you to win. Every time we played against other niggas, rather it was football, basketball, or whatever, yo ambition to win always made me play harder. We were really like brothers."

"That's crazy right," said Jarvis.

"Naw you know what's crazy? I never thought I was gone get you up here. Look cuddie. The G-Click homies they cool, it aint like you gotta prove yourself or nothing like that. Like I said, my uncle dope feed them niggas. We got beef situations with other strips, but you up here to eat not to inherit another nigga's beef.

1408 is our building number and we don't sale nothing but raw out of that bitch. The other building boys dope be cut and stepped on. Now you may think they make more money selling stepped on mud but by the time they get rid of a stepped on half a brick, you would've been done flipped two or three times selling it raw. We got all the raw heads coming to 1408!"

"You say a quarter key go for eighteen bands?"

"Yep."

"Order me one cuddie." ....

After Jarvis tried his hand with the quarter kilo, he fell in love with his new-found hustle. The profit was tremendous, and he got rid of it all in less than a week. He wasn't thinking about going back home no time soon. He soon realized that D-Bear had a vicious gambling habit. One day he might win fifteen thousand and the next day lose forty. That was the obstacle that D-Bear couldn't get around. The monkey wrench the game threw at him, to prevent him from one day walking away rich and happy. Jarvis tried to talk him into leaving the dice alone, but it was useless, so Jarvis let him do him.

27

Back at home, the KKBG Posse re-opened the projects, but the business was moving at a slow pace and the absence of Jarvis was clearly shown. M-2 was three months in on an 18-month bid and Damon was a couple weeks in on a one-year sentence.

The team thing was no more and the unity amongst themselves was dying by the day. Everybody missed Jarvis and was eagerly waiting on his return. None of them knew his plans on coming back had gotten real slim. Within two months of chilling and 3 months of flipping packs, Jarvis had a nest haven in Columbia, Maryland with a built-in tornado trap in the basement that he used as a stash away. If you didn't know the trap was an opening in the floor, you wouldn't know, so he felt safe using the house as a rest spot. He still had the lay low in the high rise. By the spot being on the block, it was beneficial to him.

On October 14th, 2016, Anton caught a quick flight out to Maryland. Jarvis invited him over, so he could spend some time with one of his best men. They gave each other a brotherly hug at the terminal happy to see each other.

"Damn nigga I like this motherfucka. Is this you?" asked Anton as they pulled away from the airport. Nobody from the KKBG knew his new-found hustle or territory.

"Yeah this me. What's been going on in the hood though?"

"Big homie you wouldn't believe it if I told you how dry the hood is. It's hard to move a pack in the hood now it's so slow.

"Straight up...........Damn that bitch a pick back up with time. I just sent Wanisha, Damon, and M-2 a thousand a piece."

"When you coming back home? The homies miss you. I need you and Imma keep it gangsta, the hood is falling apart without you. Without you, Damon, M-2 and Wanisha, a nigga feel kind of lost. I mean the original homies and KKS hoes are out there, but shit is changing bro."

In other words, Anton was telling Jarvis they need help to keep the hood alive. Jarvis felt a tight knot in his chest as he pulled into his driveway. He couldn't turn to look Anton in his face because he knew that he wasn't coming home no time soon. But Anton wasn't slow. He could tell Jarvis had his hands into something. A brand-new Jag, a nice style home, and his hesitancy to answer his last question told him all he needed to know. Anton knew that Jarvis wasn't going to be spending any money if he wasn't making any.

"So, what's up with Roxanne?" asked Jarvis once they made it in the house and got comfortable. Jarvis would only send money orders but wouldn't call because he knew she was going to beg him to come back home with his child.

"She fucking with that nigga L.K. Remember the nigga Tracy was telling us about?"

"Bitch aint waste no time huh!" Jarvis was in his gut. He felt like she betrayed him without a reason. Jarvis changed the subject.

"So how is your seed doing, Lil Anton Jr? I know that lil nigga getting big," smiled Jarvis.

"They doing good. Tracy good. Still in love with the kid."

"Look homie. I got a lot going on in B-more right now. I done hooked up with my cousin and fell in love with the heroin game. It's kind of hard for me to walk away right now. It's open arms for you Anton. You need to come up here with me. We can get right and go back home and touch them."

Anton realized that times were changing but more so coming between him and his man.

"You do what you gotta do homie, but you know me, I'm hood bound. That's where the movie started and that's where it's gone end for me. So, what do you want me to tell the homies?"

Jarvis was hurt because greed had him by the balls and no matter how he looked at it, it felt as though he was walking away from his people. He saw the hurt in his man's eyes, but Anton tried to disguise it.

"Tell them what I told you, but tell I'll be back." He didn't know if his words were true.

Later on that night, they met up with D-Bear and a few of the G-Click Homies to party at a poppin ass club in the city. A broad name Julissa who had a thing for Jarvis approached him with her game face on. She was an eight piece and her girl was a dime. Jarvis and Anton took them to the closest hotel and had their way with them. A few days later, Anton was headed back to Cleveland. Before he left, Jarvis blessed him with a free ten thousand dollars, remembering his remark a few days ago about his money being low. They hugged a farewell at the terminal before going their separate ways.

28

"Dunk it baby Dunk it," Omirah yelled.

Marco had his opponent beat on a fast break and slammed dunked it vigorously into the rim. The crowd jumped to their feet, accolading the Buckeyes come back. It was now 71-73. Perdue was up with under two minutes left in the game. Three minutes ago, OSU were down by twelve. Marco scored the last eight of their ten points in a complete zone to turn this game into a victory on their home court.

Everyone was on pins and needles as the clock was winding down. With twelve seconds remaining, down by two, a double-teamed Marco found and outlet. He drove the ball, then stopped, popped in an all net shot tying the game with two point three seconds left. The crowd went into a frenzy as Omirah jumped up and down. They were now in overtime.

This was Marco second year on the team. Last year he did excellent, averaging twenty-eight points a game. They lost in the final four against Duke and Marco promised to take them all the way this year.

It was 78-74, Buckeyes way, with two minutes and some change left. Marco, a shooting guard, had the ball in his hands. He passed it and the ball rotated around the court killing time. Then suddenly Marco made a sharp cut and the point guard passed it to him. In his momentum, Marco completed the layup but came down on his opponent's foot breaking his ankle. A silent hush swept over the center as Marco laid on his side holding on to his ankle in great pain. Omirah who couldn't take seeing her man in pain rushed the court, but security held her back. Five minutes later he was hauled off, and the game continued. They still managed to win.

The men's dorms were separated from the women and co-ed visits were 3:00pm to 11:00 pm, but much of the time that rule was broken. It was ten o'clock pm, Omirah was leaned into Marco. He was emotionally distraught about his broken ankle. Sitting out for the rest of the season didn't sit well with him. As he constantly vented, she continued to appease him by assuring that everything would eventually be okay.

"Meme everything is not okay...... Not with me. I was trying to be in the draft next year and I would've been if it wasn't for this."

"Well is it that bad that you may have to be stuck here with me for a little while longer?" she asked softening him up as she nudged him in his side.

"Huh handsome!"

"Naw baby that's the beauty in it. I'm just disappointed in my luck that's all."

"Well babe......Things happen for a reason. Just be patient okay."

"I guess I don't have a choice," he ruefully replied.

A few days later, Omirah was lounging in her dormitory room and received a call from the administrative building. It was 3:26 pm and she had just finished studying for tomorrow's exam.

"Hello," she answered.

"Yes Ms. Henderson, sorry to interrupt you, but you have a visitor here by the name of Jarvis Cooper."

An immense wave of happiness and confusion rushed over her. At first, she was at a loss for words, but she got a hold of her composure.

"Yes......um......tell him I'll be right there."

"Will do," the woman replied and hung up.

She stood there, stunned, slowly placing the phone back to its cradle. She missed Jarvis a great deal. There were so many sleepless nights as he would be her last thoughts before finally drifting off to sleep. She was honestly now in love with Marco meaning that she wasn't supposed to be having any male visitors unless they were family. Especially not Jarvis.

She knew that it was up to her to handle this situation appropriately. Deep inside she felt powerless, but once she got herself together she quickly made her way to the front of the building. As soon as she walked through the doors she spotted him sitting patiently with his elbows on his knees reading a sports magazine. He stood up and smiled as she approached.

"Jarvis... What are you........... What are you doing here?"

"I came to see you. Is that wrong in your book?"

She let out a sigh.

"Of course not," she replied as she reached out and hugged him. He let his hands fall to her hips.

"Girl you look beautiful. What is it like up here?"

They broke apart.

"Everything is good. Jarvis no disrespect but me and Marco are engaged and"----------------------

"Well look I'm in room 203 at the Sheraton. I'll be there until early afternoon tomorrow. If you can break away, then hopefully I'll see you before I go."

Without another word he turned and left. She hated to see him go.

Jarvis had caught a flight from Maryland to Columbus the previous day. His intentions were to see her first, then drive a rental to Cleveland to see his mother, a few homies, and to stop by J.d.'s grave site.

For the rest of the day Jarvis didn't have any plans as he lounged across his bed shirtless wearing dark blue jeans and socks. Thoughts of Omirah getting married weighed on his mind. He realized that it was time to let go of her completely. Three knocks at the door snapped him out of his trance. He got up and walked to the door.

"Who is it?"

"It's me J-one."

He opened the door and stepped to the side. Omirah walked in with her arms folded over her chest. He followed behind her as she turned to face him.

"Sorry if I was blunt earlier"-------- he cut her off.

"What you apologizing for? You let it be known what's what." She ran her eyes over his naturally cut up physique.

"So how long you gone make me wait for a kiss," he asked as he walked up to her and closed the gap between them. She was powerless in her ability to remain faithful to Marco when it came to Jarvis, she admitted to herself as their lips locked. They tongue kissed aggressively as he pushed her by the ass into him. Then she pulled away.

"No Jarvis, I better go."

She knew that if she stayed the line would be crossed.

"You know what... GET THE FUCK OUT WITH YOUR FAKE ASS! One minute everything is good, the next minute you switch to something else. BITCH, I aint got time for this shit!"

Omirah was stunned by his words.

"Jarvis why is you"--------- He cut her off.

"Bitch don't Jarvis me, and forget I ever made this trip! Now get the fuck out!"

"Stop cursing at me J-one. Why are you flipping on me?" She was on the verge of breaking down. He went and opened the door.

"Look, just get out and erase me from your life. I'm no good for you anyway. You got what's good for you."

She held her composure as she slowly walked pass him out the door. After the door closed, she slid down the wall and wept, totally distraught by his words.

Jarvis sat on the bed heated.

"Fuck Everybody. Imma do me. I'm coming first and everything else will be after that," he yelled to the wall. It was clear that he took a lot of stress out on Omirah.

"And fuck that bitch too. Fuck everybody."

The next day he shot down to Cleveland. After spending time with his mother, he went to see his son. He sat with him in his arms, giving all his attention to him. Roxanne sat across from him staring adamantly at him. (He didn't reveal his hand about L.K.)

"So, are you here to stay," she asked. He didn't pay her any attention.

"What's your problem. Why are you ignoring me?"

He continued to play with his son.

"Why can't you be a man and tell me what's on your mind?"

"Bitch what the fuck is wrong with you," he snapped.

"Stop talking to me Roxanne!"

"Oh okay, I get it. Your friend must have told you something. You can get out yo gut cause L.K. is nothing but a friend."

His attention was back to his child.

"You know what. You think you can just leave us for six months, send money, and everything be everything. I don't think so J-one. I haven't had sex with anybody if that's what you're thinking. I'm done tolerating you leaving us like that."

He laid his son down on the couch and stood up.

"Be looking for something in the mail for him. I'll holla."

"You know what.... Fuck you J-one and your money. He doesn't need none of your dirty ass money nigga!"

She continued to spit harsh words at him as he walked out of the house. She was right on his heels.

"I hope your ass go to jail." ....She wasn't able to finish because Jarvis turned around and slapped the shit out of her. Then he grabbed her by her throat and forcefully drove her up against the house.

"Bitch don't you ever say that again! DO YOU HEAR ME," he growled through his clenched teeth. She nodded yes, frightened by the look in his eyes. She watched him pull out from the driveway and down the street, never taking her hands away from her neck.

When he pulled the rental into the Jets, he noticed it was a lot of homies and KKS girls out. They didn't know who he was until he got out the car. Everyone displayed their happiness as he hugged and dapped his people. Angelica didn't greet him or display any emotion towards his presence, as she served the crack head and posted back up. Jarvis didn't pay her any attention. Everyone crowded around him as if he was their Martin Luther King and that touched him to the core.

"Nigga you right on time," Freeda yelled from her porch." "Wanisha is on the phone!" He went and grabbed the phone.

"What's up Y-love!" (That's Wanisha's nickname)

"Nigga don't Y-love me. Why you aint keeping it gangsta J-one. Out of all people"----------

"Hold on Wanisha. What the fuck is you saying. Didn't nothing change about me. I'm just doing what the fuck gotta be done right now. I aint about to explain myself either."

"You should nigga shit. We wouldn't turn our backs on you, so why are you doing that shit to us?"

"Y-love, I love you and I got you when you get out. Aint shit changed but right now my hands are tied. Aight shorty?" Silence followed his words.

"Come home J-one. Baltimore aint you. KKBG is you. Even if we all have to struggle to build the block back up, so what! I don't mind struggling or being broke with my people. I don't mind because I'll die for my people. I love you too J-one but come home. We need you more than Baltimore."

Jarvis didn't know what to say.

"I love you shorty and I'll see you when you get out."

He handed the phone back to Freeda. Angelica adamant behavior towards him disappeared when he walked up and hugged her. She was mad at him too for not coming back home.

"What you done found a nigga or some'em?" asked Jarvis.

"J-one I don't have time for a nigga. I just been hustling. We're all trying to build the block back up. I heard you was the man in Baltimore."

He ignored her statement.

"Are you still my ride or die Starlet or what?"

Angelica features softened. She loved Jarvis but didn't want to admit it.

"How I'm gone ride or die for you if you're not around? But yes J-one, I'm still yo ride or die."

"I won't be gone too much longer though," he assured her and kissed her in the mouth. He didn't know if those words were true, he told her what she wanted to hear.

The next day, before he left, he went to visit J.d.'s grave. He was the only visitor at the silent Cemetery. A fierce November wind was violently blowing as he stared down on his dead homie.

"J.d. what it's doing up there in heaven big homie?"........ You can't even imagine how much I wish you was still here. The world need niggas like you. I know you been watching down on the hood and as you can see it's ripped apart ever since the Feds came. Now I'm faced with a tough decision because it's like, I'm the chosen one. Where I'm at now, within two years I can be rich and out the way."

He took a second to gather his thoughts.

"You told me from day one what my purpose was. You told me not to play this game with emotions but J.d., I got love for them niggas, and it's hard for me to turn away. J.d. what would you do?" He fell silent as if he was waiting for an answer.

"J.d. you pushed me to become a made nigga and that's what I'm striving to be. You put it in my heart and I love you for that. When I see you again, I wanna be able to tell you that I accomplished that. If I can't tell you that, I would feel like a failure and I really wouldn't want to see you again. This decision placed before me is a powerful move on this chess board of life. I know it's gonna determine if I'll win or lose. Regardless of what happens, I miss you dawg, and I just needed to talk to you to get my mind right. I don't know exactly when I'll be back, all I can say is in time, and that's a promise."

29

It was in the early afternoon, the 3rd floor of the 1408 building was crowded with nod heads and hustlers transacting in business. Jarvis had gone through an ounce of heroin in less than thirty minutes. He shot to his lay low spot in the sky and grabbed another broken-down ounce and quickly prepared to make his way back to 1408. Before he made it inside the building, Vell pulled up in his E-430 cocaine white Benz. D-bear climbed from the back, and D-bo got out of the passenger seat. D-bo had on a gray jailhouse sweat suit and some black state boots. His bald head glistened from the sun, and had thick sideburns connecting into his goatee. He had to be hitting at least 455 in the joint because the nigga was solid as a rock. Six two in height with a bulldog look that was naturally painted on his face. He was eighteen when he left and now at 25, you could tell he was about to chase the years he'd lost to the system.

"Aye J-one, come meet the homie D-bo, said D-Bear. A project chick who was on her way inside the building spoke to J-one and he gave her his attention, showing he wasn't eager to meet anybody.

"Shaunna what's up with your cousin. Why she ducking me?"

"Naw she just got a nigga that's crazy, so she stays real low key with her shit. So, you gotta be low key with your approach." Her eyes fell on D-bo.

"Shit there goes my nigga. What's up yo!" She ran up to him and hugged him as some of the G-click homies started emerging from the building. While D-bo was being showed welcome home love, J-one stood in front of the 1408 building. D-Bear walked up to him.

"Yo that's the homie. Nigga put in mad work before he left. I wasn't down here yet, but I heard all about it. I hear niggas around the city fear him."

The crowd started coming their way. D-bo looked J-one up and down and asked him, "Who is you?"

"I'm J-one and D-bear is my people." Jarvis didn't like the aggressiveness of his question. Even though he didn't know D-bear, he most definitely knew his uncle Ronnie. Besides, D-bear had sent him money orders, and pictures on the regular so that he could be in D-bo good graces. He wasn't with seeing to many new faces on his block and he let that be known.

"Damn yall niggas getting soft. Yall letting niggas come eat with yall now?"

"Man, that's D-bear people he cool," said the homie shorty.

"I don't give a fuck who people he is. I bet not see another unfamiliar face or I'm knocking em out and going in his pockets. Nigga this is G-Block not everybody block."

Jarvis remained expressionless with his tech nine on his waist. The homie Nell said, "Nigga you better strap yo big ass up cuz nigga's been stopped fighting!"

"Here nigga," said shorty and handed him a bull dog four-four. Then everybody started hitting him off with money gifts. Everybody but Jarvis, who turned around and dipped back in the building to get the rest of his work off.

That night the G-click homies posse'd up in an eight-car lane and shot to D.C. to kick it at the 'Uptown Lounge' A popular night club.

Jarvis rolled in the passenger of D-bear's Cadillac and two more homies were in the backseat. The eight-car lane pulled in back to back finding their parking spaces.

When they made it inside the club the dance floor was jammed packed. The women were dancing freaky to the banging Go-Go music.

"Aye cuddie, this go-go shit is what's poppin up here yo. Damn check out shorty over there."

Jarvis eyes fell on the broad he was talking about. Dark skinned, long hair, and was hella stacked dancing by herself.

"Go see what it do nigga," said Jarvis.

"Holla back," D-bear replied and headed towards the girl.

J-one went to the bar and ordered a bottle of Ace of Spade.

"Yo J-one grab me one," yelled Shorty. After Jarvis retrieved the bottles, he handed one back to shorty. For a minute J-one sat at the bar facing the club action, turning up his bottle here and there. Then a short brown skin chick with box braids and a cute face, danced her way to him. She grabbed his hands and took him on to the dance floor. Arms up and bottle in one hand, he danced to the back of her body. Then she turned around and threw one leg up wrapping it around his and pumping herself into him. Another broad approached him from the back, sandwiching him in.

Jarvis was feeling the go-go thing. Then a beautiful jet-black woman caught his attention. She was dancing with a guy but appeared to be uninterested in who she was dancing with. As if she sensed him staring at her, she looked at Jarvis and their eyes locked. After the song Jarvis stepped off the floor. He had every intention to become acquainted to this gorgeous dark-skinned woman. He played it casual as he circled the club, bumping shoulders with different partiers, but keeping a keen eye on faces looking for the special one. Then suddenly he spotted her seated on a leather sofa with her arms folded over her chest. Two people was seated next to her, but her body language said that there was no connection between them. Before Jarvis approached, he studied her. Her beauty was one of a kind. Thick lips, a soft uniquely structured nose, oval eyes, and jet-black hair that was the same color as her skin hanging freely down pass her shoulders. It seemed to Jarvis that she didn't really match the crowd. She was older than thirty. He decided to approach her.

"What's up ma you wanna dance?" he asked with his hand out. A look that could've meant so much, but probably meant nothing at all had come across her face. Then she smirked and grabbed his hand as they hit the floor. Jarvis talked to her the entire time they danced.

"What's your name shorty," asked Jarvis.

"Why ask me my name if you already named me?"

"Did I offend you?"

"No. You probably call all the females that." Her African accent was extremely thick.

"Well I'm Kyla. Why have you been watching me tonight?"

Jarvis was thrown back by her question.

"First of all, my name is Jarvis."

"That was my next question," said Kyla.

"I was interested in the person I saw," smiled Jarvis.

"So, in other words you pursued me?"

"Well you can say that," said Jarvis.

"That's a very attractive trait in you."

"What's that?" asked Jarvis.

"Going after what you want. Do you usually get what you want Mr. Jarvis?"

Jarvis smiled.

"What's funny?" she asked

"The cute little questions you keep asking me."

"Are you gone answer me?"

They stared in each other's eyes.

"What......Oh you asked do I get what I want? It depends."

"Hmm, depends on what?"

Jarvis threw a punch of his own.

"Tonight, it depends on you."

****

The gate opened. She drove her Maybach up the long swirling driveway and parked the car. Jarvis who was in the passenger, couldn't believe his catch tonight ever since he climbed in her car at the club. Neither could D-bear and the G-click homies, who watched him leave with Kyla. Now as he looked through the windshield at her mansion, he couldn't help but display a look of awe.

"Can I trust you around expensive things?"

"Damn. You get me all the way up here then question whether or not I'm a thief?"

"No, just an honest question looking for an honest answer."

"No ma I don't steal. In fact, I'm an expensive nigga"-----------she cut him off.

"Please don't use that word. Are you ready?"

They got out and went into the beautiful styled mansion that had marble floors, crystal chandeliers, a lower level swimming pool and an overall exquisite setting all the way through.

Kyla originally was from Nigeria. She'd been living in America ever since she was twenty-two. Now, at the age of thirty-six, she was rich due to a twenty-million-dollar lawsuit she won against a hospital that gave her the wrong medicine for a kidney infection, causing her early stages of Kidney disease. As a wealthy real estate owner, Kyla commitment towards her company was intense. She remained single by choice, never allowing a man to hold a position in her life. She wasn't with the closeness of a relationship and men in her age range wasn't her taste of choice. Jarvis was about to get blessed with a passionate night of hard core sex, like various youngsters in the past. Each one she never saw again, because the next morning she would make closure between herself and her one-night lover. Of course, she knew that she was playing with danger.

She was fully aware that one of her catches could turn out to be a psychopath, but she was also enticed by danger. To her that made the sex even better. She led him down to the swimming pool area. Jarvis sat on a leather loveseat that was out of splashing waters reach. Kyla went behind the bar and came over to him with two champagne glasses cuffed by two fingers and a bottle of fine wine in the other. She sat down next to him and gave him a glass and filled them up. She held up her glass and said, "Cheers to one night between us that only we will know about and only we can share."

They clinked glasses and sipped.

"Hmm, okay, so Jarvis, are you going to get naked for me?"

'This shit is crazy', Jarvis thought to himself.

"Why don't you get naked for me?" asked Jarvis.

"Okay sure," she said and stood up.

Jarvis watched as she seductively came out of her soft material sleeveless maxi dress. He instantly rocked up, as he ran his eyes over her naked figure. She had perky breast with long erect nipples and her pubic hairs were trimmed and cut into a narrow path. Her narrow waist complimented her apple bottom, and her thighs were thick along with a nice set of French manicured toenails. She gave him her hand. He took it and stood up.

"Show me what's going to be inside of me tonight," she said softly.

He undressed himself from top to bottom, leaving everything in a pile on the floor. Only thing he had on after he was totally naked was his long white braided link, with a cross resting on his stomach. She squatted down grabbed his dick and asked," How old are you Jarvis?"

Without waiting for an answer, she started stroking him.

"I'm......eight......teen."

She focused on her job, deep throating him.

"Ahh shit...hellll yeah," he whispered. She drew back and openly licked her tongue around his head.

"Cuming?"

Without waiting, she turned and dove into the nine feet of waters.

"I'm glad I know how to swim," thought Jarvis as he dove in after her. They played in the waters doing the cat and mouse thing until he finally caught her and fucked her from the back in the shallow waters. She held on to the wall of the pool biting the air as he stabbed inside of her. She moaned in pure pleasure taking all of him. He came and realized his hardness didn't soften and that he was still horny. Kyla kept a bottle of wine laced with crushed Viagra pills for her one-night lovers. Jarvis ran through six condoms fucking her until her pussy was a bruised wound. They ended in her bed with her head on his chest while she rubbed the hairs on his stomach.

"Jarvis, what do you do? Do you sale drugs?"

"Can I take the fifth on that question?"

"Sure. So where are you from?" asked Kyla.

"Cleveland but I'm staying in Baltimore."

"So that's where I'm dropping you off at tomorrow. Baltimore?"

"Yeah."

"Let's consider tonight just an illusion in your mind because tonight was only made for tonight, not tomorrow," said Kyla.

Jarvis pride was hurt by what she said. She lifted her head and looked him in the face.

"I can dig it ma. It's whatever you want it to be."

A few seconds later they were both passed out asleep.

****

The next morning, they woke up refreshed. After they took a shower together she cooked breakfast. After she was done she sat across from him at the dining room table as they silently ate.

"How come you didn't wanna fuck this morning. I didn't satisfy you last night?" questioned Jarvis.

"Actually, your sex is the bomb but remember"--------Jarvis cut her off.

"Well look I'm ready to bounce," said Jarvis as he pushed himself back in the chair.

"Okay let's go."

They rode silently in her BMW leaving Ellicott Maryland, headed to Baltimore. She sped raced down the freeway, switching lanes repeatedly as if she was in a hurry.

"Why don't you slow the fuck down before we get pulled over."

"Why curse at me? Why even be mad at me? What have I done to make you mad except have a good time with you?"

"Kyla, I aint trying to hear that shit, and no I'm not mad at you. I just don't feel like looking in the face of the police. You work in the White House or something?"

"Please. What made you ask me something like that?"

"Shit I don't know. I just asked."

For the next hour, they rolled in silence. Once they made it in Baltimore, he could tell the poverty of the neighborhoods had her attention. He had her stop him at a store before they made it to Gilmore. Two minutes later, he came out with a bottle of spring water in his hand. She watched him through the windshield. He directed her the rest of the way to the projects. She pulled up in front of the 1408 building and saw the heavy drug trafficking going on in the building. A few G-click homies were standing outside.

"So, this is it," she said in farewell.

She could tell by looking in his eyes that he wanted more than what she offered him.

"Enjoy life ma," he told her as he climbed out of her car.

He fell into conversation with the homies as she pulled away.

30

As weeks passed, Jarvis continued flipping his paper. One day while at the house chilling, it amazed him to count a total of six hundred and two thousand dollars. He didn't even include the kilo of heroin he had broken down into fifty dollars viles that was ready to be sold.

While Jarvis focus was strong, D-bear was falling apart by the day. The dice was killing him and now he was blowing heroin up his nose. He never asked Jarvis for anything, but word had gotten back that his uncle Ronnie had not too long ago fronted him a quarter brick to keep him on his feet. Jarvis continuously tried to install words of power into D-bears heart, but situations with him was only getting worse.

One night, in the wee hours of the morning, Jarvis was out by himself hustling out of 1408. After he sold what was in his possession, he went to his lay low in the sky, grabbed more work and went back to 1408. After he finished all his work he headed back to his lay low. By it being pitch black from all the lights being shot out, he didn't see the figure hiding between the buildings until the robber jumped out and pointed the gun in his face. He was wearing a ski mask with a hoodie over his head.

"BITCH ASS NIGGA GIVE IT UP!"

Jarvis was caught off guard and froze in his steps.

"LAY THE FUCK DOWN NIGGA," the robber growled.

Jarvis complied, and the robber took Jarvis gun off his waist and money from his pockets. He also took Jarvis shoes and found more money hiding inside them. Jarvis watched in fear. Then suddenly the robber stomped Jarvis face into the ground, busting his mouth and nose, leaving him dizzy and barely conscience. Jarvis laid there after he fled trying to gather himself. A nod head came to his side bent down and asked, "Are you okay? I just saw what happened."

Jarvis sluggishly got up without answering him and made his way to his apartment. For the next two weeks Jarvis fell back at his house in Columbia Maryland. He had a fractured nose and a swollen lip three times its normal size. Angelica caught a flight out to Columbia to spend some time with him. She hated to see him hurting but he let her know that he was slipping and suffered the repercussion for it.

Two and a half weeks after Jarvis was robbed, he pulled up in the projects in his midnight blue Jaguar. A few G-click homies was socializing outside watching him as he parked his car. He was wearing a five hundred and fifty-dollar Gucci blue jean hookup with Timberlands on his feet and had Cleveland Browns skully on. He opened the back door, grabbed his coat from the seat, and walked over to the homies.

D-bear was focusing on a five-hundred-dollar side bet but still acknowledged his presence.

"Yo what's up cuddie!"

"What up Bear."

He walked up next to him and watched the crap game. D-bo was hot. Collecting and catching points.

"I've been gone for too long," said D-bo while shaking the dice in the air.

"Now it's time to crack these niggas domes!"

He let the green dice roll from his hands. Seven. Once again, him and the ones betting with him were collecting. Then Jarvis noticed something that made his blood run cold. D-bo was wearing the same air force ones the robber was wearing the night he was robbed. The same scuff mark on the top of the robber left shoe was on D-bo's. Now he noticed that D-bo's physique matched the robbers as well. Jarvis had to control his urge to blow D-bo's head off right where he stood. He continued watching the dice roll but kept a sharp eye on D-bo as he planned his move. Then out of the blue Jarvis heard a woman ask, "Is Jarvis around?"

He looked around and saw Kyla inside of her BMW with her window more than halfway down. Most of the homies attention was drawn to her. Jarvis was surprised to say the least. He hopped in her car and she pulled out of the Jets.

"What's good ma. I never expected to see you again."

"Well Jarvis let's just say, at first, my intentions were what they were, but now they're something else. Basically, I wanna know who you are. It's crazy because I usually don't wanna be involved with a person for too long but it's something about you that has drawn me to want to know more."

"Aight, and you came all the way down here to see me huh," asked Jarvis.

"Well actually I had some business to take care of. I'm the owner of a real estate company so I'm here and there. But eventually I was going to come to see you sooner than later."

He liked her conservative style. It turned him on. She was wearing some gray slim fitting slacks, a long sleeve off white color button up blouse and a gray suede material Dior jacket.

"Have lunch with me," she asked.

How could he refuse......

They went to a place on the outskirts called O-Cal. Not an expensive place, but out the way.

She ordered a vegetarian plate and he ordered a grilled hamburger with fries and a glass of lemonade.

"Answer this Jarvis, are you an on the block kind of guy?"

"I do what I do to get money. I'm my own boss and employee."

She nodded her head in understanding.

"Well, I figured you was a hustler, but what else do you do? Do you pimp chicks or whatever?"

Jarvis chuckled.

"Naw that isn't my line of work."

"Do you have a girlfriend?"

"Um, not at the moment."

She rolled her fork in her hand with her elbow on the table.

"Jarvis I'm not going to beat around the bush or play little girl games, so let me be straight up with you. I like you as a person as well as a sex partner. If we can share a relationship with no strings attached, I would be more than happy. What do you think?"

He shrugged and said, "Whatever."

"Well it's whatever Mr. Jarvis," she harmonized. "And who knows, I may be useful to you in more ways than one," she replied charmingly.

A little after nine o'clock, the business was booming heavy in Gilmore projects. Jarvis was a few blocks over at a nod head name Stacy house. Her and her boyfriend lived together but he was at work.

"You mean to tell me, you're gonna give me five viles to go over there and try to get D-bo to come over here?"

She knew all the G-click homies. They all called her auntie.

"Yeah just tell him that you got a customer from the outskirts that's spending big and he is refusing to step foot in the projects.

"Okay, but once he gets here then what? Aint no blood shedding going on in here."

"Stacy that's my nigga. Fuck is you talkin bout. He just owes me some money and I know he aint gone come if he knows I'm here."

"I don't wanna look like a damn fool when he sees I was lying about the spender. That nigga is crazy."

"Naw we just gone make it like he left. Now here take this, I know you need a quick fix."

He gave her a vile and she immediately strapped up in front of him and injected herself with the needle. He watched her draw blood and shoot it back into her vein. Three minutes later she was nodding. Then suddenly she popped up, grabbed her Virginia slim menthols from the mantel piece and blazed one. Then she grabbed her coat and headed towards the door.

"Now I want the other four viles when I get back Jay. Don't be shitting me!"

"Girl I got you. Just bring the nigga back and you got that. That's my word. Just make sure you say it exactly how I told you to. Aight?"

"Aight Jay," said Stacy while zipping up her coat.

Jarvis stood in front of the wide living room window. From time to time he would peek through the curtains to see if they were coming. His tech-nine was cocked and ready to blow as he patiently waited. Every minute or two that passed he looked at the time on his watch. It read 9:41 pm. Fifteen minutes later they pulled up in D-bo's black and grey Expedition. The moment of revenge was at hand and Jarvis could hardly contain himself. He sat on the couch and waited. A moment later they entered the house.

"Stacy you better not be wasting my time," D-bo warned her seconds before they emerged into Jarvis view.

Jarvis had both of his arms stretched out on the neck of the couch and gun in his hand but out of sight. D-bo noticed his presence but looked him off. A sign of him not being able to look Jarvis in the face.

An uncanny feeling shot through D-bo, but he tried to remain placid.

"Where he at Stacy," D-bo cried.

"Thought I wasn't gone figure the shit out huh bitch ass nigga," Jarvis hissed with the tech nine pointed at D-bo's face.

"Jay no! Not in my house. Oh my God what have I---------
'BOOM'

One unexpected shot in Stacy's forehead knocked her back into the wall, which was all brains and blood splattered.

D-bo didn't know what to do. He remained still. Then Jarvis told him, " You tried yo hand with the wrong nigga dawg!"

"Man I-I-I."

'BOOM' His body slammed into the wall and slid to the floor slumping over. Jarvis stood over him and fired two more shots into his face. He threw on his hoodie, pulled his skully down, and made his exit from the house.

A week later D-bo was being buried underground and his death was a mystery. On the other hand, Jarvis and Kyla was spending a lot of time together. They were enjoying candle lit dinners, several nights of passion and swimming at her exotic style mansion. Hanging out with a beautiful African woman was becoming a normality to him.

In April, they hit the sky in Kyla's private jet, headed to the West Indies to spend a two-week vacation off the Caribbean Sea on the Anguilla Island. Their two week living quarters was in the Cap Juluca, a posh resort set on 179 acres of two pristine beaches. When they stepped out of the jet, Jarvis was amazed at the beautiful blue waters. A few famous faces crossed their paths as they made their way to the villa. Their headquarters were immaculate. A balcony with a magnificent view of the Caribbean Sea, a private pool, along with a steamy hot tub. Exquisite furnishing, architectural paintings adorned the walls along a bar with a backdrop aquarium.

"Honey how do you like it?"

"Baby this is alright," he said pulling her close to him.

"I'm feeling the whole get away thing. It's like a fantasy or some shit that I've never fantasized about because I never thought I'd play a part in it."

She stood on her toes and kissed him.

"Do you ever fantasize about me when we're not together. Or are you getting tired of me?"

"Kyla, you're not a person I can get tired of."

"Can you love me?" asked Kyla.

He didn't answer her. Instead he swept her five six frame in his arms and took her into the bedroom. Within seconds they were naked. He kissed her body from head to toe while she spread her legs eagle style. For the first time, he allowed his tongue to taste the sweetness of pussy. Remembering Andrea's words, he worked his tongue against her clitoris with soft sensual strokes.

"Yessss Jarvis... take me now," she whispered.

He ate her until he was full then gave her pussy a viscous dick whipping.

31

It was 10:33 pm back in Cleveland. Deedra had not too long ago got out of the tub. She was now laying across the bed in a silk nightgown, deep into a good movie. She had called Anton about two hours ago, asking if he could stop by the house and put her to sleep because she was real horny. He told her that he would be over in a little while but as of yet, he hadn't showed. At least half of the two years they'd been living together, she went to bed alone. Her phone began ringing. She grabbed it off the nightstand and answered.

"Hello"

"Girl what's up!"

"Who is this Dale?"

"Yeah girl this me, but guess what?"

"What," said Deedra as she sat up on the side of the bed.

"Girl, I just saw Anton car parked at the North Point Inn. I had to tell you."

Deedra's heart missed a beat, as she heard Dale's boyfriend Mont scolding her about dipping in other folk's business.

"This is my girl, I'm supposed to tell her," Dale yelled into Deedra's ear but talking to Mont.

"Okay and that's my muthafuckin nigga. Stay outta people business damn."

Deedra heard Mont yell back and hung up on their argument. In a rush, she jumped up, grabbed her purse and keys, and left the house with nothing on but a silk gown and some slippers. She had all she could take from Anton. Her sanity had snapped. She drove at almost full speed trying to make it to 18th & Superior. Her tears were bitter as she navigated through traffic. Anton had gotten word from Mont, so he knew that Deedra was more than likely on her way. He flew pass her truck with some chic in the passenger seat. Deedra made a sharp U-turn and pursued him. She managed to get her phone out of her purse and dialed his number.

Anton answered and started yelling.

"Why the fuck is you following -----She cut his words off.

"You better hope I don't catch your ass cause I'm gone blow that bitch head off!"

Anton kept weaving in and out of traffic trying to lose her, but she was closing in.

"Deedra, go the fuck home and I'll talk to you when I get there."

"You know what Anton," said Deedra while grabbing her 380 from her purse.

"Look in yo rearview mirror because you did this to me," she yelled in bitter tears.

"You not gone stop and talk to me?"

Anton looked in his rearview.

"Deedra just go----------WHAT THE FUCK!"

He heard the shot and saw the flash all in one second as Deedra's car ran into a telephone pole. Anton parked on the side of the street and jumped out running towards the accident. Other people were pulling over to see if they could help Deedra. Anton shoved his way into a clear view of Deedra who was slumped over the steering wheel. The horn blared endlessly.

He yanked the door open and pulled her into his arms easing her to the ground, but never letting go as she stared dead eyed into his face. Once reality broke through, a scream from deep inside Anton's guts escaped his lips.........

****

Three car loads pulled into the 30th projects. They were youngsters from 88th in St Clair. The members were riding in a Delta 88 and had a black and brown brindle Pitbull posted in the back seat that was about to fight Ubie's red nose pit. The bet was five thousand dollars and both dogs were champions. A crowd of Yg members was aggregated in the heart of the Jets. Ubie was seated on a crate with his shirt off, towel hanging from his head, and dog in between his legs. He had both arms wrapped around the dog's neck as it sat on its hind legs taking fast and deep breaths. Psycho was his name and steroids kept him over the edge. When the bow-legged brindle got out of the car, Ubie pointed to it and said, "Sssss Kill'em!"

Psycho tried to break loose from his hold but Ubie tamed him.

"Hold on baby hold on." Twenty feet away, the brindle was going crazy trying to break free from the chain to get at psycho.

Baby stay strap yelled, "Psycho, you betta kill dis bitch. Don't let dat bitch make it out these Jets alive!"

The youngsters started getting loud as the brindle came closer. Customers were sticking around to see the outcome of the battle which appeared to be an unpredictable one. Foo pulled up and hopped out.

"Aw shit! It's about to go down up in dis bitch. Is bets still alive or what?"

"I got a gee say he do," said a St. Clair youngster.

"Say he do what," Foo asked back.

"Kill em!"

"Kill em," Foo reiterated in disbelief.

"Yeah," the St Clair youngster replied.

"Bet ten moe nigga," said Foo.

"Only a gee, bet."

"Bet," said Foo and turned to Psycho and Ubie who was still sitting on the crate.

"You hear this shit. He said he gone kill psycho."

Psycho wasn't paying Foo any attention. His eyes were trained on the brindle coming his way. Ubie kept his finger pointed at the brindle.

"That's food you hear me," Ubie aggressively yelled at psycho. "EAT THAT BITCH!"

Psycho answered with snapping barks. Ubie walked him to center point. The 88th youngster walked his dog up less than eight feet away. He stopped but continued to whisper words in the brindle's ear.

"Is yo fighter ready," asked Ubie. Ubie kissed the side of psycho's face and yelled, "On three!"

The heart of the Jets was packed and full of anticipation as the clock ticked down.

"HIT!"

The dogs rushed at each other and locked mouth to mouth as vicious growls echoed the block. Ubie, who was caught up in the moment screamed at psycho to kill his opponent, as the sun beamed on his shirtless body. On his right shoulder was a picture of his dead cousin Juvis and underneath his face was his birth and death year.

While Psycho had a lock on one of the brindle's legs, Ubie cousins Snatch-out, Dink, and Killa pulled into the Jets driving an 88 boxed Chevy. Ever since Ubie jumped off the porch, he been associating himself with them on a regular. When Ubie offered them an invitation into the Jets to eat a piece of the pie, they declined. Selling drugs weren't their style. Instead they offered to be Ubie's hitmen so he wouldn't have to get his hands too dirty. Little did they know, his hands were just as dirty as theirs, but he agreed considering they could be beneficial. They were officially on his payroll as hired hitmen.

"GET EM OFF YOU PSYCHO!... THAT'S RIGHT, NO PAIN! IT'S EITHER WIN OR DIE!"

Ubie continued to talk to his dog as both of them were under each other's lock. The brindle had psycho's ear and psycho managed to have a lock on the brindle's neck, only difference was that psycho's ear was coming off. It was hard for the Yg homies to watch. Psycho didn't seem as if he felt any pain as he focused on the brindle's throat. Then suddenly psycho started yanking viciously which caused his ear to become detached from his head and stuck between the teeth of the brindle. The severity of the pain drove psycho crazy. He tore into the brindle's throat shaking him with all he had. The blood from the brindle was over flowing into psycho's mouth. In a blink of an eye death took over the brindle as it collapsed to the ground with his jugular vein destroyed. Psycho continued to shake until his strength gave in his legs. Psycho had lost too much blood. He went into shock as the blood continued to pour out of the hole where his ear was detached. The 88th youngster handed Ubie the reward money and said, "Yo killer killed my killer first, but they both gone die!"

Foo paid his bill because he knew psycho was about to die. Even though Ubie won five thousand, his heart was hurt because he loved that dog. He walked up to psycho as the dog laid on his side. With blood gushing profusely from his wounds, he looked up to Ubie as if to say, "I killed him for you boss."

A tear fell from Ubie's eye from being forced to put psycho to sleep. He snatched his 357-snub nose from his waist and thumbed the hammer back, pointing it in psycho's face. Psycho never took his eyes off Ubie. It seemed as if he knew what had to be done.

"Be a warrior in your next life Psycho ya hear." 'BOOM'

Five minutes later both dogs were garbage bagged and threw away.

The crowd started to scatter while the customers pulled in and out like clockwork. Ubie walked off with his three cousins.

"Yo cuddie, we got a surprise for you," said Snatch-out as he puffed his blunt then passed it to Ubie.

"What's that?" Ubie asked solemnly.

"Caught one of the KKBG niggas slipping last night coming out the after-hour joint in the valley."

Ubie stopped instantly.

"I know that bitch made the front page, didn't he?" asked Ubie.

"Calm down young nigga I told you I had a surprise for you." Ubie quickly comprehended.

"Where he at?"

The three cousins started laughing.

"He in the trunk fool," Snatch-out replied.

"Yeah but we knew you was gone wanna be the hand to send him to his destiny," said Killa.

"Aint no question. Open the trunk so I can see which one it is."

They walked to the car and opened the trunk. Lil Tae was hog tied and badly beaten.

"Yeah good catch yall! We out," said Ubie.

32

Days after Deedra's funeral, Lil Tae's body was found floating in Euclid Creek. He was tortured to death and by it being a faceless murder, the KKBG crew was in a hopeless state of shock. They were grieving over not one, but two close friends who passed away. Anton had tried contacting Jarvis, so he could attend their funerals but was unable to get a hold of him. However, Jarvis and Kyla were at the end of their romantic two-week vacation. The last two weeks provided him enough time to gather his thoughts. He felt a sense of peace he's never felt before. Every night through the wee hours of the morning, he sat on the balcony by himself, staring out at the waters lost in his thoughts. Thoughts of realizing what he'd become. A hustler, killer, and a leader, who relinquished his responsibility of maintaining leadership towards his people back home. Of course, he was happy to have over a half million dollars and overcoming a struggle that seemed never ending almost six years ago. Although he was happy to have met a Veteran like Kyla, he didn't allow himself to become attached to her because she made tomorrow seem unpromising to their relationship. He couldn't deny his attraction for her. She carried a mysterious aura that was fascinating to him. Anything he wanted he could have, but there were a few things that opposed his happiness. The main thing was him deviating from his KKBG homies.

On their last vacationing day, they took the ferry, riding the Caribbean waters to Scilly Cay, an open-air restaurant. Once there, they ordered Scilly Cay's famous grilled lobster, side dishes with crab legs and shrimp, with a soothing bottle of Chardonnay. After eating and romantically mingling, they went to a spa resort for some relaxing body rub downs. A little after eight o'clock evening, they sat in the sand letting the waters splash against their feet as the sun was finding its way back into the ocean.

"This is so beautiful," said Kyla. "Did you enjoy these two weeks on lover's island?" She turned her head slightly to look into his face for an answer.

"I enjoyed you ma."

"And I enjoyed you Jarvis. You know I haven't been open for a person in years and I'm talking over a decade."

"Why is that Ma?"

"Let's just say a bad experience.......and I've had my share of lovers since then, but none of them had that special quality to open me back up. I guess you could say I closed my heart......that is......until I met you."

She paused to see if he was going to ask her to explain herself. He didn't so she continued.

"You're a real man. The kind of man that is so hard to find, especially in America. In your eyes, I see determination. Whatever it is, is it worth you being so determined?"

'I forgot she from Africa shit she is tapping into my soul,' Jarvis thought to himself.

"Yeah Kyla it's worth it."

A good minute of silence followed as they stared at the waters. Then Kyla said, "Remember the second time I saw you and we had lunch together?"

"Yeah I remember."

"Remember I told you that I may be useful in more ways than one?"

"Yeah Ky, I remember."

"Well do you need a connection for your hustle?"

Jarvis didn't expect that to come out of her mouth. He was stunned.

"I'm not a drug dealer if that's what you're thinking, and you better not be assuming I'm some type of cop either! Everything I've told you about me suing the hospital is true and I have documents to prove it. I also own a real estate company. I know someone and let's just say that someone is very close to me," said Kyla.

As Jarvis stared at the back of her head, he realized that he had stumbled across an uncut diamond. His words were calm as he tried not to express any feeling.

"What kind of connect are you talking about?"

"What kind do you need?" asked Kyla.

"Heroin.... You say it's someone who's close to you. Shit he must be real close for you to know his business."

"Yeah he's my brother Jarvis. An African just like me. I can acquaint you to him two weeks from now at a small gathering he's throwing at his mansion in Fort Washington. You can tag along with me but only on one condition."

"Alright what's that?" questioned Jarvis.

"We must act like we're happily in love. That's the way into his good graces."

"Won't that seem odd to him that you're suddenly in love?"

"He doesn't keep track of my love life."

"What's the occasion in two weeks?"

"His name is Adewale and if you can get into his good graces, then hopefully the rest of your determined mission will be a smooth one. I trust you enough to introduce you two. I know he's going to like you. Just please don't ever cross him Jarvis."

"My loyalty is my honor Ky. And that's all I got as a man," Jarvis replied sullenly.

"Two weeks from now is his fortieth birthday!"

33

At three something in the morning, Jarvis sat alone on the balcony while Kyla was peacefully at rest. As he looked out at the darkened waters, he promised himself that he would one day come back to visit the Anguilla Island, but as of now, he decided it was time to go back home. As the Shepard to his sheep, he was going back home to reunify KKBG, organize a setup, and redirect all the nod heads to King Kennedy Projects.

"Three years tops and I'm out the way," he soliloquized as he got up and went back inside the villa to get some shut eye.

When Jarvis returned from the Caribbean, that same day he found out that Deedra and Lil Tae was killed and already buried. He immediately shot to Cleveland. He was told that Lil Tae's death was a mystery and he found out the real reason why Deedra killed herself. Jarvis had advised Anton a long time ago, to let Deedra go before he drove her to do something crazy, but when he looked Anton in the face, he didn't have to tell him that he was wrong. Jarvis could tell that a piece of his homie had died as well. Jarvis noticed that his hood had fell apart, yet they were still together. He gave them hope by promising his return in a few weeks.

****

Jarvis met Adewale, and just like Kyla said, he took a liking to Jarvis. Adewale had watchmen on post who were all African. They were guarding the beautiful style mansion, inside and out. Jarvis was shocked that Adewale was living like he was in a movie, amongst a society of white people. Jarvis realized that he was a bigger fish than he thought. He figured he had to have some major connects to live like this and live on the other side of the law. Adewale's manner was very polite, but the seriousness in his eyes told Jarvis that his polite act was just that. An act!"

Five eleven, medium build, black as night with teeth as white as snow, he and Kyla resembled favorably. There were only 12 attendees which included Jarvis and Kyla. There were six men and six women whom all were couples. He figured these were his five best men and their wives. After he was introduced to Adewale as Kyla's fiancé, he introduced Jarvis to everyone else.

Kyla sat on his lap amongst other couples and for a little over an hour, everyone discussed politics and the disasters being caused by mother nature. Jarvis even added his opinions while sipping Hennessy pure white cognac from a glass.

Kyla purposely focused most of her attention on Jarvis. She knew that by her brother seeing her with a man was pleasing to him. For years she had been telling him that she was in an active relationship because she knew that he was hoping that she would soon get married. He wanted a niece or a nephew but truthfully, she didn't want either. After a while her lies became transparent because he never saw or met the person, which gave him reason to believe his sister was a lesbian. One day he confronted her which forced her to tell the truth. She had no desire for a husband or children but assured him that she wasn't gay. He was hurt about the possibility of never having nieces or nephews, considering she was his only sister. That was a case he couldn't argue. Now tonight, even though her fiancé seemed a lot younger than her, she was right. Adewale was very well pleased to see Kyla engaging in a relationship with a man.

As the night wore on, Jarvis realized that he was having a good time as he and Kyla joined other couples on the dance floor.

"A couple more shots gone send you over the edge ma."

She giggled.

"As long as you're not drunk cause you gotta drive us back," said Kyla.

"When are you moving back to Cleveland," asked Kyla.

"In a few weeks," Jarvis replied.

"Is this transition going to come between us?"

"Not at all. As long as there's transportation you gone be seeing me on the regular. Besides, I'm still keeping my crib in Columbia Maryland."

"Jarvis, I'm not understanding why you're putting distance in between us. You don't tell me much. I just hope it isn't to avenge your friend's death. Don't get yourself in any trouble." The liquor had her open. "Promise me!"

"Promise you what ma," Jarvis serenely replied back.

"Promise me that you're going to be careful."

Jarvis couldn't deny that his love for her was getting stronger.

"I promise Ky."

"I talked to my brother too. Just be patient babe," said Kyla as she laid her head on his shoulder. He didn't bother to ask her what his reaction was, although his curiosity wanted him to. He decided to leave the situation in Kyla's hands.

Within a month Jarvis had relocated back in Cleveland, renting a condo on the outskirts. He left his jaguar in his garage in Maryland. That was his get around car for when he was there. The day after his return, he bought an all-black Audi, paid in full cosigned by Kyla. That night Angelica threw a welcome back get together at her house for Jarvis, but he intended to utilize this gathering for an important meeting.

As everybody socialized in harmony, Jarvis acted as though everything was good, but he was really analyzing his homies altered characters. All the KKS girls were there but he could tell there wasn't a connection anymore. Then after Tasia got drunk, she started crying in remembrance of Deedra. Her crying caused a chain reaction against the girls then Lil Bit started pointing the finger at Anton.

"Nigga I hate you. If it wasn't for you---------------

"BITCH I WILL BREAK YO MUTHAFUCKING JAW!" A few homies held Anton back from fulfilling his threat.

Then Jarvis stood up and said, "Yo what the fuck is this. Man look at you muthafuckas!"

The noise level reduced instantly.

"She dead yall. Dead! Keep her in your heart but let that other shit go cause he aint put the gun to her head. Man, this shit looks pathetic and I aint just talking about the block cuz we finna do some'em about that. I'm talking about yall niggas. It doesn't look like yall ready for what I got in mind!"

A complete silence fell over the adjoining rooms.

"Look yall, I stopped what I was doing up in Baltimore for one reason and one reason only..........to finish where we left off. Before I even get into that, I gotta know where we stand as one."

"As one?" asked Beatrice. "These niggas is for themselves J-one."

Jarvis listened as they went back and forth. Then Freeda said, "J-one it's gone take more than just you to clean this mess up. When J.d. died, that was the beginning of the end. Then once they took J-rock and all of them, the projects fell apart. It aint none of our faults, we just don't have what it takes to keep things alive. Especially after you left."

"Damn Freeda, now that's the realist shit I've heard since I been back," said Jarvis. "But yall niggas need to hear me out cause it's about to go down. What I'm bringing to the table is more than what it takes. What we did before I left was jumping off the porch status. Yeah there was money to be made, but this move right here, is going to birth some serious jealousy throughout the city, bring about death and cause murder. Niggas is gone do bits for they slip ups. Some of us might even die for what it's worth. What we're about to do is build a foundation stronger than any others in the city. A dynasty. I'm willing to die for that. What are yaw niggas willing to do?"

Lil Hurt said, "J-one, you know it's whatever with me!"

"Whatever means nothing. It holds no significance. Is yall ready to make history? Create a dynasty to be talked about even after we're in our graves?"

Suddenly the youngsters felt inspired to represent whatever cause Jarvis was bringing to the table. The energy in their responses convinced him that they were paying attention and motivated. Out of all the voices being spoken, Marlo's voice out spoke theirs.

"I'll never walk again because of what I chose to rep. Aint no question I'm willing to die for that!" Beatrice walked over to him and took the half empty bottle of Hennessy out of his hands and softly said," Boo I understand you're happy J-one is back home, but you aint ready to die and you aint gone die on me."

"Girl give me back my........Dawg let me hit the weed," said Marlo, and grabbed the blunt from Lil Hurt, causing a chaos of laughter.

After the laughter settled Jarvis Continued.

"Aight this is what it is. We started out pushing the white, now we're moving on to bigger thangs that will produce bigger profits. Only four hoods move heroin in this city, yet its nod heads everywhere. As long as we got the best shit, which I believe we do, my aim is to redirect all the nod heads to the Jets. Outside panhandling is dead, operations are being ran out of the buildings. I'll go further in detail with that but first let me enlighten yall to the beauty of how this hustle works.

When Jarvis was through he left everybody in an enticed state of anticipation. Everyone knew there would be positions but didn't know what their positions were. He told them that in no more than a months' time, positions would be set along with the motion of the hustle. He asked the girls did they want jobs and they were more than eager to work. Before he left, Angelica asked him were things going to be like they were between them before he left. He gave her a satisfying answer, seeing that she had put her life on hold until he got back, but truthfully Jarvis had out grew her.

A little after two in the morning, Jarvis and Anton was back at the condo. Jarvis was pacing the living room and Anton was seated listening intensely.

"The Puerto Ricans on Clark's Westside, the Cedar boys, 10-5 boys and the Jamaicans down in Garden Valley are our only opponents. All their big time Willie niggas is about to be copping from us. You, Damon, Wanisha, and M-2. I need yall to be my lieutenants. Everybody else is up under yall."

All of them were still locked up and soon to be free in a matter of months. They were Jarvis four most trusted, so he had to wait for their return. However, their absence wasn't going to stop the ball from rolling.

"Now I see its a few new faces, but I aint really tripping. I'm willing to give them a chance just like J.d. gave me one, but a lot of them niggas is taking the front line. My lieutenants and me as captain, faces should rarely be seen. Of course, we gotta push the ball to get it rolling but after it takes off, they work to eat. All or nothing nigga, now let's reach to the sky."

34

Two weeks later Jarvis was still waiting for the big connect to fall in his hands. Him and Kyla would talk long distance and she seemed pleased with just hearing his voice. Jarvis was contemplating hooking back up with his connect from Baltimore and while contemplating, he received a call from Kyla.

"He wants you to visit him at his mansion in Pensacola Florida in two days. I already have the airline ticket for you, but I need to see you tonight."

Hours later he was at Kyla's getting his dick rode by a champ while the maid was preparing a dinner for two. She threw her head back in pure ecstasy bouncing up and down on Jarvis, circling her hips with perfection.

"Yessss Jarvis... You fuck me so good baby!!!! I love it... I love this shit!"

Jarvis aggressively switched positions in one motion. Kyla on her back and him on top. Her pussy was so good to him he kept a bite lock on her neck while stroking her deeply.

"Damn baby, I could do this all-night. This is some good loving baby," smiled Kyla, as she started moving fast, meeting him in the middle of the stroke and staring deeply into his eyes.

Once they were through, they laid there sweaty and out of breath.

"Is this a permanent sucker bite or what," she asked rubbing the same spot on her neck.

"My fault Ky but sometimes the feeling be unbearable."

"I know honey. You can bite me whenever you need to," she uttered kissing on his chest. After their breathing calmed, Jarvis asked her a question that she wasn't expecting.

"Ky, answer me this honestly. Why would a beautiful woman like you be single?"

She was slow to respond, turning over to give him her backside to look at.

"I told you a bad experience."

"Yeah I remember you telling me that, but you also said that was years ago."

"I know what I said Jarvis, but do we have to talk about this.........like right now?"

"I mean it's on you Ky. I'm just curious to know more about you that's all."

She turned over and was now staring him in the face.

"If I tell you more than enough, will there be a tomorrow for the relationship we share?"

"How could you ask me a question like that. I fucks with you the long way Ky. The past can't come between that."

"How far should I go back?"

"Do yo thang ma."

"Well when I was fifteen my mother and father passed away from a car accident in Nigeria. That left me in the care of my brother Adewale since he's 4-years older than me. For reasons of his own, we moved over here when I was twenty and two years later I developed a kidney infection. Well the hospital's nurse wrongfully administered medicine prescribed from my doctor, and it almost killed me. They drained my kidneys before they completely locked up which saved me temporarily. They said if I continue to take my medicine for their fuck up (mind you) then I can still live a long life, but there's a thirty percent chance that my kidneys can lock up at any moment and there goes my life. Thirty percent is a high chance of something happening to me so do you see why I was single the day you met me?"

Jarvis didn't respond as he stared deeply into her fearful eyes.

"Tomorrow is very unpromising to me."

Jarvis stepped off the plane into the blazing hot weather in Florida with light baggage. He was met by a familiar face that he remembered at the gathering he attended almost two months ago. Once he gathered Jarvis attention, he tore the sign in two, dropping it in a garbage can a few feet away. The back door of the cocaine white Rolls Royce awaited Jarvis as he approached.

"So, we meet again Jarvis, it's a pleasure," said the tall bulky man as he shook Jarvis hands. "The boss awaits you."

Jarvis climbed in the back and a few seconds later the Rolls Royce was making its way from the airport.

As Jarvis drove up the swirling driveway of the Victorian Romanesque structured mansion, it dawned on him that a blessing was in the making. A beautiful waterfall caught his eyes along with a huge unoccupied swimming pool with the sun rays reflecting off its clear blue water. Jarvis in his Gucci shorts, short sleeve, unbuttoned Dior collar shirt, revealing a white wife beater with Gucci sneakers, felt cheap walking up to the mansion steps. The sound of a piano being played in the first guest room welcomed Jarvis. Adewale appeared to be in meditation as his fingers punched into the keys. Bag in hand, Jarvis and the body guard remained standing until Adewale finished. Right when it seemed to Jarvis as if he would play nonstop, the room became still. Adewale turned to face them and smiled.

"Jarvis my friend, how are you?"

"I'm good Adewale how about yourself?"

"Things couldn't be any better. Toney show him to his lay. Jarvis after you're situated, come back and have a drink with me out in the swimming area."

After he was showed to his room Toney turned and left. Jarvis placed his duffel bag in the corner and sat on the edge of the bed unable to shake the feeling of awe. Everything seemed like a dream to him since the day he met Kyla. Not only was she an outstanding catch but she led him to an outstanding connect whereas though if it wasn't for her, he would've never had the chance of coming across Adewale's presence. As these thoughts ran through his mind, he knew things happened for a reason. Just like he knew that whatever his destiny was going to be, it was already set.

Toney led Jarvis onto a spacious steel gated fenced balcony where Adewale was seated at a round table, looking down on his elegant property.

"Come," said Adewale. Jarvis walked over and sat across from him. Toney turned and left. Adewale popped open a bottle of Costa Russi wine and filled both of their glasses. While blazing his diamond cigar he then offered one to Jarvis who accepted thinking, 'why the hell not.'

Adewale reached over and lit Jarvis cigar and said, " So tell me Jarvis, how is your relationship with my sister and what is it worth to you?"

Kyla cajoled him to exaggerate their relationship as if it were a permanent one, but he kept it honest.

"It's worth having. Well actually to me, it's worth more than she'll ever know."

Jarvis realized that his answer portrayed deceit when really there was none.

"Okay and why may she never know what's on your heart?"

Jarvis could tell that he was trying to read him by looking under the surface of his words. A quick answer fell off his tongue.

"Well she has this little insecurity of wondering do I look to her as a vet. Adewale she's a beautiful woman that I've fallen in love with. Not for her money or nothing else but for who she is as a person, but I don't know if she realizes."

"How old are you?"

"Eighteen."

"Listen to me, I want to see my sister truly happy. If it's by a younger guy or, some guy a hundred years old, I don't care. So be it. You give her that and I extend my hand to you!"

"Imma give her that regardless of whatever come between me and you."

Adewale was satisfied with his reply and for the next few minutes, they sipped and puffed in silence. Then Adewale said, "So how much does a kilo run and what's the powder worth?"

"Sixty thousand. The powder be good enough for me to step on it, so I don't complain," Jarvis replied.

"Hmmm. So, as I see it you're looking for a better connection. If I became what you're looking for, should I need to worry about you ever crossing me," asked Adewale.

"I'll tell you this as a man with honor, you would never have to worry about that."

"In order for us to do business you have to solidify that by giving me a list of relatives addresses. At least five of them starting with a parent."

Jarvis just realized why the small notepad and pen was at the center of the table and he pointed to it for his permission to use it. Adewale nodded.

He gave him four addresses.

"I don't have a fifth address."

Adewale ripped the paper off the notepad and looked at it for a second, then folded it.

"These will be checked into, but I trust they are substantial. Are you established?"

"Yeah, but I'm about to open up in a city where heroin is rare."

"Where might I ask?"

"Cleveland. That's where I'm from, Cleveland Ohio."

"I don't know how you were planning to transport from Maryland to Ohio, but lucky you I have a base in Akron, Ohio so it shouldn't be a problem."

"I had a way to------ Adewale cut him off.

"No time for careless mistakes. Are you ready financially?"

"Yeah I'm ready."

"How does forty thousand a key sound at ten to twenty a purchase. Twenty kilos or more, thirty thousand a kilo will be the price, and I guarantee my product is absolute pure, therefore you'll be able to step on it as much as you like."

Jarvis gulped down the rest of his wine then smiled. "Adewale that's beautiful. And if you need me to assist you in any way, I'm here for you."

Jarvis first purchase from Adewale he spent over half of his stash leaving him with two hundred thousand dollars to his name. He copped ten kilos which was picked up in Akron by Angelica. Jarvis showed Anton how to cut a kilo using banita and quinine. After he stepped on it and packaged it all up in twenty-five and fifty-five-dollar viles, the product was still taking an eight. Something that the nod heads in the city of Cleveland wasn't used to but would die to have. Jarvis opened the projects with the first broken-down kilo. Mildred, a nod head from King Kennedy over dosed her first time shooting the high purity product into her veins, along with a few others, who quickly spread the word that the King Kennedy projects had the name tag drop dead and there was nothing else in the city that could compare. Word spread like wild fire and just like that the projects had awakened.

Jarvis nineteenth birthday was a month and a half away but wasn't any time to celebrate. Nod heads were pulling in like clockwork, looking for the drop-dead product and nothing else. By the time September rolled around, business was crazy. Jarvis had fronted every KKBG member a healthy pack through the hands of Anton. Not only did Jarvis bring some knock out dope to the city, he was also changing the way prices were being ran in Cleveland. Grams were cheaper than usual and the dope that Jarvis had couldn't be emulated by a long shot. It didn't take no time for the KKBG crew to put the city on lock.

September 27th was Damon's release date. Jarvis and Anton were sitting on the hood of the Audi when he emerged from the building. They were happy to see him and vice versa, but Damon instantly detected a serious aura from his two best friends, as they climbed in the car and pulled away. On the way back, Damon was told of his position as a lieutenant and asked if he could handle it.

"Aint no question. You don't doubt that do you," he asked back.

"How could I ever doubt my man," Jarvis replied but little did Damon know, Jarvis had established a dynasty that would soon prove to be one of the biggest establishments ever ran out of the city of Cleveland.

****

When Wanisha touched down a month later, she was eager to get her hands dirty and thirsty to stack some bread. Anton picked her up with instructions to take her straight to Jarvis condo where Damon awaited. Jarvis had drove out to Columbia Maryland earlier that morning to stash away a ton of money. From there he took an hour and a half drive out to Kyla's to quench their thirst for each other before they went their separate ways again. Kyla had to attend a business meeting and Jarvis was headed back to Cleveland.

"I heard we got the city on smash," said Wanisha.

"In a major way. Yo check this out Y-love. He told me to shoot you to the condo first, but I don't even think he's back from Maryland yet. You want me to shoot you to yo peoples house first so they can see you?"

"Naw if my nigga said shoot me to the condo then take me there. Didn't nobody say much to me over the phone because that aint how it go, but the streets talk and I know the hood is back up. I'm so happy Jarvis came back home. I'm about to turn up out here."

"Bitch calm down, you bout to be up too!" smiled Anton.

"I know that's right," Wanisha replied. "Ewww this is my shit!!!!" She grabbed the remote control and turned up Yo Gotti song 'Fuck you' and started nodding her head to the beat. Then she turned it down and said, "This my shit nigga. So, what's up. How good is things for you?"

"Oh, I thought you was finna tell me to shoot you to one of these hotels out here and break you in."

She nodded her head in dissatisfaction.

"Anton get it through that big head of yours, I will never fuck you because I feel like that will destroy our friendship and I'd rather be ya nigga for life than yo bitch for a year."

"I'm just fucking with you Y-Love damn, but you are looking good as a muthafucka baby!"

"Thanks nigga but is you gone answer my question?"

"What's that," Anton smiled.

"How good is things going for you?"

"Things is real good right now but first let me tell you my intentions wasn't never to hurt Deedra. I never thought she would do what she did. Some of the KKS girls feel some type of way about me ever since that happen. But it's good to know that you aint had a change of heart for ya boy."

"How can I be mad at you. I'm disappointed in her for her going out like that. Reason why I didn't bring it up is because I know that's the last thing you wanna talk about but, rest in peace to her."

"Yeah doe, all the big Willie heroin boys copping they dope off us cuz we keep that china white, and we the only connect with it. Who J-one connected to, I have no idea right now, but on the panhandle side of things a nigga can step out there amongst other homies and make three bands a day......... easy."

"I know how they be needing it. My auntie shoot that shit she be all-------Anton cut her off.

"Hold on let me finish telling you. Jarvis don't do shit. We his lieutenants. Me, you, Damon. and M-2 when he come home. Everybody else is up under us. First, he started off giving me a key and I would have to bring him back fifty gees. At first, I was serving it all in weight without getting my hands too dirty. Then crazy money started flowing through the projects, so now I sell half in weight but still hit the block and move work like that too. Jarvis prefer his lieutenants to stay behind the scenes but I'm a greedy nigga."

"But aint that like going against J-one strategy?" Wanisha skeptically asked. "If he wants us behind the scenes then that's the way it should be."

Anton overlooked what she said and began giving her insight on what Jarvis expected out of his lieutenants.

"Ma you know it's only a handful of heroin blocks. Me and Damon supplying all the big boys. You gotta get in where you fit in."

She chuckled. "Boy don't you know these hustle hands are certified?......... That's the least of my concerns."

35

Not only did Jarvis have her seventy thousand dollars in hand, he took her shopping and spent countless gees on her. He also had her three-year-old truck tuned up and ready to go, not to mention, her gift from him was a brand-new infinity. Wanisha also had a $25,000 check from the money she made in the joint, so she was prepared for her fresh start. Jarvis continued to coach her on their way back from the mall about her position as lieutenant.

"The money you got, put that up. My lieutenants don't need to do no re-upping. I put the work in your hands and you make a quick and easy profit. We're passed the level of panhandling Y-love you feel me. We don't need to catch cases, we need to be out here getting this money."

"J-one baby you know I'm following yo lead regardless."

"I just got a huge load in last week, but Imma give you a few days to get yourself together before I bless you. You can stay at the condo for as long as you need to. Shit I'm hardly there. I'll be back and forth from here to Maryland."

"Good looking J-one. I'll have a spot in a few days. My lil boyfriend wants me to come and stay with his ass but you already know I aint on that shit."

"Is he that same little lame you used to bring through the Jets before you left?" asked Jarvis.

"Yeah J-one. That's my heart though. He rolled that bid out with me. Every other week he was in that visiting room and not a day went by without me receiving an email from him."

"Damn that's a good nigga. So yall was on that Remi and Pap shit huh. Aint to many niggas gone ride like that sis!"

"Yeah that's my baby. Even though I had to send him money off my books here and there cuz his hustle hands are dead weight."

Jarvis started laughing.

"What's funny?"

"You gotta love this nigga, you're taking care of em."

"J-one you know me. Money, that shit tear, loyalty means everything. It's unbreakable."

"That's right sis," said Jarvis as they went back and forth until they made it to the Jets.

Wasn't anyone in the parking lot when they pulled in but nod heads coming and going out of the operating buildings.

"What the hell!" Wanisha blurted as they got out of the car. Shonte was standing on top of the building's roof looking down on them with a pair of binoculars to her eyes.

Then suddenly Shonte shouted," Ayyyye girl... Ayc yall look, that's Wanisha with J-one!"

A few of the KKS girls who was on watch commenced to climbing down the rooftops trap to meet Wanisha.

"J-one, what is them hoes doing?"

"That's their job Y-love, and them hoes is getting paid some decent money to be watchwomen."

Marlo came busting through the entrance of the next building over.

"There goes my other half," he yelled.

At that moment, she felt a cherishing feeling for her freedom. Not ever wanting to be away from her twin brother again.

"Heyy nigga you look good," she said while hugging him. She noticed he was sporting a rose gold figural diamond chain around his neck with a diamond hand gun emblem hanging from it.

Although he couldn't walk he still dressed in quality fashion.

"Girl how much you weigh now?" he asked perusing his eyes over her.

"125 pounds, why?"

"Cause your ass done got a little thick!"

"Boy shut up. How is Ma?"

"Still smoking like a rock star, but she misses your ass. You need to go see her."

The parking lot was getting jam packed, and everyone was in harmony. It had only been five months since they opened shop and brand-new whips littered the parking lot. Day and night KKS girls patrolled the roof tops alternating shifts. Before task force could successfully hit the projects, the girls would radio in on their walkie talkies informing the hustlers of the adversaries' approach.

Two months after Wanisha's release date she had made her mark. She was now switching cars like panties. Her latest purchase was an all-black 635 Coupe BMW. She was renting a condo not too far from Jarvis and it was elegantly plushed. She was enjoying the good living in the fast lane and stayed draped in the finest of clothing and jewelry. She continued to send Rhonda pictures and money orders on a regular, awaiting her return to the streets. Rhonda only had twenty months left of her bid. As a whole, the KKBG crew were being watched by every neighborhood in the city. Eyes of jealousy, envy, and hate were looking upon them. Which solidified a fact, that niggas were about to be tested and caskets were about to start dropping.

✷✷✷✷✷✷✷✷✷✷✷✷✷✷✷✷✷✷✷✷

Snow was falling hard on this cold winter day in December, and it was a traffic jam of nod heads in the projects waiting to purchase and go. Traffic jams were a regular and police were working on cracking down King Kennedy's drug operation.

"Damn nigga yo sister told me ten minutes. That was a half hour ago," said Cho-cho.

"I'm waiting on her too," Rio uttered.

"What yall niggas copping?" Marlo asked while organizing his money that was sprawled over his lap.

"Four and a half," said Cho-cho.

"That's what she's bringing me," Rio confirmed.

"Damon just left not too long ago, why yall aint holla at him?"

"Nigga you know yo sister got them holiday prices. Twelve grand for four and a half ounces shit you can't beat that with Bud Crawford's hands my nigga," smiled Cho-cho.

"Shit it's only a five-hundred-dollar difference. That compensate for being on her time. Yall niggas cheap, that's why yall missing all this money," said Marlo.

Eric and Mont came inside the building.

"Aye dawg, that nigga Trell just pulled in," Mont told Marlo.

Marlo restored his money back into his pocket and said, "It's time for me to take a break and kick it with my East Cleveland nigga."

He put his bag of heroin inside of his leather coat pocket and wheeled himself out of the building.

"Here she goes right here," he yelled back to the homies waiting for his sister. Rio and Cho-cho hurriedly made their way to her truck and climbed inside.

Trell's forest green candy painted Porsche truck was thumping loudly. He saw Marlo approaching the car.

"What's good nigga. Let's get into some'em."

"Aight let me holla at my sis for a minute."

"Cool tell her I love her," said Trell smiling.

Marlo wheeled himself up to her driver side. She rolled down her window.

"What's up Y-love," said Marlo tucking his twin nines on his waist. Something he always did before he climbed out of his wheelchair.

"Shit.... What you about to do?"

"Hit some corners with Trell, blow some trees and probably shoot over one of my lil hoes spot for a lil bit."

"I hope that nigga got his license since you wanna ride around with them flame throwers, acting like you got a license to carry."

"Sis I'd rather get caught with em then without em. He legit though sis. Oh! He told me to tell you he love you."

"Tell 'em I love money not lames from E.C."

"Stop getting beside yourself now, you used to go with him in elementary."

"Okay well I'll see yall later," Wanisha said to Rio and Chocho and gave her attention back to her brother.

"Why you be wearing all them jewelry pieces out here?"

"What you mean, because they mine!"

She hated that she asked him that because she knew why. Ever since he been paralyzed he stayed draped in expensive clothing and fine jewelry to compensate for his lameness.

"Sis I'm gone cop a quarter brick from you probably tomorrow. How long yo holiday prices gone last?"

"Until after the holidays. Just give me eighteen grand. You know for you the prices are sweeter than everybody else."

"I love you sis. You coming back through today?"

"Only if I'm dropping off some'em. I'm chillin with my man all day."

"Now Mel's a lame," Marlo laughed and headed towards Trell's car.

"Shut up punk Mel's that dude."

Marlo and Trell rolled around the city blowing trees, with the power hole cracked to alleviate the cloud of smoke.

Marlo and Trell been friends for a long time. Trell lived half of his childhood a few blocks over from King Kennedy and went to elementary and junior high school with Marlo and Wanisha. When he was thirteen, he and his family moved out to East Cleveland. Although its considered a suburb, it's among some of the worse ghettos of the town itself. Back in the 80's it was upper class. By 1992 it was drug infested and the murder rate was sky high. Trell was from a block called 'The Tribe,' a one-way street full of action. Trell stopped the car in the middle of the street on the side of the dice game on the sidewalk. He rolled down his window.

"What it's looking like Chubb?"

"Ah I'm only up about eight hunned, but you know these niggas sweet. It'll be eight thousand in a minute!"

Trell turned to Marlo, "Let's hit a few pockets real quick and dip."

"Shit I'm dirty. I got some raw on me------before he could finish Trell said, "Put that shit under the seat."

"Fuck it lets hit some pockets then."

Trell put Marlo in his wheelchair and they got in the dice game. While Marlo was engaging in a huge side bet, his phone started vibrating. It was Tom, a nod head lawyer and one of Marlo's dedicated customers. He quickly called his number back and gave Tom instructions to where he was at, then he focused back in on the dice game. Almost an hour later after Tom had come and gone, Trell asked if Marlo was ready. Marlo who was rolling a blunt said, "yeah shoot me back to the hood."

Before they made their exit, two figures emerged from the cut with masks on and guns aimed at the crowd of dice shooters.

"GET THE FUCK ON THE GROUND BEFORE I SMOKE ONE OF YOU NIGGAS!"

"Aint this a bitch," said Marlo in disbelief as the crowd complied including Trell who was shook. Everybody was caught off guard. The robbers quickly stripped them of all their money and jewelry.

"Take that shit off nigga. Right now!" The robber barked at Marlo after he took away his money. By Marlo never zipping his leather coat back up, his chain was in plain view. He took it off and gave it to him.

"STAY FACED DOWN," one of the robbers' ordered as they back peddled their way through the alley. Marlo slowly reached to his waist for both of his nine millimeters, that somehow went unnoticed to the gunmen. As soon as they turned to flee, within seconds, Marlo had both guns in his hands, letting off excessive rounds in the direction of the men.

"AYE DAWG throw me in the car and let's go hawk them niggas," Marlo shouted as everybody retreated to their cars. Deep slabs were being laid in the street as the cars violently pulled away from the curb.

The gunmen had managed to get away.

"Hurry up and shoot me to the block. I know one got damn thang, Imma find out who got my muthafuckin chain and watch what happen. If a nigga buy it he gone die wearing it!"

While Trell continued to dwell back and forth about everybody slipping, Marlo analyzed his behavior and the moments before the robbery took place. It didn't look like it was any foul play on Trell's behalf, so he wrote that out of his mind. But he believed in his heart that somebody on his block had to know something.

A circle of homies were standing in the parking lot when they pulled in.

"Pull up to them," he told Trell.

Marlo opened his door and told Dae-dae to grab his wheelchair and help him out. Then he said to Trell, "If you hear word about whoever was behind this, make sure you holla at me."

"We gone find out who, it's a small world. But I don't know if they gone be alive by the time I come tell you."

"Be safe nigga," said Marlo.

"What the fuck was that nigga talking about?" Dae-dae asked after Trell pulled off.

"Somebody just robbed me for my shit!"

"What! Where at?" asked Lil Hurt.

"On the Tribe block in E.C. Some niggas laid the whole fucking block down. Can you believe that shit?"

"I can believe that nigga set you up dawg. You don't think so?" asked Trey.

"Naw that's my man."

"But one of his homies could've set it up," Lil Hurt replied.

"Man, them niggas soft. Aint nan nigga have a strap out over there shit I was the only one dumping!"

"What all they take?" asked Dae-dae.

"Everything I had on me but my twin babies.".............

Jarvis, Anton, Damon, Wanisha, and Marlo were in the guest room of Jarvis condo, listening to Marlo tell what happened earlier.

"So, when you was bussing yo gun, they didn't bust back to get the heat off they ass?"

"Does it matter?" Marlo asked irritably.

"Nigga you better start using yo head. Hell yeah it matters, them niggas set you up. They didn't wanna make a mistake and hit one of their peoples," Wanisha yelled. "You posted over there with eighty thousand dollars' worth of jewelry on gambling and shit. You think them thirsty ass niggas aint have nothing to do with it?"

Marlo didn't respond, because he realized that he had put himself in a vulnerable position earlier. Wanisha quickly calmed her temper, softened her expression not wanting to hurt her brother feelings about his mistake, but she also wanted him to learn from it.

"Look Marlo, you already know how I am about you. I just hate that you keep putting yourself in situations that's costing you everything but your life. I'm not gone just sit and tolerate things happening to you and you know that. Something has to be done."

"Leave that shit alone until we find out exactly who," said Marlo.

"Hell naw they guilty by association and it's gone be repercussions,"--------Jarvis voice cut her off.

"Do yall understand what we got going on... What's in the making?" He looked at each lieutenant, then at his soldier.

"A dynasty. This shit aint to be taken for granted and it's damn sho aint to be took lightly. When all this is said and done, our money should be long enough to touch our great grandchildren. But how can that be possible if we gone continue to make careless mistakes. I shouldn't have to call shots that result in death, for no other reason other than we received a threat to our establishment. Now I feel like your sister feel because your sister is like my sister, we just didn't come from the same womb. And you're her brother which means you're mine to. What happen to you can't and won't be tolerated. Murder is the only example that we display when it's this kind of drama. But Wanisha, you as my lieutenant will have no part in this move." He silenced Wanisha with a motion of his hand and continued.

"You nor Damon. Anton, I need you to round up a team of four to complete this shot. But first I want you to roll through their strip in the wee hours of the morning and peep the area out. After you do your homework, kill on sight."

Wanisha stayed behind after everybody left. She didn't understand Jarvis shot call, so she reasoned that he was trying to show his authority and had to confront him about it. She locked the door behind them and went back into the guest room. Jarvis was leaned back on the sofa smoking a Cuban cigar, a habit he picked up since the day he established his connection with Adewale.

"Jarvis, why didn't you put me in charge of the shot?" she asked with her arms folded over her chest standing over him. He patted the cushion next to him.

"Sit down Y-Love. Let me talk to you."

She reluctantly complied.

"Was I wrong for giving you the position as a lieutenant?"

"How could you have been wrong? What made you ask me that?"

"I never said I was wrong, but I'm asking you."

"No J-one of course not."

"Well then show me you can think like one because that's what all this shit is about. Even a situation like today must be thought out and I'm trusting in my lieutenants to be absolute thinkers. Front line action is not for us. We move behind the scenes. If it's ever a hit to be handled and I feel like it may be bigger than our soldiers, then that's when we move. I know that's your brother but we're an organization, so we must move like one. Let the soldiers handle it okay."

She took a deep breath and exhaled. She now totally understood her strength and limits to her position.

Twenty-four hours later at two thirty-three in the morning, five Tribe hustlers was agglomerated in a circle taking turns serving customers. In a blink of an eye, rapid gun fire caught them off guard, as four masked men ran towards their targets from out of a yard a few feet away. Screams and pleas sounded, but within seconds the scene was silenced.

36

February 12, M-2 came home and got blessed from his click with pure love. A nice home, a brand-new Chevy Tahoe and a huge shopping spree, not to mention his position as a lieutenant. He was so happy to be a part of a click so dominant. He hugged Jarvis tightly and told him that he was willing to die, kill, and testify his love to the judge if it came down to it......All for the KKBG clan.

Winter came and went, and spring had settled in. Jarvis was now moving eighty kilos a month and he and Adewale were very good friends. Although he found a way to make a sufficient amount of time for Kyla, she could never get enough of him. His relationship with Roxanne was nothing more than a parental one and she hated herself for messing up a good thing. Not because of how rich he'd become, but because she still loved him more than anything. However, Jarvis remained adamant about not becoming her lover again.

Jarvis mother was doing well. This was her third-year drug free, and she was now living in a beautiful home in Shaker Heights Ohio that Jarvis purchased. Her and her boyfriend Joseph was engaged to be married but a date wasn't set. Wanisha took a trip out to Columbus to visit Omirah at the campus a few times. Each time, Omirah was overly happy to spend some time with one of her closest friends. Wanisha had put her up on everything good in the hood and especially about Jarvis prosperity. Omirah was in denial because she constantly told herself she was over him, but her heart always made her face the truth. She realized she would always love her some Jarvis.

One afternoon on a hot day in June, Jarvis noticed a white card stuck between one of his windshield wipers. He retrieved the card. It read, "Sam 4370201-immediately."

Jarvis heart rate quickened from the notion of being followed and the smell of trouble. He quickly pulled out of the driveway and off down the street. He waited for an answer. After the sixth ring he was about to hang up when a male's prude voice spoke into his ear sounding like a hundred percent white man.

"Hello."

"Speak," Jarvis insisted.

"Hey Mr. Cooper. How are you?"

Jarvis didn't answer. A still silence lingered.

"Mr. Cooper, we need to meet if you want to last in the world you're living in."

Jarvis didn't answer.

"I assume you know what's going on so let me be frank, meet me at T & A Bar and grill. It's in Elyria on Foster Ave. Rather you show or not, that's on you. I can either help you or hurt you, now either we make alliance today or I'll crush you within a year. It's your call."

"What time?" asked Jarvis.

"Six o'clock sharp."

Without another word Jarvis hung up and checked the time on his fifteen-thousand-dollar Roger Dubuis watch. It read 2:26pm. He shot to another low-key house he had in

Cleveland and parked the brand-new beamer in the three-car garage and pulled out his Audi. A half an hour later, he and his four lieutenants were having a meeting at Lake Erie. Everybody was sitting on the huge rocks right off the shore.

"So what you think. Think we should shut the Jets down until you find out what's what?" asked M-2.

"Naw that aint necessary but I know one thing, shit is real and I'm sure he wants on the pay roll. But for what it's worth, he could prove to be very useful."

"Hell yeah shit a heads up is always a beautiful thing," said Damon.

Jarvis walked into the small bar and Sam beckoned him to a table for two. Jarvis made his way over and had a seat. He slid his badge across the table. Jarvis opened it and perused over his identification before sliding it back discreetly. Jarvis had gotten nervous, never expecting Samuel to be a Federal agent. Samuel Mccroy cut straight to the chase.

"Who am I? I am the corporal of my team of investigators. I receive orders from my sergeant to investigate, then my team and I will go out and observe the situation. Since I'm the corporal it's my responsibility to report back to the sergeant. Basically, all the specifics of what we come across. If I give him vital information, the investigation gets deeper. If I tell him that there's really nothing, he reports that to his boss and the investigation disappears. Now, my team have just recently been assigned to investigate your operations, but it doesn't start until Monday. If you want your way of living to remain intact, give me one hundred thousand dollars tomorrow and bring it here tomorrow same time, same place. Once that happens, I'll call the dogs off."

"Well what about for future references?" asked Jarvis.

"It's on you. My sergeant is the boss over me and he's a part of this connection, but his face will never be shown. I pay him. After the one hundred thousand tomorrow, I expect twenty-five a week and me and my boss guarantee that you and your associates will never see a federal court.

Twenty-five thousand a week was chump change to Jarvis and although it was a slight gamble dealing with a crooked official, it was more than a relief to Jarvis to have a federal agent on his team. He agreed to the deal and Samuel Mccroy was placed on Jarvis payroll.

※※※※※※※※※※※※※※※※※※※※

"THE LOS ANGELES CLIPPERS SELECT.......... MARCO HANKINS, FOURTH PICK OF THE FIRST ROUND OF THE NBA DRAFT!"

Omirah who watched from the crowd was happy to see her fiancé's dreams come true.

"It's such an honor to be given a chance to play for the LA clippers," Marco said into the microphone. "But all respect and praises go out to my parents and future wife who have inspired me in so many ways."

Omirah who still had a year left of college was two weeks away from becoming Marco's wife.

※※※※※※※※※※※※※※※※※※※※

The opening of Jarvis Club "Platinum G's was jammed pack. Gold diggers and ballers came out to party, trick, and splurge. The clubs were adjoined to a bowling alley that could be seen through the ceiling glass windows of Platinum G's. The admission days were different but both establishments were owned by Jarvis and set up for success.

Downstairs under the party floor, were rooms for pool playing and a food serving concession area.

KKBG members congregated amongst the crowd, celebrating the opening of the Platinum G's. Jarvis and his lieutenants were relaxing in the glass office.

Wanisha sat conservatively with one leg over the other, and a glass of champagne in hand. She was sporting a John Varvatos black silk collar shirt, that ran her $3,520 dollars along with a pair of $895 Agnona wool and silk slacks. She always stayed on top of her shoe game sporting a $485-dollar pair of Jimmy Choo heels. She had close to five thousand on in clothes not to mention her ladies Rolex watch and Mikimoto Pearls that were worth thirty thousand dollars. From the gutter to a butterfish life style, they were all on top, touching and living amongst the finer things in life.

"Nigga I got the best retained lawyer in Ohio....... Tommy Tito. Send him at your mother, I guarantee he get her back in court on an appeal," Jarvis assured.

"Yeah, I'll call him tomorrow then," said Anton. "I wonder why she just now telling me that it was all these technicalities in her case."

"Well damn Anton, today is your first time going to see her since she left. Give her a break," Wanisha chided.

"Man.... I gotta get her up outta there. It took for me to go see her to realize how much I miss her."

"I can dig it," M-2 replied, never taking his eyes off the chess game he and Damon were playing.

"How can yall niggas concentrate with all this noise going on?" asked Jarvis.

"It aint a thang J-one," said M-2. "But the question you should ask him is how he gone save his bitch cuz dat hoe trapped!"

"Fuck that bitch," Damon retorted. "Take the queen nigga. I aint get this far in life cause no bitch!"

"I heard that," Wanisha uttered while studying their moves.

"Come on Y-love, lets show our face around. Brush shoulders for a minute," said Anton.

Wanisha put down her champagne glass and looked at the time on her Rolex.

"Come on," she replied.

As they commenced to circle the dance floor, they were continuously accosted by faces too eager to show their respect for them. After a full go around, they stopped at the bar and mingled amongst a few of their homies.

Then Bujo, a Jamaican from the Garden Valley Community, one of Anton's famous wholesale purchasers, came out of the crowd. After he and Anton embraced they sat at the bar.

"So, is it still a delay?" Bujo asked in his thick accent.

"Naw naw everything good, just came in today. I was gone call your man fab tomorrow to let him know."

"Same product as always?" asked Bujo.

"Yeah it's the same thing. Top quality as always."

"Tomorrow I'm going to cop eight kilos from you. Am I worth a deal?"

"Four hundred and fifty thousand is a deal. I can't go lower than that and expect to be happy."

"I see.... My man fabulous will do the transaction because in a few hours, I have to fly out to Jamaican and won't be back until late night tomorrow."

"Aight just tell him to call my main man Trey whenever he ready to get the package delivered to him.

While most of the action was upstairs on the party floor, Beatrice was downstairs at the food concession, buying a few items for Marlo and herself. After paying for the items, she headed back upstairs but was stopped in her tracks by an unfamiliar face.

"Slow down shorty."

"Excuse me you're in my way."

"I know but only for a second."

"A second is too long when my man is upstairs."

She tried to walk around him, but he cut her off.

"Would you please move."

"Not until you at least tell me your name."

She exhaled irritably.

"My name is Beatrice. I take it yours is crazy. Now unless you want this food all over you then I advise you to move out my way."

He could tell that she liked him, but his mission was yet to be completed.
"I don't got you doing that," he said while going into his pocket pulling out a small piece of paper. "But I do got you

using this number for whenever you get lonely and things get a lil tight. You can call me, and I'll come loosen it up for you."

"Don't you see my hands are full."

He walked up on her and stuck the piece of paper inside of her back pocket. She let him. Something about the two tear drops tattooed under his eyes, gave her the impression that nothing scared or mattered to him. He seemed dangerous and she perceived him to be a good lover. Somebody she could possibly creep with considering she hadn't had sex ever since Marlo stopped walking.

"By the way, you can call me Snatch-out."

37

Through the wee hours of the morning, Anton sat in his crib, pondering over a deceitful motive. What would be a quicker way to reach his five-million-dollar mark before he could retire. At a little over a million he realized that he was still far away and didn't know how long the ball would continue to roll in his favor before things began crashing down. He analyzed what the profit would be if he only sold Bujo four kilos and kept the other four to himself.

Originally taking an eight the product would only be taking a four after he stretched it. If Bujo didn't cut it, the dope would be weak when it hit the streets. However, if he did cut it then after he get finished putting his touches on it, the dope would hardly be any good. He remembered Bujo saying that he was about to catch a flight and wouldn't be back until late tomorrow, meaning by the time the dope gets in Bujo's hands, it would've been done marinated in Fab's company long enough for him not to know who crossed him. He knew that if Bujo believed in his man then it was going to be a war. Anton only concern was being accused by his peoples of starting it. But by him putting the dope in Trey's hands to deliver it for him, he figured that he would be completely out of blames way. If the blame made it pass Fabulous, he was going to make sure it didn't make it pass Trey.

Early the next morning, Jarvis drove out to Maryland to stash some cash and spend a whole day with Kyla. Around 9:30am Wanisha pulled up on Mont and Dae-dae in the Jets parking lot.

"Aye yall let's roll to the game out in Pittsburg so I can watch my babies kick the Steelers ass."

It was the third week of the season and she was a die-hard Browns fan. They hopped in with her and started rolling up back to back blunts preparing for the two-hour drive.

At one in the afternoon, Beatrice and a few other KKS girls were standing on the rooftop waiting on their replacements since their shift was over. Beatrice found Marlo in one of the buildings working and told him that she was about to drive across town to her mother's house. She kissed him and left. Once she made it out of the parking lot, she dialed Snatch-out number. His deep voiced answered.

"Who's this?" he asked.

"A stranger!"..........................

Snatch-out was silent.

"Damn how many girls did you give your number to last night?"

"It aint that. It's just that I forgot your name, so remind me."

"Just call me B. Are you busy?"

"It depends."

"On what?"

"What's at hand," he told her.

"Remember what you said last night right?"

"Um hm."

"Well it needs some loosening so I'm taking you up on that offer," she said yet admitting to herself that she was wrong. She was feening for what she needed but didn't realize it was that serious up until now and didn't have the power to turn back.

Twenty minutes later she was walking into Snatch-out's house, who had on nothing but a pair of boxers. Her eyes went from his dick print back to his face.

"You don't cut any corners, do you?" said Beatrice.

He walked up to her and started kissing her. She lost control of herself, bent down and unleashed his penis.

"Oh my God," she uttered and started sucking it like a pro. He didn't want her to stop, but she couldn't wait any longer. They made it to his room and she quickly got undressed. Snatch-out knew why she was feening, because he knew who her man was. Her actions confirmed that she had been faithful to him up until now. Snatch-out's mission was completed.

She felt like a Virgin getting re-split and it took her a while to adjust to his pounding strokes, but she soon found his rhythm and matched it. After a half an hour of sweaty sex, she quickly got dressed.

"Can you let me out?"

"Fa show, but is we gone be doing this again?" asked Snatch-out.

"Just keep the same number and I'll make sure not to lose it."

"Damn that felt so good," she thought to herself pulling out of his driveway.

As she drove the twenty-minute drive home, she was already dealing with her guilty conscience. Plenty of times she could've cheated on Marlo since he's been in a wheelchair, but her love for him was too strong for her to do it. Now that she finally did it, she questioned herself, wondering what was happening to their love. She once vowed that no matter what his condition turned out to be, she would never turn away from him. Although she still felt that way, today she had allowed a stranger to have his way with her. She stopped at a red light and slammed her fist against the steering wheel.

"Damn Marlo, I need you to walk! Walk again baby please. Walk for us!"

Distracted in her thoughts, she never noticed the gray Regal tailing her.

It was four in the morning when Bujo finished. He added a quarter kilo of cut on each kilo that he purchased from Anton. Dope fiend Mary sat at the table with her works laid out ready to test the product they assumed would be thriller. He put a half of a gram in front of her and told her to get to work. She quickly strapped up. Bujo sat across from her, and grabbed his blunt out of the ashtray, expecting her to give him thumbs up like always. He watched as the needle poked into her vein, waiting for her chin to hit her chest. After two minutes, Mary blurted out, "Something is wrong."

Bujo spit the weed smoke out and leaned up in his chair.

"This isn't thriller," said Mary.

"What! What you mean Mary?"

"Exactly what I said. This most definitely aint thriller. Matter of fact this aint shit!"

Bujo jumped up and got on the phone. First, he called Fabulous and ordered him to come to him immediately. Then he called Anton's cell phone. While waiting for an answer, he put more stuff in front of her to try.

"Hello," Anton answered.

"Bomba clot this some foof you give me. No good. Give,"--------Anton cut him off.

"Who is this?"

"Motherfucker this Bujo. Take this shit back and give me my money.

"What is you talking about?" asked Anton as if he didn't know what was going on.

"Don't fuck with me......... Give,"----Anton cut him off.

"Nigga what the fuck is you talking about, I gave you what you requested. You better check yo man!"

"YOU WANNA FUCK WITH ME! WATCH YOU DIE FOR IT MUTHAFUCKA! YOU AND EVERYTHING AROUND YOU!"

He ended the call and turned to face a half sober Mary.

"Nope, it's no good Bujo."

38

Something much deeper than beef itself was at hand, and Anton realized that, after he hung up the phone.

"What's did is done," he thought, but the feeling he was receiving told him that four bricks wasn't worth what was about to come with it. At four something in the morning, he managed to get a hold of Wanisha, Damon, and M-2. He told each one to meet him in the projects immediately. During the drive there, he continued making back to back calls to different homies, ordering them to get to the Jets. Surprisingly he got a hold to at least fifty percent of the clique, and when he made it to the Jets, he noticed twenty five percent of the clique was still out grinding. A half an hour later, twenty-two soldiers and all four lieutenants were gathered in one of the buildings. Only ten people were absent not including a handful of KKS girls.

"What the fuck is going on Anton........what happened?" asked Wanisha.

"Hold on let Beatrice and Marlo get in here," said Anton.

A minute later they entered the building.

"Yo what's up?" Marlo instantly asked.

"I don't quite know. Trey, you aint fuck with that work I gave you to deliver to the Jamaicans did you?"

"Fuck naw nigga!"

Anton stared into his face for a long second.

"On everything nigga. That's on Tae and Deedra," Trey stated veraciously.

"What the fuck is going on?" asked M-2.

"The Jamaican nigga Bujo just called me making threats. talking about I sold him some foof, when I know damn well what I gave him is what I always give em. Now I remember him saying something at the club about not being back from Jamaica until late tonight. Then, Trey and the nigga Fabulous transacted business early in the day and what it looks like to me, is his main man crossed him and is trying to put the blame on me."

"How much did he buy from you?" Damon asked seriously.

"Eight bricks."

"And what did he say to you?" asked Wanisha.

"He threatened my life and everything around me. Shit, he declared war."

"Shit he better redirect his aim and take back what he lost from his mans and them," Lil Hurt strongly replied. "Cause the only thing he gone get this way is a toe tag and a closed casket."

"Hold on. Hold the fuck on.... he said what?" Wanisha asked disgustedly.

"Just what I told you Y-love. Now this is what I think is going on. I don't think anybody crossed him, I think he infiltrated us and now that he sees we're here for the long haul and want us out the way. I mean look at how many toes we have stepped on. We got this shit on lock. We reduced the quantity prices of heroin and some moe shit. You know niggas want us out the way."

Damon looked deeply into Anton's eyes.

"Where J-one at?" Rio asked.

"He in Maryland, he'll be back tomorrow," said Wanisha.

"Look, yall stay strapped and play it real safe. When J-one come back we'll calculate our move. One thing for sure they aint coming over here, but hopefully and for everybody's sake, dude will come to his senses," said Wanisha.

"I don't know Y-love, that nigga was talking real reckless."

✶✶✶✶✶✶✶✶✶✶✶✶✶✶✶✶✶✶✶✶

It was now five forty-eight in the morning as Marlo and Beatrice headed home from the projects. The streets were free of traffic and snow continued to fall heavily onto the ground.

"Boo, do you really think it's about to be a war between us and those Jamaicans?"

"That's what it looks like," Marlo replied deep in thought. "But for some reason it seems like it's more to it than what Anton is telling us. His body language was saying something different than his words."

"Do you think he really sold Bujo bad dope?" Beatrice asked not giving it much thought until now.

"B, I don't know what to think but I damn sho wasn't feeling his vibe tonight. But if we gone war with these muthafuckas, then I just hope it's for the right reasons, and not because he did some snake ass shit."

"Are you gonna tell J-one about the bad vibe you're feeling about Anton?" asked Beatrice.

Marlo blazed a blunt.

"It aint factual that he's in the wrong so imma let the situation take its course. If he did some snake shit then the truth will unfold."

Five minutes later they were pulling into their driveway. Beatrice killed the engine. They sat in the car and talked until the blunt was gone then she got out and put him in his wheelchair. Hours later they were both in bed, deep in thought and sleep was closing in. Beatrice guilty conscience was getting the best of her as she laid next to Marlo who was now softly snoring. A tear fell from her eye into her ear as she stared at the ceiling. Then suddenly she heard a noise in the hallway outside of the bedroom door. She quickly raised out of bed and listened intently.

She heard another creak in the floor and tried to shake Marlo awake. Before Marlo was fully awakened the bedroom door was ferociously kicked opened, causing Beatrice to scream out in horror. Marlo quickly sat up as the three intruders emerged with their firearms trained at their targets. Neither one was wearing a mask.

"BITCH YOU SCREAM ONE MORE TIME AND IMMA FILL YOU UP WITH SO MUCH LED THEY GONE BE ABLE TO WRITE WITH YO ASS!" Ubie sneered, standing between Snatch-out and Killa.

Snatch-out started laughing, then he said to Beatrice, "See what being unfaithful get you?"

"How in the fuck did yall get in my house?" Marlo barked, while slowly trying to reach underneath his pillow. "And what the fuck you mean she was being unfaithful," he asked trying to buy time.

"Just take the money and go," Beatrice pleaded.

"Oh, we got that now we want......him," said Ubie and fired two shots into Marlo's chest. He fell back onto the mattress gasping for breath and made a desperate attempt for his gun. Before he could squeeze off any rounds, his body and face was bullet riddled.

"OH MY GOD NOOOO!" Yelled Beatrice as she covered her man's body with hers. Snatch-out fired two shots inside of her, silencing her screams.

"Now that's a Kodak moment to be remembered right there," Killa joked.

****

Garden Valley was one of the most poverty-stricken ghettos in the city. A Jamaican populated community, they were all natives of Kingston. Garden Valley Posse were known for inflicting the most atrocious casualties upon their enemies. Through the history of G.V.P. along with the flipping of generations, they have been feared by many because of their heartless acts. In the mid 90's, a dominant member in G.V.P name Machette was gunned down by the police in cold blood. For the following two months after his death, severe killings were imposed on family members of various police officers. Victims were killed in their homes, jobs, etc. Although the finger was pointed at the Jamaicans, the chain of murders went unsolved yet the G.V.P. crew had birthed a new sobriquet by authorities called, The Treacherous Jamaican Posse.

Bujo, Perry Shaw, and a few G.V.P. members, were gathered in Bujo's apartment. Perry joined forces with Bujo a short while after he cut his ties with Gianni. Their business relations was beneficial on both ends.

"I want you to touch everything he love. If he got seeds, I want them buried. The mama of his seed, I want her dead. If he got a mama or grandmama, kill em both! He's gone hate that he had the heart to even think to fuck with me!"

Perry stood up, anxious to fulfill his assignments.

"I'll keep you informed as I go, but you can rest assure everything will be taken care of."

After Perry Left, the five G.V.P. members started to plot their executional plans against the KKBG Posse.

Jarvis made it back from Maryland a little after eleven in the morning. While away he purchased a purple GT Bentley that he drove back. Once inside his condo, he sent a text message to his four lieutenants, to come to him asap. After he got comfortably situated, he sat back and blazed up his forbidden cigar, not yet knowing the problem that was already inherited into his hands.

"J-one, you know damn well I would never jeopardize this dynasty you put together," said Anton.

"I'm not saying that you're jeopardizing anything, I'm asking your opinion as to why this nigga would go about declaring war in such a cowardly way."

"I can't call that J-one, but you do trust that I wouldn't do no shit like that right?" Jarvis stared deeply into his eyes for a lingering moment along with his other lieutenants.

"Of course, I trust you," said Jarvis, breaking the silence.

"This Bujo character. He got to die."

While Jarvis was in Elyria, Ohio having a meeting with Samuel Mccroy, Marlo and Beatrice bodies were discovered by Wanisha. Twenty minutes after she found them, paramedics, detectives and coroners were scanning the scene. Beatrice who had been shot in her back and in the head still had a weak pulse and was now being ushered away to the hospital. Marlo was dead on arrival.

"I have no idea who would do this," Wanisha cried to the detective who continuously questioned her.

"Well ma'am, we're going to have to ask you to come downtown with us for further questioning." Unable to stop from crying, she agreed.

Later that evening, all the KKBG and KKS members were ganged up in the projects. Each one was very emotional, and they believed the Jamaicans were responsible. Nevertheless, they were all ready to ride. Jarvis too was in an emotional trance, but he knew that he had to stay smart for everyone's sake. By the end of the night, the first hit was set, and Jarvis put Wanisha in charge of it.

Friday night was reggae night at the Double Nickel and like every Friday, it was packed to capacity. A sufficient amount of G.V.P members were inside mingling amongst the partiers.

"We're gonna kill every last one of them Bomba clot bitches. They don't know I'm the Don Dadda!" Bujo boasted.

"Four hundred and fifty thousand I piss on, just like I'm gonna piss in his face before I destroy him."

Bujo and a handful of his men were in the VIP section along with some other Jamaicans, who were on boss status from different areas around the city. They too were teaming up with the G.V.P. crew to help exterminate the KKBG Posse.

"So why isn't he dead yet?" asked Slice, one of the allied Jamaicans.

"Because I want him to see some of his family members go underground first. Torture his soul you know."

While Bujo and some of his boys were at the Double Nickle, his right-hand man Fabulous was being tortured. Limb by limb was being chain sawed off until he confessed his guilt. Although Bujo didn't know if he was guilty or not, he felt that he had no other choice but to make sure. Fabulous last words were, "I didn't do it!" Before his body was chain sawed in half.

A little after two in the morning the last call for alcohol was announced by the D.J. Twenty minutes later, the club was emptying as the sidewalks and parking lot was littered with Jamaicans. Wanisha who was parked across the street in a stolen car, keyed in on Bujo who was amongst a huge circle of Jamaicans. She whipped out her cell phone and dialed Angelica's number. Without a greeting Angelica answered her phone and asked, "Is it time?"

"As soon as yall bend the corner, they're the circle standing behind the stop sign."

Angelica hung up, put on her helmet, and cranked up the motorcycle. Her pursuers followed suit. Each of the four motorcycles were paired up with all KKS girls. Each passenger was intending to be a shooter. After the girls cocked back their mac elevens, they sharply pulled out of the darkened alley.

A Jamaican broad walked up to Bujo's circle wanting a minute of his time.

"Why are you bothering me Tasha. Don't you see I'm discussing some business?"

"It will only take a second," she responded.

He passed the blunt to Geno and he and Tasha walked a few feet away.

"What is it you want to talk about and make it quick!"

"Bujo, I just want to apologize for the way I've been acting lately and from this point on I swear that I will play my part in your life the way I'm supposed to play it."

"I don't wanna hear that. You's a jealous bitch. Always have been and always will be."

While she continued to beg for his forgiveness, four motorcycles sharply turned the corner. Before the Jamaicans could react, rapid gunfire chopped down the circle, instantly sending the majority of them to their maker. Bujo went unscathed as he ducked and took cover. The girls continued to spray as they rolled by, not only focusing on the circle that they chopped down, but everything moving. Sixteen people was shot, eight was dead, and the girls had made a safe getaway.

Bujo made it to his Lexus and sharply pulled away. Wanisha pulled out and followed in his direction. She tailed him from a distance until he turned down a side street and parked in front of a house. As he walked up the pavement, he cautiously peered into the stolen car before she stopped abruptly, and open fired on him, knocking him clean off his feet. She then aimed at his stretched-out body and fired more rounds at him before pulling away.

"It was them, I know it was them," Bujo barked. "They killed five of my men who the fuck do they think they are!" He looked down at his bullet proof vest thinking about how it saved his life.

"I can't answer that," said Perry. "But I do have information to move off of."

"Talk to me what's good."

"Anton's mother has just been transferred to Marysville prison. I have a niece locked up there. She's a money hungry heartless bitch. I'm going to go and visit her tomorrow and offer her twenty thousand dollars to put her to sleep for eternity. That's a bill you must cover."

"Is it a sure thing?"
"As sure as my motherly given name."

"What's his mother's name?" asked Bujo.

"Angie Deevers."

"As soon as her death is verified, she gets the money."

"Sure enough. I also have an address of his child's mother. Tracy Green."

"Kill 'em both!"

"Enough said." Perry stood up.

"Is fifty thousand a sufficient amount? asked Bujo.

"Most definitely."

After Rhonda came back to the unit from visiting her uncle, she immediately started her investigation on finding out who Angie Deevers was. Twenty-four hours later, Angie was discovered. She lived in the thirty-five and older unit on the other side of the compound. Three days later the plan was set. At five-thirty in the morning when the cell doors unlocked, she got herself together and left the unit, as if she was headed to the chow hall. Instead she made her way to Angie's unit. Once she made it to her unit, she noticed that only a few inmates were in the common area. She realized that nobody was paying her any attention, so she made her way to room 217. She didn't have to worry about any cameras because there weren't any. She just hoped that her bunky went to breakfast. She peeped in her window and to her favor, Angie was on the top bunk, alone in the room. She cracked the door open and creepily slid in. Angie didn't stir. Rhonda hovered over her as she laid on her back softly snoring. Rhonda pulled a steel blade shank out of her inside coat pocket and held it high over her head. Angie's last dream was of her being free inside of a church with her one and only son who she loved dearly, Anton. In her dream, she told Anton that she was sorry for leaving him for so long, but her thoughts died with her life, as Rhonda plunged the blade deeply inside her neck. She would never see her son nor freedom on earth ever again.

The same day, Anton and other relatives were notified of Angie's death. Anton couldn't bear the painful truth of knowing his mother was killed in jail. The back to back casualties caused the KKBG members deep sadness and confusion and things were destined to get worse. The KKBG members found themselves attending back to back funerals while on the other hand, Beatrice was still comatose fighting for her life.

A few nights after Angie's funeral, in the wee hours of the morning, Anton was headed home. Once he arrived at the house, he noticed the door was off the hinges. Immediately his heart fell. He ran through the house yelling for Tracy but didn't hear a response. Thoughts of his baby mother and child being in danger caused a dizzy spell to wash over him. As soon as he barged into the bathroom the bloody scene dropped him to his knees. Tracy and Anton Jr. were the only two precious pieces left in his life. Both were laying in a bathtub full of bloody water with a bullet hole on each of their foreheads.

Anton's mind had snapped, and he wanted to kill everything moving. He didn't give a fuck about life anymore or the outcome of his.

The KKBG members had found out that someone had spray painted the words 'Rest in piss, Tracy, Angie and the kiddo,' on the brick walls of the Garden Valley Projects. Bujo wanted them to know that he was the executional shot caller. Anton already believed that it was him who had killed Tracy and his son, but he never expected Bujo to be behind the killing of his mother as well. On April 30th, Beatrice awakened out of her coma. Friends and family members were there to welcome her back. She couldn't stop crying, remembering what happened on that fatal night. Jarvis and Wanisha had not yet arrived and she was anxious to see them, so she could tell them who killed Marlo. She didn't know who the third person was, and she wasn't going to tell them about Snatch-out. She wanted to kill him herself.

"Who is it?" asked Rere, making her way to the front door.

"Rere it's me......Ubie." She reluctantly unlocked the door and opened it.

"Hey, Ubie....Foo's not here. He left about an hour ago."

"Oh yeah. I need to holla at him, he's not on the block. Let me use the bathroom right quick."

Rere wasn't used to anyone coming to the house because Foo didn't allow that unless he invited them over. She knew that Foo would have a fit if he knew that she let him in.

"Hurry up Ubie because Foo will have a baby if he knew I let somebody in here without his consent.

"It' will only take a second," he affirmed. He ran his eyes over her curvy body as she stepped to the side. At a little after two in the afternoon, she still had on a black silky night gown, revealing her natural sexy. She recognized his eyes roaming and started to feel uncomfortable.

"Damn Rere you are doing a whole lot in that gown."

"I'm in my house and why are you looking at yo boy's girl anyway?"

"Yeah you right, I'm tripping."

"Yeah you are but I know you don't mean no harm. Now hurry up before I get in trouble."

While Ubie was using the restroom, he was thinking about Rere in that gown. When they were younger, before her and Foo were a couple, at times they would play house in the projects and she would be Ubie's wife. They used to have pants up play sex but to them it was the real deal. They were attracted to one another, but truthfully Ubie never stopped liking her. When he came out of the bathroom, he found her seated on a sofa in the living room. She stood up.

"Don't tell Foo I let you in here because I won't hear the end of it."

"It's on, you know I aint gone tell' em no way. As a matter of fact, we can share more secrets than one," he told her as he walked up to her.

"Ubie you are tripping. What the hell are you talking about?" She couldn't believe he had the audacity.

"Just think about what I said Rere, and if you aint with it then let it go. But don't stir up no bullshit cause it aint no telling what it could lead to."

"I thought you really had love for my dude," said Rere.

"This aint about my love for your nigga. This is about what I want."

"Bye Ubie."

"I mean it aint like I'm trying to come between yall, I just wanna fuck you Rere. Finish where we left off at when we were younger."

She realized he had been smoking wet.

"Can you leave now?"

"Aight....I'll holla at you"

"WANISHA, CALM THE FUCK DOWN!" Jarvis yelled, pinning her up against his car in the hospitals parking lot. Wanisha tried to resist his hold, before breaking down in his arms. Jarvis held her for a good two minutes until she calmed down.

"Now listen to me Y-love, I understand how you feel, but you gotta control your feelings in order for us to focus on what we need to do. These muthafuckas can't escape our wrath. Let's not forget it's still money to be made and I need you to stay sharp, you hear me?"

She wiped her face.

"Yeah J-one I hear you."

A WEEK LATER

Business was booming tough in the King Kennedy projects despite all the chaos. Jarvis had just distributed eighty kilos of heroin to his four lieutenants, when he received a text from Roxanne. Ever since Tracy was killed, she's been a wreck. She believed her sister was murdered on the strength of Anton. Instead of Jarvis calling her back, he drove straight to her house. When she answered the door, he could tell she'd been crying.

"What's wrong?"

"Somebody has been across the street watching this house. He just pulled off about two minutes ago."

"How do you know he was watching this house though?"

"Because he was there for about two hours yesterday, but today I put two and two together. Jarvis I'm scared. Your son is in here. What if they are the same ones who killed Tracy?" She started crying again.

He grabbed her and tried to console her with a tight hug. He didn't know if her suspicion was accurate or not, but he couldn't take any chances.

"Where my lil nigga at?"

"He's upstairs taking a nap," she cried.

"I'll get him. You pack yall things and stop crying. Everything will be alright."

"I took a picture of the car, but its blurry, and you really can't see his face."

"Give it here," said Jarvis, and they headed up the stairs.

Jarvis studied the picture while driving them to one of his low-key spots on the outskirts of Cleveland.

"Don't drag us in to whatever's going on. I don't want me and my child to end up like." ......She couldn't finish what she was about to say.

"Trust me Roxanne, yall is okay out here," he assured.

"What about you? Is our child about to lose his father because of some street war you're in?"

"Daddy, daddy, can I sit on your lap while you drive?" Jr. asked.

"No, you sit right here," said Roxanne.

Jarvis grabbed him out of her lap and sat him in his lap while waiting at a light.

"You don't know, is that it?" asked Roxanne.

Jarvis continued to study the picture until the light changed.

"Listen Roxanne, stop asking me these kinds of questions. Now I said everything is going to be alright and I'm gonna make sure of that."

She exhaled deeply.

"Jarvis, you need to start thinking more about yourself and your son and let them streets go before it's too late."

39

It was Friday night and the YG members were posted in the neighborhood bar, getting toasted. Then out of the blue, Foo said, "What's up Ubie. You stopped over my house looking for me last week huh. What were you looking for?"

Ubie took a second to respond.

"I was looking for you."

"So why is Rere telling me something different?" The noise level between everyone had reduced.

"Fuck is you talking about. She let me use the bathroom and I bounced."

Foo jumped up.

"Bitch ass nigga you wanna stab me in my back after everything we been through!" He was now walking up on Ubie who was still sitting down. He then stood up.

"Nigga aint nobody trying to stab you in the back. What did she------.

He never finished and never saw the left hook coming that broke his jaw. Ubie collapsed to the ground. They tried to restrain Foo but he started stumping Ubie.

"Bitch ass nigga I made you and this is the thanks I get!" He broke free and kicked Ubie one last time in the face. Foo was hurt because his right-hand man had tried to cross him, and he would put his life on the line any day for him. Foo broke free from his homies and exited the bar.

Samuel McCoy stared at the picture.

"Do you think you can get me a clear visual of the guy in this car?" asked Jarvis.

"Give me a few days," he said as he placed the picture in his shirt pocket.

"Do you need my assistance in any other way?"

"As a matter of fact, I do. There's a guy from the 30th Projects who calls himself Ubie. He killed one of my peoples. See if he has a stable address. If not then an address of someone he holds close to his heart."

"Will do boss," said Samuel and the meeting was dismissed.

****

As soon as Jarvis and his son walked inside Crystal's house, he ran up to his grandmother and she scooped him in her arms.

"How's my handsome little grandson!" She kissed him on his cheek.

"Grandma can I have some ice cream?"

"Sure, you can," she replied while staring at her son.

"Baby are you okay, you look tired."

"I'm good Ma, it's just hard being me sometimes." Jarvis made his way to the sofa and sat down letting out a deep breath.

"Where's Joseph?"

"He had some errands to run but he'll be back shortly."

It felt good for Jarvis to see his mother so happily wrapped in another man's love. He saw a spark in her eyes he thought he'd never see again. After she fixed little Jarvis a bowl of ice cream she sat down beside her son.

"Baby is everything okay?"

Jarvis ignored her question.

"Why is it so hard for you to answer the question, and why is Roxanne worried that her and my grandbaby may be in some type of danger?"

Ma, she is still shook up about what happened to her sister and nephew that's all."

"Jarvis listen to me.... I didn't bring you into this world as no damn fool, and you most certainly weren't raised like one. Now its obvious something is going on. Ask yourself is it worth jeopardizing you or Jr. and everything you've become. At the end of the day, when this game that you're playing is all over with, all you gone have is us. So, baby come to a conclusion and in that conclusion, know that you're gonna have to let go of one or the other. The streets or your life!"

Jarvis leaned over and hugged his mother. He knew that for the love of his crew, he was in too deep and things were completely out of hand. Even the "All or Nothing" advice J.d. once gave him held no significance anymore because he was serving more than one purpose now. She sniffled in his arms.

"I can tell you're not happy baby. What good is having all the money you have and not being happy?"

"Ma, I'm happy enough just having you as a mother, now stop crying. On another note, have yall two decided where yall getting married at?"

"Don't be trying to change the subject Jarvis," she uttered while wiping her face.

"Naw Ma I need to know so I can take care of all the expenses. I already told you to tell him that yall are not paying a penny towards this wedding and I mean it. This is my gift to you."

"Well we haven't decided but we're debating on having it at the duck pond off Chester. That's a beautiful area for a wedding wouldn't you say?"

"Yeah Ma that's a beautiful spot."

"Well I'll let you know our decision soon enough."

****

Foo broke Ubie's jaw in two places which caused a detrimental confliction. He also band Ubie from the projects and turned all the Yg members against him. However, Ubie had a personal vendetta against Foo that he couldn't let go. For an entire month, he laid low until his jaw healed. Then him, Snatch-out, Dink, and Killa, went on the hunt to retaliate on Foo. While Foo was standing outside of a car wash watching his Benz get dried off, a car sharply pulled up and an Ak-47 protruded out of the back window. Before Foo could take cover, he was knocked clean off his feet, as midget missiles penetrated his face and the bullet proof vest. Before he took the first bullet he thought it was Ubie and his cousins behind the masks, but it wasn't. It was KKBG members, Lil Hurt being the shooter.

Ubie and his cousins were shocked that somebody had killed him before they could. The Yg members were like lost sheep about the death of their leader, taking Ubie back with open arms. Rere who was barely able to cope with Foo's death was consoled by Ubie. After three days of playing consoler, Ubie took advantage of her by forcefully having sex with her. Although she realized it was rape, she gave in, letting him do what he wanted. As he continued to pound her, she thought about how cruel life really was.

Thoughts ran through her mind about Foo. She couldn't believe that while he was laying up in a morgue, his best friend was lying on top of her. At that moment an ugly reality dawned upon her. She realized that she was deceitful and untrue, and just a product of the world's madness....

✣✣✣✣✣✣✣✣✣✣✣✣✣✣✣✣✣✣✣✣

"His name is Perry Shaw, He's a retired detective," said agent McCoy.

"Why in the fuck is a retired detective watching my baby mama house?"

"Jarvis, I don't know but I do know that his history as a detective was corrupt. He killed two people in the line of duty and was only suspended without pay. It was also rumored that he was affiliated with Drug Lord Suckay, who is now awaiting the death penalty. However, although it was never proven of his affiliation, six months after Suckay's arrest, Perry hung up his badge. It's a mystery what he's been up to lately, but I doubt that's he's living happily ever after.

Jarvis sat in deep thought, then blurted out, "That muthafuckas working for Bujo!"

"My thoughts exactly," said McCoy, going into his worn wallet.

"Bujo is listed under this address." He passed Jarvis the written info. "There wasn't a direct address for this Ubie character, but his father name is Antonio Wright."

His name and info were on the same piece of paper. Jarvis cuffed the information in his pocket.

"Bujo owns a restaurant on 69th and Cedar but he doesn't run it. The Hogy Castle, you familiar?"

"It aint nothing in my city I aint familiar with."

"Well sometimes he's there, majority of the time he's not. Do you need me to force him in a web for you, that way he's out your hair?"

"No offense but that's a coward act. I can't do that. I gotta do this thing my way.

A little after nine o'clock at night in LA, Omirah was comfortably inclined in the bath tub watching the Cleveland news on her cell phone. She had finished college successfully and married Marco, who together they shared a beautiful mansion paid in full. Not only was his prosperity huge in basketball, but he was also up under a one hundred-million-dollar endorsement with Nike, not to mention the other endorsements deals in the process of negotiation. When they got married, she recommended a prenup to verify her love was for only him and not his money, but Marco trusted in her love enough, so he decided they didn't need one. Although she had her degree in communications he didn't want her to ever have to work. Only thing he asked her to do was stay true, bare his children and be a good house wife. Although she vowed to fulfill his wants, she never got over Jarvis. She would watch the Cleveland news everyday hoping there wasn't any terrible news about her ex-boyfriend. Tonight, as she sat in the tub missing her husband who was away training for the upcoming season, the blog of Foo's death caught her attention. After perusing over the article, she placed her cell phone on the floor and stared blankly at the ceiling.

"Damn that's crazy," she uttered remembering Foo very well. Suddenly she had the urge to call Wanisha to see how she been doing. Ever since her style of living changed, she had been out of touch with her family and friends and she realized that it's been almost a year and a half since she had last talked to her. She hadn't heard from Yasha in three months and although she was happy to be able to have anything she wanted, she was unsatisfied living long distance away from loved ones. After she got herself situated she dialed Wanisha's phone number. After the fourth ring, she was about to hang up when Wanisha answered.

"Hello."

"Hey girl this is me Meme." A quick silence followed.

"Hey stranger. How's everything going down there?"

"Decent but what's up with you? Are you staying out of trouble up there?"

"Meme so much has happened since the last time I talked to you but let me start off by telling you that my brother is dead."

"WHAT! Oh my God what happened?"

"He got killed Meme, a little over a month ago."

Omirah felt Wanisha's pain through the phone and wished she could reach through it to hug her.

"I look at the Cleveland news every day on Facebook so how could I have missed that. I would've called and more-so attended his funeral."

"It's cool girl and besides, aint no reason for you to come back down here unless you're visiting your people. It's ugly out here and it's about to get even uglier. You know I got mad love for you girl so I'm gone tell you what's good. And what's good for you is to follow the path that God have paved for you and try not to look back this way. This way is for the birds. Birds that can't fly and you are flying girl. I don't wanna see you break ya wings for the wrong reasons.

"I don't understand Wanisha, what are you saying?"

"Look, we will always be road dawgs in the heart, but let's leave it in the heart okay. That way I won't have to worry about you breaking a wing. Take care Meme." Click.

Omirah stood frozen with the phone to her ear and tears running down her face. Marlo and Foo's death gave her clarity on what was going on, and at that moment she was determined to save Wanisha from destruction by any means necessary.

40 (Sunday Morning)

Jarvis and his four lieutenants were at his condo, going over their missions at hand.

"As you all can see, we have adversaries to our right and to our left, and each clique have taken away from us a loved one. Y-love and Anton, I admire yall for being able to stay focused and patient behind the loss of yall peoples. But this morning its eye for an eye, meaning the innocent must die."

He looked each one of them in the eyes.

"Before we built this dynasty we all knew it was a high chance that some of us would die and some would get lost in the system. We chose this life yall. Now we have to accept what comes with it."

Wanisha cocked back her 40 Caliber as everybody stood ready to fulfill their task.

"I accept it boo," said Wanisha. "Let's see if these hoe ass niggas can accept what they got coming as well."

****

Wanisha turned down a one-way street and parked the rental in the first opening on the curb. She cut the ignition all the way back, so the music could still play while she finished what was left of her blunt. After she finished, she climbed out, dressed in Jehovah witness attire with a fishnet veil covering her face. Handbag in hand, she made her way to the assigned address.

 Antonio, (Ubie's father) was twenty minutes into his run on the treadmill when the doorbell rang.

"Shit!" He hissed, irritated about the disruption. A bachelor for over a year now, he still wasn't used to having to run to the door, cook and clean behind himself and so on and so forth. He grabbed the towel off the table and wiped the sweat from his chiseled body, making his way to the door in nothing but his shorts and Nikes.

"Who is it?" he asked sounding similar to Barry White.

"Hi, my name is Ciara. A witness of Jehovah. Can I share a few minutes with you if you don't mind?"

Antonio wasn't big on religion and was about to turn her away without opening the door but didn't want to disrespect a servant of God, so he opened the door to turn her away politely.

"Hi, how are you. If I were in to religion, I would be happy to indulge in a religious conversation with you, but I'm an agnostic."

Wanisha quickly reverted to plan b. Him having his shirt off made it so much easier. She sexily ran her eyes over his body back to his face.

"Oh, excuse me, what did you say?"

Antonio chuckled as his ego rose.

"I said umm......of course we can share a moment with each other in the name of God-Jehovah that is." He unlocked the screen door for her to enter. Once the door was shut, she turned to face him while reaching inside her hand bag.

"So, Mr. Wright, are you alone this morning?" ....

Mrs. Carter, Bujo's 66-year-old grandmother and her son John opened Hogy's castle five minutes before Anton and M-2 walked in and were the first two customers of the day. It seemed as if they were still getting situated behind the counter when the two homies walked up. Mrs. Carter turned and greeted them with an innocent warm smile.

"How may I help you two handsome young men?"

"You can't," said Anton.

"Excuse me!" She quizzically replied. John immediately smelled trouble.

"We're not here on a robbery," Anton said as both homies quickly drew their weapons.

"We need you to call Bujo and tell him to get here immediately for whatever reason you can think of." John made a desperate dash to the back covering the back of his head. Three shots from M-2 Glock 380 penetrated his back causing him to fall on his stomach.

"God Noooooo, please don't kill us!" She screamed.

They quickly climbed over the counters. M-2 pursued his victim. Anton grabbed Mrs. Carter and led her to the back as well. John tried to squirm away from M-2 who was on his heels.

"I'll call him. Just don't kill us.... please," he begged, spitting up a mouth full of blood. Once they had them in the back room, Anton made her give him the camera film.

"I can't get up," John blurted in pain.

"Just stay on ya back and breathe easy," said M-2. He grabbed the cordless phone off the desk and gave it to him.

"If you sound abnormal I'm gone blow ya head off," M-2 warned. "Tell him that this old lady is having a stroke."

"No John don't bring my grandson into this. They're going to kill us anyway."

"Ma'am you're not going to die as long as you cooperate. We need to talk to your grandson face to face," said Anton.

"God is going to punish you for this,"--------

John cut her off.

"Ma, just let me call him. It's our only chance."

"Oh my God my son is dying," she cried.

John started dialing Bujo's cell phone number. While waiting for an answer, Anton put his finger to his lips demanding her to remain silent. They all heard Bujo's deep voice break the silence.

"Nephew this me, come quick. I think Ma's having a stroke."

"Nooo Bujo DONT COME THEIR GONNA KILL,"-------------- POW!

Mrs. Carter body slumped to the floor. Anton bent down and shot her in the face again.

"Bujo we're dead," John cried before M-2 opened his head wide open. M-2 picked up the phone but Anton snatched it away and put it to his ear.

"Was it worth it nigga. Answer me bitch ass nigga!"

   Without saying a word, Bujo hung up.

Andrea hadn't seen Perry in a few days, something she became accustomed to. Perry needed a lot of space to himself for various reasons and she understood why. Most nights, he would occupy his other home in Cleveland Heights. This morning she had a list of things to be done which included grocery shopping, an oil change, and then to the beauty salon to get her hair and nails done. She tried calling Perry before she left but there was no answer. Traffic was light as Jarvis tailed her from a distance.

"Damon nigga that's her, I can never forget that broad or that night," Jarvis told him excitedly.

"Hold on let me get this straight. That's the broad that gave you yo man when you left with J.d. years ago?"

"I'm telling you dawg that's her," Jarvis replied as memories of J.d. and that night came rushing back overwhelmingly.

"Since she is sleeping with the enemy, how we gone play this?"

"We gotta go with the flow on this one," said Jarvis.

At the same time, his phone started vibrating with a text message. The code read 1-187. That was Wanisha confirming her hit was complete. Twenty minutes later 2-187 came through, while Jarvis was trailing Andrea in the grocery line. It was Damon and M-2 confirming that the hit was complete.

When Jarvis was passing her their eyes met and he began acting as if he was surprised to see her.

"Do I know you?" she asked hesitantly.

"Andrea, right?"

"Yes, but where do you know me from?"

"Six years ago, remember you told me you didn't know if you would ever see me again?"

For a long second, she didn't know what the hell he was talking about, then suddenly her eyes got big.

"You were......J.d.'s little friend!"
Jarvis nodded his head in unison. Her eyes became watery.

"Oh my God. You're so big and handsome, give me a hug." They embraced both feeling the painful loss of J.d.

"God, I miss that man so much," she said in his arms, more so to herself. They broke apart. Jarvis still saw the tears in her eyes. She really loved my nigga," he thought to himself.

"Jarvis how you been doing." She wiped at her eye to prevent a tear from falling.

"Damn you still remember my name?"

"I never forgot about you. How could I?"

"I see you're still beautiful," said Jarvis.

"Well I wouldn't say beautiful, but I do take care of myself." She was indeed beautiful with and outstanding body. Damon turned down the aisle.

"Yo J-one, my son done got sick we gotta go get him from school," he lied. "Wassup shorty, how you doing?"

"Her name aint shorty homie its Andrea, and she's a special woman to me." Andrea blushed admiring Jarvis courtesy.

"My bad homie, I'll be in the car. Hurry up dawg." Damon walked away.

"Andrea is it a chance that I can see you again, or have a number I can reach you at?"

"Jarvis I'm under restrictions, so I can't give you my number but if you can give me yours I can call you. Is that cool?"

"That's what's up," said Jarvis and gave her the number.

41

Perry had been parked down the street from Jarvis mother's house for half of the day. When finally, a moment happened in his favor. Crystal and Joseph were pulling out of the driveway. He immediately called his friend Cheryl at ADT and had her dis-activate the alarm to Crystal's address. His goal was to tap her phone and await Jarvis call to get a location where he stayed. It only took him ten minutes to quickly get inside and complete the job. A couple minutes after six, he was pulling away.

Bujo had went into a state of madness behind the death of his uncle and grandmother. He never expected the KKBG crew to be a strong threat to him, but now he realized that he was terribly wrong. He knew who the head was of their crew, and with him dead, he knew the body of his posse would surely die with him. He wanted Jarvis dead as much as he wanted Anton.

Ubie, Snatch-out, Dink, Killa, and six other Yg members were in Ubie's living room. Ubie was emotionally distraught about his father's death. Tears streamed down his face as he spit hate words towards KKBG.

"Dem bitch ass niggas smoked my muthafuckin father! I don't give a fuck if I go down for murder, I'm finna blatantly kill all them muthafuckas!"

Wanisha had left a message on the wall in his father's blood that read: 'Eye for an eye til the day you die......Them killers is at you. U Bitch.'

"Deez muthafuckas then already killed Foo, Coupe, Karmen, and now my father."

He turned and pointed his finger in Jerome's face. "And now yo bitch ass talking about you moving to Illinois next week!"

"I just wanna be here to see my seed grow Ubie." ....

"Nigga fuck you and yo seed!" Ubie barked, snatching a nickel plated 357 off his waist. "You think I'm gone let you turn yo back on the hood, the hood that made yo soft ass!"

"Come on Ubie get that gun out my face man."

Snatch-out blazed his blunt and leaned back on the sofa as if he was watching a good movie. Ubie thumbed the hammer back.

"Bitch ass nigga you running because you scared! What you scared of. You scared to kill one of dem niggas, or you scared one of dem niggas gone kill you.... answer me nigga!"

"I'm just tired of the game dawg," Jerome solemnly replied.

"You tired huh," Ubie mocked. "Well get you some sleep dawg. I'll be the one to tell ya seed that he won't see you no more."

Two powerful shots went into Jerome's face, causing it to explode on sight.

"Any more of you niggas wanna turn yall back on the hood? Raise ya hand if you need some rest too!"

Killa and Dink was quickly preparing to dispose of Jerome's body.

"Aight then.... it's killing season."

Day after day members from KKBG, Yg, and G.V.P. were getting killed. A month later, 16 deaths were totaled between the three hoods and seven of them were KKBG members. Caught in two wars, it looked as if their ship was starting to sink.

****

Crystal and Joseph wedding ceremony was being held at the duck pond in another week. Jarvis had taken care of all the expenses, yet he didn't feel comfortable with his mother having an open ceremony, but considering it was being held in a suburb on the outskirts of the city, he went along with his mother's wishes. It was a little after midnight and he had just got off the phone with Andrea, who finally agreed to see him again, when he received a call from his mother.

"Hey baby."

What's up Ma."

"Nothing, just making sure you're okay before I go to sleep."

"I'm good Ma. As a matter of fact, after we're done talking I'm going to bed too."

"If I knew that you were at home, I would've called your home phone instead of your cell," said Crystal.

Perry was listening and fuming because if only she would've called his home phone, then he would've had Jarvis address. He continued to listen. Jarvis and his mother talked back and forth as the conversation led to her new-found joy with Joseph.

"Jarvis, I never thought I could remarry another man after your father. I didn't think there would ever be another man for me, but I guess God proved me wrong."

"Yes he did Ma. Anyway, my father aint deserve a woman like you. What you deserve is what you feel today. I hope the feeling last forever for you."

"I hope so too sweetie. I love you Jarvis."

"I love you to Ma."

"Jarvis, I wanna say something before we hang up. For those years that I was on drugs, I know you saw a side of me that disappointed you heavily. I'm sorry that I took----------"

"Ma stop. Life is what it is and we all make mistakes in it. Let that go because those days are over. You're a good woman and next Friday you'll be marrying a good man. Focus on your blessings and for the record Ma, I don't hold nothing against you."

She sniffled.

"I went to the duck pond earlier, you know just to overlook the area and I wouldn't want to hold the ceremony no place else."

****

An hour later Perry was in Bujo's living room revealing what he had just found out.

"Are you sure it's taking place at the duck pond?" Bujo questioned.

"Unless they redirected their plans but right now I'm one hundred and one percent sure."

Suddenly a wide grin came across his face.

"Friday is our day to kill the head and I just might have a solid enough plan to make it all happen."

Omirah caught a flight to Cleveland to spend a few days with her mother and to talk with Wanisha face to face. She pulled her rental into the projects of King Kennedy. Nod heads were lined up as if it was an assembly. She spotted Anton climbing in his CLK 430 Benz and drove up on the side of him. After a quick second he recognized her. Anton rolled his window down. "Yo what's up shorty. What you doing down here?"

"Hey Anton. Can you do me a favor and give me Wanisha's cell number. The number I have doesn't work anymore."

Instead of Anton giving her the number, he told her to hold on and pulled out his phone and called her himself.

"Hello."

"Y-love, what's going on."

"Not a damn thang."

"Where you at?" asked Anton.

"At M-2 house. Why what's up."

"Who all over there?"

"M-2, Tasia, and Angelica."

"Well I'm in the Jets and guess who down here looking for you?"

"Boy you know my nerves is bad don't play with me...Who?"

"Meme, I'm finna give her my phone hold on."

Anton got out of the car and gave her the phone through her window.

"Hello."

"Girl what the hell is you doing down in them projects." Omirah's eyes fell on the rest in peace tattoos on the brick buildings.

"I need to see you Wanisha."

"How long you been in Cleveland?"

"I got here this morning."

"Meme you know it's dangerous for you to be down there."

"I don't care."

Wanisha exhaled. "Girl you are crazy. Go to your mother's house and I'll be there in about twenty minutes.

"Okay bye." She handed the phone back to Anton.

"Thanks Anton."

"There go ya boy pulling in right there," said Anton as he flagged Jarvis down.

"Oh my God I don't need to see him," she said to herself not making any attempt to pull away.

Jarvis yanked the 760 Beamer on the side of her car but didn't notice Omirah. Anton nodded his head in her direction and Jarvis peeked in her window. They both stared at each other for a still moment, then Jarvis got out and walked up to her car.

"What's your reason for coming in these projects. I thought we made closure."

Omirah wondered if he had any feelings left for her.

"You made closure not me, but I was looking for Wanisha."

"Really," said Jarvis sarcastically.

"Yes really. You know what Jarvis, you're not my man, I don't have to explain to you why I'm anywhere. Last time I saw you I was a bitch and everything else."

"Naw I was in my gut because you let ole boy come between us plus I had a lot on my mind."

"I didn't let nobody come between us you did. So don't blame me for your actions. You broke my heart and it's still broken."

"How is it still broken when you're living amongst the rich and famous?"

"Jarvis some things just can't be replaced."

Her words made him realize how much he really missed her. He opened her door.

"Step out and give me a hug." Without hesitation she complied. She was even more beautiful to him than before, he thought as she wrapped herself in his arms.

"You know I still love you right," he whispered in her ear.

Her heart fluttered.

"Do you?" she asked softly.

Omirah was waiting on her mother's porch when Wanisha pulled into the driveway. She climbed out and made her way up the stairs as Omirah stood up prepared to hug her.

"I'm sorry about what happened to your brother."

Wanisha didn't respond. Omirah saw pain with so many other things in her eyes that she had never seen there before.

"Are you okay?" asked Omirah.

"Yeah girl I'm just high as hell right now!"

"You're not okay Wanisha, you look good but you're not okay. I see it in your eyes. Girl what are these streets doing to you?"

"Meme tell me what's on your mind because you aint fly down here for nothing," asked Wanisha.

"The last time we talked you said you were a bird that couldn't fly and that bothered me ever since. It just seems like streets have made you turn cold!"

"Girl these streets aint done shit to me," Wanisha said defensively. "Understand what's going on and stop taking things the wrong way."

"Okay well try telling me then," said Omirah.

"I don't have to tell you, you know. They killed my brother and for that, tomorrow aint promised to none of them niggas. Only place safe for them niggas over there is jail."

Omirah knew that trying to save her was worthless. She saw a look in Wanisha's face that stated she was ready to die if it came down to it.

"No Wanisha, I'm not gonna let you throw your life away!"

"Meme, Marlo was my twin, my other half. He didn't die he was murdered. Nothing else matters to me anymore."

A tear fell out of Wanisha's eyes that she didn't bother to wipe away.

"Wanisha I can give you the money you need to start a business, you don't need these streets. You could move out to L.A. with me," Omirah pleaded.

"Meme, I got so much money I can't even spend it all, but girl thanks for caring."

Without another word she turned and left. Omirah didn't know if she would ever see her again...

42

Jarvis sat patiently waiting for Andrea at an expensive restaurant outside of Cleveland. She chose this place outside the vicinity because she had to be discreet about seeing another man. Right when he was starting to have doubts about her coming, her beautiful body emerged through the restaurants door. She spotted Jarvis seated at the reserved table and strutted his way. His eyes went to her beautiful toes that was displayed in her steel plated open face high heels. The Givenchy skirt covering her juicy thighs stopped at the knees, but her ass in that skirt had half the restaurant's attention.

"Hi J-one."

"Hey what's up girl. I didn't think you were coming."

"Sorry for holding you up, my boyfriend had stopped by."

The waitress approached and took their orders.

"It looks like you're doing really good. Do you always wear expensive jewelry around like that," she asked, not believing he could afford what he was wearing?

"Ma this aint nothing."

"Nothing," she blurted. "J-one I'm a jewelry fanatic, and that Roger Dubois watch you're wearing cost at least twenty thousand dollars if not more."

"Put it like this, if it wasn't affordable then I wouldn't be wearing it."

She assimilated the meaning of his words. They talked casually back and forth until their food arrived.

After swallowing a few bites of her lasagna she said, "I'm thinking about something J.d said to me about you and now looking at you, I guess he was right."

"Right about what, what did he say?"

"He said one day you would be a made dude, and that he didn't know if he would be here to see it happen. He felt like it was his job to nurture those qualities within you."

"He told you that?"

"Yes J-one he did." Jarvis turned and gazed out the window as a mournful pain cut through his soul. He looked back at her and cut straight to the point.

"Is Perry Shaw ya boyfriend?" The question caught her off guard.

"How do you.... know Perry?"

"Listen to me Andrea. I don't really know if I can trust you or not, but I'm about to be honest with you and reveal to you some things."

She didn't respond as her eyes studied him intently.

"J.d. installed it in me to become what I am today. I guess you can say a made nigga. The neighborhood he was from is the hood I'm from, King Kennedy. We're at war with another hood and I believe your man Perry is on the other side."

"Other side of what?"

"The war." He went into his pocket and pulled out a photo.

"This is a picture of him watching my baby mother's crib. Two weeks before this picture was taken, my homie baby mother and child were killed home invasion style."

Andrea posture was now rigid as he continued.

"Do you know a guy named Bujo?"

"I--I heard of him."

"Perry's connected with him, right?" Jarvis didn't wanna give her time to think.

"Hold on, so how did you find me because now I'm convinced that it wasn't a coincidence."

"I had somebody on my team do a check on the guy in that picture, that's how I got his name and address. It was your house.

"So you followed me that day?"

"Yes, I did, and I was surprised at who I was following. You went from a guy like J.d. to a nigga like that. A fucking cop!" Jarvis emphasized with disgust.

"Hold on don't you dare criticize my situation, you don't hardly know what I've been through behind the death of that man," she snapped.

"I will never love another man like I loved J.d, but yes Perry's my man and I'm sorry about yall little beef thing but------" Jarvis grabbed her left arm as she got ready to get up.

"Andrea don't turn your back on me for a nigga like that. If you really loved J.d. then understand I'm his protégé, and his protégé really need you Andrea. Dude aint right and he's trying to kill me."

"Can you let go of my arm please?"

Jarvis did and she got up and left without looking back.

Crystals wedding was three days away. Bujo, Perry and Dre, were in Bujo's headquarters putting a lethal plan together. Dre was a Jamaican born in America, from the Garden Valley Projects. Three years ago, he tested positive for HIV and ever since then he felt like he had nothing to live for. He would do anything in the world for Bujo if he asked, and he was very well willing to complete Friday's mission. Only stipulation was that he wanted to give his mother the seventy-five thousand Bujo offered the day before the hit. Bujo agreed.

It was a beautiful day in the sky, Friday afternoon as relatives and friends were gathered at the duck pond along with some unfamiliar faces who had decided to pay respect to the couple and their soon to be union. Jarvis four lieutenants were amongst the guest, each one decked out in fine clothing and expensive jewelry. They were also working security, each one in their own section scanning the crowd looking for abnormal behavior. Wanisha's eyes fell upon Joseph and the priest who were standing at the alter and she imagined Joseph being Mel, waiting for her to walk down the aisle. 'Maybe when all this is over with', she thought to herself as she started to rescan the crowd. Suddenly the violins commenced...... The ceremony started.

Jarvis and Crystal were in the limousine at the top of the hill of the duck pond waiting for their cue to make their way to the alter. Jarvis was taking the place of his deceased grandfather giving his mother away. He was proud that she was marrying a successful man that helped her kick the drug habit and he was highly thankful for that to say the least.

"Jarvis I almost feel complete today, but until you finish whatever it is you're doing out here, I can never fully reach that point. I know that's something you have to overcome but you have no choice son. You have more than yourself to think about. Don't you dare give another man the pleasure of raising your son, by depriving him of the gift of having his own father in his life.

Jarvis glanced at the time on his diamond framed rose gold Phillipe watch.

"Ma, you look absolutely beautiful in that dress. Ole Joseph is gone drool when he sees you."

She lifted the veil over her face and stared deeply in her son's eyes.

"Can you promise me that you are almost through, at least?"

At that moment the wedding coordinator rung the bell signaling for Crystal to make her descent down the aisle.

"I'm not getting out of this car until you promise me Jarvis."

"I promise aight. As soon as I'm through, it's over and it shouldn't be much longer. Now come on before you make ya husband nervous."

Dre sat patiently amongst the crowd, discreetly looking for Jarvis. By his dreads being freshly cut off, he didn't look Jamaican and each lieutenant looked him off, not recognizing who he really was. Under his arm, hanging from a sling, was a sawed off 4-10 shotgun. He felt sweat trickle down his back as he anxiously waited for his moment to strike. Then suddenly Jarvis emerged into his view.

Jarvis and his mother carefully made their appearance, walking down the huge stairwell as everybody looked upon them. Once on ground level, Jarvis cautiously studied the crowd while walking Crystal down the aisle. When Jarvis released her at the altar, he saw a joyous look in her eyes that he would always remember. As soon as Jarvis turned around to make his way to his seat, Dre jumped up and pumped two slugs into Jarvis, knocking him backwards into the alter. Everybody went into a frenzy. Crystal hysterically bent down over her son right when the third gunshot blasted.

Anton who was four rows back from Dre, shot him in his head a second too late. Crystal's blood was all over Jarvis who was still struggling to catch his breath. The four lieutenants desperately rushed the alter and was relieved to see their man alive, but devastation ensued. Jarvis was flat on his back still halfway out of breath holding on to his mother who was flaccid on top of him.

"Not my......not my mother...God Nooo. Not my mother," he said breathlessly unable to see her face because of the awkward angle she was laying.

"J-one are you okay. Talk to me," said Wanisha after securing their safety.

"My mother, yall help my mother."

Joseph pushed his way through the lieutenants, saw Crystal's body and fell to his knees sobbing helplessly. Jarvis knew that she was dead and wish he would've died with her.

Anton blended in with the chaos and disappeared before police arrived. Jarvis was rushed to the hospital where he was told that he had a fractured sternum. He cursed the bullet proof vest for saving his life. Within twenty-four hours, he forcefully checked himself out of the hospital.

Jarvis sat alone in his condo trying to find the strength to cope with the loss of his mother. Earlier he had went into a raging fit and even contemplated ending his own life but realized that would defeat all purposes. As he sat all cried out, he got on his knees and talked to his mother as if he was talking to God. When he got up two hours later, eternal hell was in his heart. A hell his surroundings couldn't escape from....

Jarvis had no choice but to have a private funeral for his mother where only a few close relatives attended. He knew that he had to recover from his sternum injury so after the funeral he and Kyla took a flight out to her place where he went into recovery mode. He appointed Damon to be the overseer and shot caller until he returned, and Damon didn't waste any time assigning missions against G.V.P. members. While KKBG's main goal was retaliating on G.V.P, the Yg's wanted revenge in blood from any member or anybody associated with members from the King Kennedy Projects. However, Wanisha was Yg's deadliest threat.

She was determined to kill Ubic at all cost.........

43

The two laid in bed naked after making passionate love.

"That was breathtaking poppy. You always please me well you know that," said Omirah. She started planting soft kisses on his chest as they laid on their sides in one another arms.

"Do I Ma?" The sound of his response made her look at him quizzically.

"Marco that shouldn't even be a question for you to ask, you know that you do."

"But Meme it's a lot of things that I don't know," he countered.

"What don't you know about me that I haven't told you?"

"Let's start with J-one. You still love him, don't you?"

For a second neither blinked as they stared in each other's eyes as a loud silence hung in the air.

"Why is it hard for you to answer me?"

"Poppy you're tripping. I wouldn't have married you if I was still in love with someone else."

"When you found out about his mother, you took that kind of hard. Who was you crying for, her or him?"

"Marco she was killed in cold blood what did you expect," she snapped.

"But you hardly even knew her Meme. Who the fuck is you fooling!"

"Look don't accuse me of loving somebody else Marco. You,"--- his quick movement cut her off and in a split second he was on top of her aggressively opening her thighs, pushing himself inside of her.

"Get em out ya mind Meme and I mean it," he warned her while stroking her at the same time.

"You are my wife and this is my pussy, something you better not ever give away. Do you hear me?" Omirah nodded yes. He vigorously pushed himself inside of her and held it there.

"Do you hear me?" he reiterated.

"Yes Poppy I hear you," she replied softly, and then the two made love until sunrise.

✷✷✷✷✷✷✷✷✷✷✷✷✷✷✷✷✷✷✷✷

A little over a month had went by since the death of Jarvis mother and he was yet to return, but his lieutenants had enough dope to last for at least another month. Their drug business was successfully flowing, yet the murder rate in the city was sky high due to the ongoing wars between the KKBG's and their opposers. Youngsters were dying and mothers were crying while bullets continued to fly day by day which showed that these youngsters were gonna war until the last casket dropped.

It was 10:52 p.m. Damon and M-2 were at their stash house that they shared on the other side of town. Stacks of money covered the entire bed while the two homies sat in front of money machines exhaustedly counting stacks after stacks. After the last stack was counted, M-2 blazed a 12-inch cigar filled with dro and stared at the money on the bed.

"We can actually say we rich fool. Shit crazy aint it!"

"Yeah we did it big my nigga. We hood rich," Damon replied. "And all these soft ass rappers who claim they been where we at now, are faking. This is it dawg, and the streets love us."

"Why because we certified rich niggas?" M-2 asked.

"Yep, just what the streets love." Damon replied.

M-2 grabbed the blunt from Damon and walked out onto the balcony staring down at the streets.

"So this is what it's all about," he said out loud as he took a toke.

"Yeah I guess this is it my nigga," Damon replied as he emerged onto the balcony. "This is the feeling that most niggas chase but only a few of us get the chance to actually feel."

M-2 passed the blunt and gazed out at a lingering star in the sky. Then suddenly the star fell. M-2 shook his head and said, "damn I must be tripping."

"You aint tripping. I saw that shit to. It just fell."

"Maybe that meant that somewhere, this world just lost one hell of a person."

"Or...... this dro is playing tricks on us," Damon shot back and both homies burst out laughing.

"Yo, what all J-one say earlier?" asked M-2.

"He asked was we financially ready. I told em yeah. He asked about you and Y-love and he told me to get ready, he will be back in a few days.

"I wonder how he gone move on this nigga Bujo cuz shit we can't catch em."

"Leave it up to the God my nigga."

"I don't believe in no God homie," said M-2.

"Not that God fool, I'm talking about J-one nigga!"

"Oh that God. Yeah. Now I do believe in him."

✳✳✳✳✳✳✳✳✳✳✳✳✳✳✳✳✳✳✳✳

It was a little after midnight when they left their stash house. They were now driving to the projects in M-2's steel gray Maserati as another 12-inch blunt rotated back and forth. They stopped at a light and a police cruiser pulled on the side of them. Although the windows were tinted, both homies seemed unconcerned as they continued to smoke. The light changed green and M-2 blew smoke out the window and passed the blunt.

"Yo Damon."

"What's up homie."

"We only about what, fifteen deep now? Half of us dead my nigga. I hope they died for the right reasons and not because Anton really snaked that nigga," said M-2.

Damon didn't respond as he thought about that foreign look he observed on Anton's face when he enlightened them about the situation a while back.

"You believe he did?"

"I'm not gone answer that," M-2 replied. "But I want you to analyze this. When me and Anton killed that nigga's people in that restaurant, Anton made a statement to the nigga Bujo that left me thinking."

"What you mean homie. What he say?"

"He asked the nigga was it worth it. What kind of question was that considering that nigga had already killed his mother, his seed, and baby mama. To me it sounded like he was asking him was the money he took from him worth retaliating for."

"Damn is you serious," asked Damon as a new reality began to set.

"As a heart attack and if it's true then he caused his family to get killed. Not to mention a lot of our homies and J-one's mother and aint no end to this shit," M-2 replied. Damon remained silent. "And all over some dope," M-2 continued.

"Anyway, he in a helluva position, why would he do some shit like that knowing them Jamaicans gone take it to the grave?"

"I don't know," said Damon. "But we gone find out what's real!"

Once they made it back in the hood, M-2 realized he was at a half tank of gas and decided to fill it up. Damon was on his phone with Shonte when they pulled into the gas station.

"Grab a couple house of Windsor's nigga."

"Nigga you know that goes without saying," said M-2 and got out and made his way to the window.

Damon's phone reception began to fade in and out.

"Is that your phone or mine?"

"That's yours," said Shonte.

He got out the car to see if he could get a better reception. He noticed the more he walked away from the gas pump, the clearer the line got.

"Look Shonte, I give you more of my time than I give Yasha so why the fuck are you tripping?"

Bujo's around the clock hit men who were strictly KKBG hunters spotted M-2 pumping gas into his car. They didn't notice Damon standing almost ten feet away from him as they quickly circled back and pulled the stolen van in a vacant pharmacy's parking lot across the street. Two Jamaicans quickly jumped out with Ak-47's in their arms.

"Come on nigga why you all out there on the sidewalk slipping and shit!" M-2 yelled as he sat the pump back in its place.

Damon began to walk back to the car when the fusillade erupted. Damon dropped to the ground, unable to take cover, but M-2 was the target caught in the enemy's wrath. Then suddenly a huge explosion occurred, leaving the gas pump in flames. M-2 never had a chance at survival.

44   MARYLAND 1:35 AM

Kyla watched Jarvis struggle to finish his last set of pushups. She winced as if she felt the pain he was feeling on his sternum. It was not yet healed but she couldn't convince him to seek medical attention, he was determined to heal alone. Ever since his mother passed, Kyla had been worried about his well-being. The whole month and a half in recovery, he had not been himself. He was distant and many days it felt to her like she was invisible. Sometimes he would break down and cry for hours and her attempt to console him never helped any so they cried together almost every night. Kyla was unsure of him ever overcoming this sorrow and she didn't think that she'd ever see that sparkle in his eyes that once held so much life. She was determined to stay by his side through it all....

He got up off the floor, sat on the sofa across from her, leaned back, and closed his eyes. Kyla watched the sweat drip down his torso. After a long silence Jarvis cell phone started to ring on the table in front of him. At first they both stared at it because that was the first time it rung since he's been in recovery. In his heart, he felt it was something wrong so he grabbed the phone.

"Speak."

He heard the sniffle.

"J-one, its' me, Y-love."

"What's wrong?"

"M-2 just got killed."

Jarvis put his elbows on his knees and clenched his teeth tightly together.

"Who was behind it?" he asked curtly.

"We don't know. Damon was with him but I'm at the hospital now waiting for them to release him so hopefully I can find out exactly who."

"They hit Damon up too?" Jarvis asked with stinging tears in his eyes.

"They shot M-2 up at the gas station. One of the pumps exploded and Damon got hit by the explosion."

A still silence followed, both lost in their thoughts.

"J-one I don't even know if I'll be alive by the time you make it back because I'm finna move on everybody against us, but in case I never see your face again, I want you to know that I love you my nigga. Even though our dynasty is broken, I wouldn't erase a day of what you created."

Jarvis lifted his head up and Kyla saw that his face was wet with tears. He looked at his watch.

"It's one-fifty-two, I'll be at the condo before the sun come up. When they release Damon yall go straight there. No soldiers just you, Anton, and Damon."

Suddenly her voice came alive.

"Okay J-one we'll be there."

Kyla begged him to stay as he quickly got dressed but her efforts were useless.

"So, I take it you're ready to die too. Is that it?" Kyla asked ruefully. Jarvis zipped up his coat and grabbed his keys and headed towards the bedroom door. Then suddenly he stopped in his tracks and turned to face her, realizing that she was at least entitled to an answer.

"Kyla I'm ready to die, kill, or jail over the death of my mother and now my friend who was just killed tonight. Sorry for the stress that I caused you and I appreciate how much you care but shorty I gotta do what I gotta do. I'll be back when the smoke clears. If I drown in that smoke, I'll always remember you."

Without another word he turned and left, both unsure if they would ever see each other again.

J-one made it to the condo a little after six in the morning. His three remaining lieutenants were already inside. Damon had his head bandage wrapped because of second degree burns on his head and face. Everybody stood up and embraced Jarvis when he walked in.

"Samuel Mccroy is on the way. It's time to let it all hang, is yall ready to move?" They definitely were and assured him they were ready as ever.

"I don't know who was behind the hit J-one we never saw it coming," said Damon.

"Look it don't even matter who was behind it, this is how we gone do it. We gone have the pig bring Bujo to us. It may take a minute, but I got faith that he gone deliver that bitch to us on a silver platter. While he's in the process of doing that we gone hunt down Ubie and whoever in the way of that gone catch it too.

"Now that's what I'm talking about," Wanisha blurted.

As they went back and forth, Damon continuously thought about what M-2 had told him before he died. The more he cut his eyes at Anton the more he saw the truth.

Pain and hurt was in everyone's eyes but he observed shame in Anton's and it spoke volumes. Damon couldn't hold it back any longer.

"Let me ask you a question Anton. Our peoples, yo peoples, the ones that died behind the Jamaicans, did they die because you were in the right or because you were in the wrong?" Everybody's eyes were on Anton. He tried to remain calm, but he believed they saw through his act.

"What you think I sold them niggas some foof for real?" He looked at each one then back to Damon. His eyes told the naked truth and his deceit was now apparent.

"You did didn't you," asked Jarvis.

Anton couldn't hold it in any longer. He burst out crying as all of the shame and guilt came to a head.

"Oh my God," Wanisha cried, not wanting to believe what she now knew was true.

"My mother, yo mother, yo seed, and yo seeds mother died behind this shit. Not to mention some of the homies and M-2. and now all you can do is cry.. WHY MUTHAFUCKA WHY!" Jarvis screamed.

"I didn't know it was gonna be like this," Anton cried.

"You didn't know! Fuck you mean you didn't know?" Jarvis got up and went into his bedroom. Five minutes later he came out with a plate in his hand. On the plate was raw heroine. He sat it on the table in front of Anton and sat down on the sofa across from him.

"I thought we once made a vow not to ever cross one another. I thought we made a vow to be friends until the end. How could you break those vows my nigga!"

"Greed took control over me J-one but I never meant to hurt our peoples. I never meant to place them in harm's way."

"But you did my nigga. You broke up our dynasty and you sent the queen of my life to her grave."

Jarvis pulled a nine-millimeter off his waist and pointed it in Anton's face.

"About some got damn dope! Now pick up that plate and blow that shit up ya nose since it meant that much to you!"

"I know you can't find it in your heart to forgive me but don't do me like this J-one, please homie," Anton pleaded.

"Don't make me ask you again."

Anton looked at each one then scooted to the edge of the couch. Silent tears ran down Wanisha's face.

"Pick the tray up and kill yoself like you killed everybody else!" Demanded Jarvis.

Anton reluctantly complied. He realized that his desire to live was absent as he grabbed the plate. Jarvis sat expressionless.

He put his nose to the straw and froze as his life flashed before his eyes. A flash of Tracy and his son lying in bloody water flashed in his mind and that's when he snorted the first portion of raw dope. His nose instantly started bleeding as an overpowering feeling quickly washed over him. He put his nose back to the straw, anxious to get it over with.

The plate fell from his hand as he lost all sense of control. He put his hand to his heart and leaned back. Then suddenly he started jerking violently as foam gushed from his mouth. Then he froze, eyes wide open, death had taken him away.

When agent Mccroy arrived, Anton was still on the couch dead. Sam was ordered to dispose his body after everyone left.

"I'm offering you three million to capture this Bujo character and bring him to me alive. I'll give you half now and the other half afterwards."

Samuel wasn't expecting a proposition worth millions and was very excited to receive the first half. Jarvis handed him the bag.

"After I grab him where do you want me to take him?"

"I'm giving you three million, I'm gone let you figure that out. Take him somewhere secluded because torture is a must."
"I got you. As soon as I dispose this body I'm gone track him down."

"It's on," said Jarvis and him and his remaining lieutenants left the condo.

45

Daylight invaded as the three friends drove in silence. Then Jarvis said, "I know its early yall but aint no telling what lies ahead for us so how about we each spend a half hour with family one at a time."

They agreed.

Their first stop was at Shonte spot. Jarvis and Wanisha waited in the car while Damon spent his time giving Shonte a few 'just in case' orders. Their next destination was Wanisha's mother's house. When they pulled in her driveway, Wanisha noticed that her mother's bedroom light was still on. She got out and made her way to the door. After continuously knocking, she turned the doorknob and the door opened. The house was a mess and hadn't been cleaned in weeks. She found her mother in bed sprawled out with a framed picture lying face down on her chest. On the dresser was a crack pipe and drug residue. At first Wanisha studied her to see was she breathing, after she saw she was alive she took the picture out of her hand and looked at it. It was a picture of Marlo blowing out the candles of his 12-year birthday cake. Wanisha sat in the chair and silently wept for the loss of her twin brother and the self-destruction of her mother. After she was all cried out she kissed her mother's cheek and quietly left.

Jarvis woke Roxanne out of her sleep.

"Hey, when did you get back?" asked Roxanne.

"This morning," said Jarvis and sat on the bed.

She propped herself up on her elbow.

"Did you hear about what happened at the gas station last night in your neighborhood?"

"Yeah," he replied.

"Your friend M-2 was killed. Did that have anything to do with you and those other people," she inquired.

He didn't answer her, but she knew the truth.

"What are you going to do Jarvis because I know that I can't talk you out of anything, especially after all that has happened, but let me say this, you haven't lost everything yet. You still have us, and that boy needs you in his life more than anything. Jarvis don't cheat him by taking that away from him."

He looked her in the face and she saw a ton of pain in his eyes.

"I wish it was another way Roxy but it aint. If the outcome go against me keep him close to me, bring him to come see me from time to time.

"And what if you die Jarvis?"

"If I die, then you gone let him know why I died when he get older."

When Jarvis got back in the car, Damon and Wanisha was passing a blunt back and forth. Jarvis called Ron-Ron, a KKBG soldier on his cell phone.

"Hello."

"Where you at?" asked Jarvis.

"Who the hell is this?"

"It's me J-one."

"Oh shit my bad, I didn't know it was you."

"Where you at?" Jarvis reiterated.

"I'm in the jets big homie."

"Good that's where I'm headed. Have a hotty waiting for me aight."

"No problem," Ron-Ron replied. Ron-Ron specialized in stealing cars.

"I guess you heard about what happened last night right?"

"Yeah now hurry up and get on that," said Jarvis.

"Okay but before you hang up, some broad slid through here a few days ago looking for you. She said her name was"....... He took a second to remember her name. "I think she said her name was Andrea or something like that, but I got her name and number in my glove compartment. She said it's really important that she get in touch with you."

Jarvis heartbeat quickened.

"My car in the parking lot, you want me to go grab that for you?"

"Hell yeah man hurry up."

A few minutes later he had her number and quickly dialed it.

"Hello."

"Hello is this Andrea?" asked Jarvis.

"May I ask who's calling?"

Jarvis hesitated for a second.

"It's J-one."

"Oh, how are you?"

"Does it matter to you?"

"Yes. I'm sorry for not helping you when you needed me to but at that time I was totally confused, but I'm here. Do you still need me?"

"Tell me what I need to know," said Jarvis.

"The same day the attempt was made on your life, he had a fit that you survived but he was happy that his friend killed your mother."

"So what you gone do Andrea?" A still silence lingered.

"Deliver him to you."

"Where you at," asked Jarvis.

"At home by myself."

"When can you meet me in the projects?"

"When do you need me to be there?" asked Andrea.

"In twenty minutes and I'll be in the parking lot waiting for you."

"As soon as I get dressed I'm on my way," she told him and hung up.

Jarvis grabbed the blunt from Wanisha and hit the gas as the Bentley smoothly sped down the freeway.

Samuel Mccroy discreetly dumped Anton's body in a huge dumpster in a dark alley and then sharply pulled off. He knew it wasn't going to be easy capturing Bujo and one mistake could cost him his life. He had a plan that could make this mission much easier, but he knew it would take a lot of persuasion. 'With one point five million in my possession who can't be persuaded,' he thought to himself and headed over an old friend's house...

Roy Johnson was a black Ex-Fed agent that's been retired for seven years now. Him and Samuel were partners for almost ten years and were still good friends. Despite Roy being gay, Sam always admired his expertise as an agent and he never allowed Roy's lifestyle to come in between their friendship. Occasionally they would still go on fishing trips and hunting adventures together, but it's been almost a year since they've seen one another.

Sam didn't know if Roy was still sleep or not when he pulled into his driveway. Before he could ring the doorbell, the door opened. Roy stood in front of him smiling from ear to ear happy to see his friend.

"Look who the wind blew in," said Roy and hugged his ex-partner.

"Come on in let me fix you some coffee before you tell me what's on ya mind."
Samuel chuckled.

"Why can't I just be stopping by to see my friend."

Roy looked at his watch.

"Because its nine twenty-three in the morning and there's something in your eyes that's telling me that you're up to something or on to something but have a seat. Let me go get us some coffee."

"Cool," said Samuel and made himself at home.

Three minutes later he returned with some fresh coffee.

"You look like you're headed to the gym or something," said Sam.

"Actually, I was just about to take my daily jog but forget about that, why haven't you called in almost a year?" asked Roy.

"Conspiracies and court appearances kind of got me out of touch but let me reverse that question. Why haven't I heard from you?"

Roy stared at the black liquid he was drinking as his expression turned solemn.

"Me and Shaun broke up early in the year and it's been kind of tough for me to get over it, but I don't want to talk about that, tell me what's going on."

"Sam took a swig and sat the cup on the table.

"First let me ask, if you don't mind, how is everything financially?" Sam asked.

"I'm living but sometimes I feel like I retired too soon. Why what's up?"

"A whole lot if you're willing."

They stared at each other for a brief moment.

"Willing to do what?"

"Before we discuss that let me put you up on what's really been going on for the last seven years of my life."

Sam enlightened him about his ties in corruption and Roy appeared to be at a loss for words. He was a hard man to surprise but he would never believe that his ex-partner was a crooked agent if he didn't just hear it from the horse's mouth.

"What!..........Don't fucking look at me like that. So what that I chose to secure my future instead of being loyal to a government that doesn't give a crap shit about me. You think they'll shed a freaking tear if I get jammed up in some undercover operation and get my fucking head blown off!"

"Since when did you start feeling like this because last I remember, you couldn't see yourself being nothing else but a soldier for the law."

They stared eye to eye.

"Truthfully speaking that feeling died seven years ago when I lost a loyal partner."

Roy stood up and walked over to the window.

"If I knew it meant that much to you I would've stayed."

After a minute of silence he turned to face Sam.
"So you say this Jarvis character already gave you one point five million?"

"Yep and he's going to give me the rest once we capture Bujo for him. Now I'm not only offering you five hundred thousand just to help me capture this man, but also because you're my friend and I wanna make life a tad bit easier for you."

"And what if we don't catch him?"

"Oh we will........By any means necessary."

46

Bujo, Perry, and a few other Jamaicans were at one of Bujo's spots smoking weed and discussing matters at hand. At this moment the room was silent as the extraordinary weed pipe went from man to man. Then Bujo spoke.

"What was a five-headed monster has now become a four headed one and they will soon die too. After what happened last night, I want every G.V.P. member to lay low for a while. I don't want a soul out there in them projects."

"I'll put the word out asap," said Death.

"Don't get too comfortable," said Bujo. "As soon as it cools down we gone finish this war altogether."

****

Jarvis took Andrea into an apartment where his two lieutenants awaited. As soon as she sat down she said, "Perry called me before you called and told me he had a lot of down time on his hands and wanted to spend some with me. Later on we're going out to his house in Willowick. It's a place that's secluded by itself."

"Perfect. We gone put him to sleep out there," said Jarvis. "But I need you to go straight there when you leave here. Take my girl Y-love with you, she's going to handle the business."

"This man is dangerous!" she warned. "Why leave it up to her?"

Jarvis chuckled and looked over at Wanisha.

"Honey he may be dangerous, but I am thee epitome of danger. Don't judge a book by its cover," Wanisha advised her.

Realizing that Wanisha must be a dangerous woman, she shrugged her eyebrows and looked back at Jarvis.

"So, I guess it will be safe for me to move back to Columbus when this is over."

"What's in Columbus?" asked Jarvis.

"My family. Ever since I moved up here to be with J.d. I've never went back home... I'm sorry for not being there when you needed me."

"I can't hold that against you Andrea besides, everything happens for a reason. When you get to Columbus, put all this stuff behind you aight."

She nodded her head and looked at Wanisha.

"Are you ready?" Andrea asked her.

Wanisha stood up.

"Let's ride."

Andrea followed suit. Jarvis gave Andrea a hug.

"Give me a hug before you go and be careful," he told Wanisha. She walked over and embraced him and caught the soft whisper as well.

****

Roy stared out the window at the worn-down Garden Valley communities as they cruised by.

"Why is it a ghost town over here," Roy asked.

"'They're probably ordered into hibernation because of all the killings going on. Shit they're behind half of them."

Sam, you know what man, my gut is telling me that word of mouth is the only way we're going to get close to him. Unless you're contemplating a better idea."

"See these fucking crazy ass Jamaicans live by a code of honor, and will die by it, so that's not the route we should take," said Samuel. Then suddenly a character came to mind. The character was not a GVP member, but he certainly stayed in the thick of things and it wasn't nothing in these streets that he didn't know about. His name was Samoj, an American Jamaican who was a Deejay at the Double Nickel, a club where the Jamaicans hung out on the weekend.

Samoj had his share of run-ins with the law and authorities knew him well. He had not too long ago served a three-year sentence in the feds for a gun case. Considering he wasn't a soldier to none of the Jamaican gangs, Samuel wondered if a nice amount of money could convince Samoj to help with tracking down Bujo. He quickly filled Roy in on the plan and Roy used Samuel's Laptop computer to see if they could come up with an address under the name Samoj Winn. Minutes later they had one.

****

"Aye Samoj baby wake up, some pigs are at the door!" He popped up quick and jumped out of bed.

"Shit hide the guns in the drawer!"

His baby mama Rachael quickly complied.

"Now go answer the door. Shit I aint done nothing."

"You didn't violate your Fed papers did you?"

"Hell naw. I aint been selling no dope or nothing. Just go and answer the door. If they want me tell them to hold up."
She followed his orders and went and welcomed them into the sitting room while he was upstairs getting dressed. He looked down upon the sleeping toddler in its baby crib.

"I promised I wouldn't leave you son and I meant that. Daddy aint going nowhere."
She came back up and told him they were waiting in the living room. He reluctantly headed downstairs with Rachael in pursuit.

"Mr. Winn! How are you doing today sir?"

"I'm aight what's up?"

"We need a few minutes of your time and I hope we didn't inconvenience you, did we?" asked Samuel.

"Well I aint used to no cops popping up at my door. What's all this about anyway?"

"Mr. Winn let's just cut straight to the chase. It's about putting some money in your pocket. A nice figure to say the least."

Samoj looked at Rachael, then back to the detective.

"Do I look like a fucking snitch to you!"

"We're not asking you to snitch on anybody," said Samuel. "We're offering you twenty-five thousand dollars to find out a person's whereabouts."

Samoj was suddenly bemused.

"And who yall looking for anyway?"

"Bujo!"

"BUJO!" yelled Samoj.

"That's right! Can you lead us to him or not? If you can I'll even raise it fifteen gees."

Rachael and Samoj became enticed with the amount and it showed clearly.

"Listen I know there's not much you can't find out in these streets. Find out where he's at and the money is yours. You don't have to worry about nothing falling back on you, it's not that type of party. You won't have to see a court or nothing of that nature."

"So If I agree to do this, we won't have any discrepancies when it's time to get paid right?"

"As soon as you give me the information I need, I'll turn the money over to you. Just don't try to play any games with us because then it will cost you."

Samoj thought for a long moment. Then Rachael said, "Baby we definitely need this money and you know I can help you." Suddenly she became an interest to Mccroy.

"Give me your number officer," said Samoj, redirecting the officer's attention back to him. "It shouldn't take me long to find out."

"Good because we need to catch up to him as quick as possible."

****

Perry didn't make it to the country house until 8:42pm. Andrea had called him earlier in the day and told him that she would already be there. He didn't rush to get there. He scratched a few other things off his schedule first. When he got out the car he lazily stretched his limbs, then he just stood there staring in the blackened sky as the stars stared back. He loved the peaceful vibe he always received when being there. He called this place his heaven.

When he entered the house a still silence greeted him.

"Baby it's me," he said out loud as he made his way to the kitchen grabbing a can of Budweiser out the refrigerator. He cracked it open and downed it on the spot.

'What's wrong with this picture. She aint cook me nothing to eat. This heffa done got lazy as hell,' he told himself as he grabbed another can of beer and headed upstairs.

He stopped at the doorway of the master bedroom and looked at Andrea's body that was cover with silk linen. Only the back of her head was visible as she was lying on her side. He figured she probably went to sleep upset because he was hours late and that was the reason for an uncooked meal. After he sat his gun on the dresser, he took off his vest and dropped it on the floor.

"Daddy's home now baby." He crawled up behind her and planted soft kisses on the back of her neck but Andrea didn't stir.

"Baby I had some errands to run that's why I'm late." He pulled the blanket back and froze in panic. Two bullet holes was in her forehead as she laid dead-eyed. Perry didn't want to turn around because he felt the killer's presence behind him. Suddenly he had the urge to jump through the window which was not too far in front of him. He looked back and saw Wanisha in the doorway watching him.

"What do you want......Money?"

"You bitch ass pig. I want you to have the heart to die like you had the heart to go against my squad!"

He turned all the way around and looked her in the eyes. She then pointed both guns in his face and walked a step closer.

"Look at you.......... you can't even embrace your death.. You's a coward with a million more deaths to come."

Twenty rounds followed her words, but Perry was dead from the first one.

✲✲✲✲✲✲✲✲✲✲✲✲✲✲✲✲✲✲✲✲

Juju and Mouse was in Ubie's Lexus, with two dime pieces in the back seat. Juju and Ubie had switched cars earlier for no essential reason. The windows had midnight tint as the four of them kicked it in harmony while the music blared. They were all on their way to the hood bar where the Yg's hung out. Mouse who was in the passenger, passed each one two ecstasy pills and everybody popped them right then and there. The girl in the backseat blazed a blunt and passed it to Mouse.

"Don't burn no holes in my nigga seats," said Juju and grabbed the blunt.

"Yall hoes bet not be back there fucking up that Luis Vutton leather," said Mouse.

"Right they asses a be selling pussy for months to clear up that debt," Juju replied.

"Fuck you Juju aint nobody fucking up Ubie seats. Now when are we going to the hotel. Me and my girl tryanna get some action," said Trena.

Then Sasha said, "Yall......... fuck the bar. My pussy is too hot and too moist to be sitting around."

Juju and Mouse looked at each other and started laughing. They were two blocks over from the bar.

"Yall calm down we aint going in unless it's necessary," said Juju.

It was a crowd of homies standing in front of the bar when they pulled up and stopped, causing the traffic to go around their car. Mouse rolled down his window.

"Where yall niggas been all day," one of the homies asked.

"Just killing time," said Mouse.

"That nigga Ubie aint been through yet?" Juju asked.

"Nope not yet, but yall niggas need to get out and kick it. It's a lot of hoes from across town in the bar tonight."

Juju rolled down the back windows to display the two horny chicks.

"Shit we good for the night fam," said Juju.

"I see," the homie replied.

A car stopped abruptly on the driver's side and a chopper protruded from the window. In a split second everything turned chaotic as the tinted windows shattered, and Juju's head exploded on sight. The girls in the backseat screamed in terror as they watched both homies in the front get slumped. Jarvis (The shooter) thought he had killed Ubie no doubt. Damon the driver hopped out and chased another Yg member down killing him execution style.

As he jogged back to the car, he eyed the girls through his skully mask as they screamed to the top of their lungs.

Shells and a deep slab in the street were the only traces left behind.

A little after Ubie left from one of his girl's house, he noticed a blue Lincoln following him. He drove and watched as the person in the car continued to follow.

"Whoever this is following me must think I'm Juju," he said out loud. When he was convinced that he was being followed, he grabbed his cell phone and dialed Snatch-out's number. He immediately answered.

"This me...... Ubie.... where you at?"

"Just left Killa's crib. We're looking for something to get into. What's up?"

"I wanna know who's following me so we can set they asses up. Where yall at?"

"In front of Wendy's on 59th."

"Good I'm on 40th at the light in front of the plaza. I'm about to direct you to me as I drive. Is yall strapped?"

"Is we? ....Never leave home without them cuz! Aight direct nigga."

Wanisha called Jarvis and he quickly answered.

"I handled it baby, it's done. But look here, guess who I'm behind right now?"

"Who?"

"Ubie hoe ass and I'm about to kill his ass J-one. Please don't tell me different. This is my chance for what he did to my brother."

"I just hit that nigga at the bar. I got him already Y-love."

"You couldn't have. He right here in front of me, I'm looking at him and he's in Juju's Lexus."

"Fuck!" Jarvis hissed as reality set.

"Damn I thought that was Ubie. It must have been one of his homies. Where yall at?"

"We turning off 40th and Quincy, I think he headed to the Jets. When the moment opens up I'm taking it," said Wanisha.

Jarvis didn't like the moment at hand. He wanted to be there to oversee Ubie's death plus he didn't want Wanisha to move with carelessness, but he knew he couldn't talk her out of it.

"Look don't do nothing in traffic, let him make it to the Jets. We'll hit him over there. Me and Damon on our way there now Y-love don't move crazy. Let him make it to the Jets aight?" Jarvis pleaded.

"Okay," she replied and hung up. Only thing on her mind was everything Ubie did to her brother.

"It's a bitch homie and she is tailing the shit out of you. What you wanna do?" asked Snatch-out.

"I think it's that KKBG hoe. This bitch finna get it," said Ubie as he turned down a one-way street. He wasn't expecting a broken-down car to block him off a little up the road, and it alerted him when he noticed it because of the possibilities of what could transpire if the girl was Marlo's sister. Instead of stopping behind the car, Ubie whipped in a driveway and quickly got out of the car, hating himself for leaving his strap on the block. Wanisha pulled to a halt directly in front of the driveway and hopped out with her strap in her hand. Ubie darted in the back of the house but not before a bullet hole went through his back and slowed him down. He ran to a fence and threw his body over it and fell to the ground. He struggled to get back on his feet, realizing he was vitally wounded. Unable to escape, he tried to crawl, as Wanisha ran up and jumped over the fence.

"Hoe ass nigga you lucky I can't torture yo ass but this is for my brother. Rest in piss nigga!" She shot him five times in the head and hoped that was torture enough, never giving a thought to her surroundings as she stood over him.

"I got him for you Marlo, you can rest in peace now," she said to the sky.

Then suddenly more gun shots brought her back to reality. She was being attacked by Ubie's cousins who was using the house for coverage. Thus far unscathed, she tried to retreat while ripping the 40-cal in their direction but wasn't nothing but open field. She continued to fire and back pedal as the twenty-two shot extended clip warded off her enemies. As soon as she let up, they went back in attack mode, but Wanisha had vanished into the night.

****

Yg members Levar and Solo were in crack head Linda's apartment in the 30th projects when Levar received the shocking message that his partners had been killed.

"WHEN?"

"Just now about five minutes ago," K-rocc told him.

"Who did it? Was it them bitch ass KKBG niggas?"

"Probably but they was masked up. I was inside the bar when they got hit."

"Me and Solo on our way now. Get ready homie cuz we bout to ride on them niggas tonight. Some of theirs got to die," said Levar with tears in his eyes.

"No doubt. In a minute homie!"

"We on our way," Levar said and hung up.

"WHAT HAPPENED?" yelled Solo.

"Mouse and Juju just got shot up at the bar. They said they both dead."

They both jumped up and hurried out the door.

****

Damon and Jarvis pulled into the 30th projects after circling the block a few times noticing it was empty. They parked and waited. A few minutes later Jarvis cell phone rung, it was Wanisha.

"I got him J-one but I'm stranded."

"You got him? Where you at?"

"I'm on 39th in Central, in the backyard of an abandoned house. The address is 2653."

"Is you aight?"

"Yeah I'll tell you about it."

"Aight stay where you at until I blow. Here we come now."

"Okay bye."

"39th in Central," J-one told Damon. "She said she got that nigga."

Before Damon could pull off they saw Levar and Solo emerge from the apartment.

"Hold up," said J-one. "Let's down these two niggas in memory of the dead homies.

"Let's do it," replied Damon and they got out of the car. Levar and Solo never noticed them creeping between parked cars. When they felt like they were close enough, they rushed their targets and slaughtered both of them in a matter of seconds. A few seconds later they were pulling away.

****

Considering Rachel and Bujo's niece Char were close friends, she went over her house with a deceitful intention to try and find out Bujo's whereabouts. What Samoj didn't know is that it would be easier than he thought because Bujo had a thing for Rachael and have stopped by Char's house on several occasions to get a quickie off with her. If Samoj would have ever caught wind of her cheating on him with Bujo, he would've probably shot her dead. Luckily, he had no idea and Char was someone she trusted with her life.

They sat around and smoked a few blunts as they talked and gossiped back and forth. Then finally she made her attempt.

"Girl, I am so tired of the same dick that I don't know what to do. I mean it's still good but right now I need a different stroke in my life. Do you get like that at times?"

"Girl I know exactly what you mean, that's why I does me. I aint gone never dump James but I definitely gotta have more than one dick girl."

"You the wrong one to be asking that question," said Rachael.

"I'm hip. Girl you know I'm serious about getting my issue."

Rachael passed her the blunt while exhaling the smoke. "As a matter of fact, I need Bujo to make my night. Think I can get him to come here?"

"Girl please," Char chimed. "So much been going on between him and them KKBG niggas, I'd be surprised if he is answering any of his calls. His ass gone fuck around and get locked up."

"You aint lying. They think they in the middle east don't they. Well look Char, hit him up for me anyway and let's see what it do. I just might get lucky."

Without giving it much thought she grabbed her cell phone and sent him a text message. They continued to kick it. Five minutes later the phone started ringing which immediately brought their conversation to a halt.

"Damn is that him," Char blurted and grabbed the phone.

"Hello."

"Hey Bujo, bout time you called somebody back."

Rachael got nervous in her anticipation to fulfill this mission.

"I know uncle, but somebody practically begged me to call you, so here talk to her for a minute."

She handed the phone to Rachael and said, "girl I don't think this gone be one of those nights."

"Hey sexy!"

"What's up... Not tonight baby. When I'm available I'll see you okay," he said in his thick Jamaican accent.
"Okay daddy," she pouted. She could tell he wasn't in the mood for soft talk, so she gave the phone back to Char.

"Are you straight?" Char asked him.

"Most definitely. I'm finna put my son to sleep and kick back."

"Oh, you over Cheryl house?" she asked. After a slight hesitation he replied, "Yeah... and keep that between us. Shit is crazy right now so I'm out the way for a minute."

"Okay you be careful, and I'll talk to you later."

"Fa show," he replied and they both hung up.

Two hours later Rachael was back at home delivering the news to Samoj. They both knew his son mother considering they all had grew up in the same neighborhood as kids. Now it would be up to the detectives to locate her address.

Samuel answered after the first ring.

"Hello."

"Mccroy this me......Samoj."

"At this moment he is over to his baby mama's crib, but I don't know where she live at."

"What's the lady name?"

"Cheryl Tipler. She's between thirty and thirty-five years old and mixed with black and white."

"Are you sure he's there?" asked Mccroy.

"Positive... and gone be there for the rest of the night," he added.

"Okay look. If everything checks right, I'll be by your house with the money first thing in the morning, so be there. If this is misguided information you will hear from me tonight. Do not. I repeat DO NOT discuss our business with anyone. Is that clear?"

"I got you. As long as I get what I'm entitled to you don't have to worry about me saying shit," said Samoj.

"It won't be a dollar short. You're using the cellphone I gave you right?"

"Yeah this it."

"Ok well keep it charged. Never know when I may be calling."

47

It didn't take Roy long to come up with Cheryl's address on his laptop computer. As soon as it was discovered they quickly left Roy's house, hoping that this mission didn't involve any technicalities. Cheryl lived in Warrensville Heights Ohio, s small suburb outside of Cleveland. Her neighborhood was very clean and quiet, and the crime rate was low. Both men knew they had to move quick and discreetly as possible.

They monitored her house from their car which was parked a few doors down. The one-way street was quiet on this cold winter night as the howling wind continued to break the silence.

"Roy, I know you've been out of commission for a while, but I also know that you're still one of the best. Now this motherfucker is dangerous so utilize your special instincts, and also, we can't kill him. It aint our job to do so."

"Enough said…. Now let's grab this motherfucker," replied Roy as they got out and headed towards the house…

Cheryl and Bujo sat cuddled on the sofa, watching an intense porno flick as the next-door neighbor's dog continued to bark furiously. Bujo didn't pay it any mind but it started to annoy Cheryl.

"That dog hardly ever barks. What's wrong with it?" she skeptically pondered.

"Is that right," Bujo thought out loud and quickly sat up.

He studied the dog's bark and suddenly something didn't feel right.

"Boo do you think something is wrong by it barking like that?" she asked as fear quickly ruffled her hormones.

"I don't know but let's cut all these lights out," he demanded. A minute later all the lights were out, and he was gripping a 40 caliber. They sat in the living room silently listening as the dog continued to bark. Again, Bujo peaked through the curtains but only nature stared back. Then suddenly a gas bomb came crashing through the window. Then another one crashed another window.

"OH MY GOD!" Cheryl screamed.

"Go get the baby and run out the front door. HURRY UP!"

As frightened as she was she quickly complied realizing there was no other alternative. She grabbed the crying child from the bed, wrapped him in her arms, and ran out of the front door and down the street. She was too terrified to look back. Bujo knew he couldn't exit from the front or back door so he climbed through a side window just as a dizzy spell washed over him. Before he could get completely out the window, his adversaries had the drop on him."

"DROP THE GUN MOTHERFUCKER! DROP IT!"

Halfway through the window he was forced to obey the order. Mccroy yanked him out the rest of the way and quickly hand cuffed him.

"What the fuck is going on," said Bujo while trying to figure out their motive. Neither man responded as they forcefully directed him to the car.

By the midnight hour the streets of Cleveland were littered with police cruisers and unmarked homicide vehicles. Things were in a complete disarray and until some significant arrest were made behind all the recent slaughters, the authorities were prepared to shake and shut the city down. Jarvis and his two remaining lieutenants checked in at a shabby motel and quickly settled in. At first neither person spoke as a blunt rotated amongst the three. Then Wanisha spoke for the first time since they picked her up.

"All went well on my end Jarvis.... Of course, nobody survived."

"I already know Y-love," Jarvis replied knowingly.

A tear rolled down Wanisha's face.

"And J-one, it doesn't matter to me if my number falls next, I just needed to silence Marlo's tears from his grave.... Now let's silence your mothers."

Jarvis got up and walked over to the window staring out at the streets.

"We created a dynasty and made millions but lost a whole lot in the process." He turned and faced who he felt like was the only two people he had left.

"Although, I knew we would lose some, I never thought it would end like this. My mother, your brother, M-2, Anton and his entire family and the rest of homies......they all gone."

Damon walked up to him.

"If we could rewind the hands of time then we would, if that meant bringing our peoples back, but we can't J-one. We can only go from here."

"I know Damon but its killing me homie, I can't accept this," Jarvis admitted and broke down in his man's arms unable to hold it in any longer.

A few hours later, while the three were dozing off, Jarvis cell phone started ringing. Each one quickly popped up. Jarvis snatched it off the table and answered.

"Who dis?"

"Jarvis. This is me.... Mccroy."

Jarvis heart beat went crazy.

"Is everything good or what?"

"Everything is beautiful! We have him and he's secured safely. My friend owns a bar on 152nd in lakeshore, on water gate. You can trust him, he helped me accomplish tonight's mission."

"So that's where yall at right now?"

"Yes! Come without deceit, I expect our relation to end that way," said Mccroy.

"We're at a point where I have no other choice but to trust you... and you have to trust me as well," said Jarvis. "If it's a trap...I'm willing to die in it. But be willing to die as well."

"Well enough," Mccroy replied.

After circling the location, they spotted Mccroy's truck in the parking lot of the bar. Wanisha parked two blocks over. Jarvis read the time on his watch. It read 4:07am.

"Y-love, listen to me. If you don't receive the awaited page by six, take the money, put it with everything you got and go. Leave the city and don't come back. You and Omirah been friends for years, she will do anything for you. Go out there with her. Start a life in LA."

"But J-one, what if yall need me. I can't just sit here like this, not knowing if yall okay."

"You played yo part Y-love and we love you to death for being you all the way through.... But it's time to wrap things up, and this is how we gone close out. When you get that text, you know what to do aight."

She nodded with assurance and hugged J-one with pure love. Then she hugged Damon who was in the back.

"Don't slip in there... I mean it yall," said Wanisha.

"We won't," Jarvis assured as he and Damon got out and began their walk. Neither one of them looked back to see a teary-eyed Wanisha.

Mccroy let them in from a side door entrance and led them to the heart of the bar where Roy awaited sitting at a rounded table.

"Where is he," Jarvis asked.

"He's here but first let's have a seat and discuss matters. Jarvis and Damon cautiously scanned the room as they both pulled out their weapons.

For a second Roy and Mccroy froze before understanding their actions.

"Don't panic," said Jarvis. "We only intend on killing one person. We just rather have these in our hands."

"I understand," Mccroy replied. "This is my old friend, a good man. He helped me capture Bujo, and he's going to help me dispose of him."

"How are you," Roy spoke.

Both homies nodded.

"So, you gave me 1.5 million, when will I receive the second half?"

"Five minutes after we leave this bar. I'm going to call your phone and direct you to what's yours."

Mccroy analyzed his statement and realized he had no choice but to trust him.

"Sure enough," Mccroy agreed.

"I have all sorts of torturous equipment in the basement where he awaits. Follow us fellas," said Roy.

Bujo was held captive at the center point of the room. His arms were held high with each wrist was hand cuffed chained and bound to a ceiling pipe. His ankle was rope tied and they barely managed to touch the ground

A few layers of duct tape were over his mouth. Jarvis calmly descended down the stairs, followed by Damon. Once on grounds level, Jarvis and Bujo locked eyes. Scattered on the floor was torturous weapons of all sorts. Jarvis stood directly in front of him, and Damon at an angle. Roy and Mccroy posted up and watched the situation. Jarvis snatched the tape off his mouth.

"What's up boy. How did you feel when you killed my mama?"

Bujo looked him in the eyes and said, "The same way you felt when you had my grandmother smoked."

"I definitely know the feeling," Jarvis shot back.

"Tell me something J-one. Did you know yo man Anton was gonna gank me out of my bread. Did you order him to do that to me or did you not know?" asked Bujo.

At that moment Jarvis realized that he was standing in front of a man who had created a war based on principle. A man who had no fear of his forth coming death. In his heart he felt like he did what he had to do.

Jarvis answered him honestly.

"I don't move like that and truthfully I never expected him to do no such thing, and when he confessed to me this morning of crossing you, it broke my heart.

"Where is he?" Bujo asked flatly.

"He's dead."

"Good," Bujo blurted and spat on the floor. I'm ready to die now."

Damon quickly picked up a hammer. Jarvis stepped back. He swung the hammer ferociously as the rounded steal crushed Bujo's front teeth. He then dropped the hammer and grabbed the drill.

"Noooooo!" Bujo screamed as he drilled into his sternum, but not enough to kill him. While Damon afflicted atrocity upon Bujo, Jarvis texted Wanisha the awaited code. Twenty minutes later, Bujo had taken his final breath, yet Jarvis didn't feel any self-gratification as he stared upon the lifeless body. Mccroy walked up to him knowing that their relation was at its end.

"After today where do we go from here?"

"This is where it ends for me. I gotta disappear," said Jarvis.

"Mccroy nodded concordantly.

"That's the right thing to do. This city will either be a trap for you or a place to remember," said Mccroy.

Jarvis shook his hand.

"Let it be a place to remember," Mccroy advised.

Wanisha received the text in advance and quickly followed instructions. Afterwards, she returned to the spot where they left her. Suddenly she spotted two figures approaching from a distance who she recognized as her two best friends.

"Thank you God thank you," she soliloquized as she quickly cranked up the car and drove up to them. They climbed in.

"Did you handle that?" asked Jarvis.

"It's there," she confirmed. He quickly dialed Sam's number.

"Look under ya truck."

Without another word Jarvis hung up unsure of what tomorrow would bring.

****

Two weeks later Jarvis and Damon mug shots were on Americas most wanted for murder. Anton's body was found, but there were no leads on the case. Fortunately, Wanisha wasn't under the police radar but she was deeply worried for her partners who she hadn't heard from in weeks. Jarvis and Damon were in Maryland buying as much time as possible at Kyla's mansion, and she was going to harbor them for as long as possible and do whatever they needed her to do.

Jarvis and Damon were going to need a team of great lawyers and Kyla knew the perfect man to assist them in that matter. Her brother! After arranging a meeting with Adewale she took a quick flight out to Pensacola, Florida where a chauffeur awaited her. When she arrived at the mansion Adewale embraced her in his arms and then led her out onto the balcony. He poured them both a glass of Chardonnay and sat next to his sister who took the glass and sipped in thought. Neither one desired to rush into conversation about Jarvis troubles but he knew that Jarvis situations were causing his sister deep grief and for that reason alone he was going to provide help for Jarvis. He didn't think that Jarvis would try to bring him down to overcome his adversity but to eliminate the possibility of that happening he was going to be Jarvis hope, strength and savior. Nevertheless that possibility was impossible to happen because Jarvis didn't have a rat bone in his body.

"He needs you Adewale. He's about to be in a fight for his life with the system and I don't want to lose him. Not like this at least," she sadly admitted as she struggled to hold back tears.

"Sis I understand his troubles and I definitely feel your stress. Tell him to turn himself in as soon as possible. Tell him he doesn't need to worry about any lawyers, I got a team of grade A lawyers on standby ready to take his case as we speak. Also, I have an ace of spade up my sleeve that should prevent him from doing a day in prison. So, just tell him to turn himself in and let me handle the rest. Okay!"

A joyful smile expanded across her face.

"Thank you thank you," she exulted and hugged her brother tightly. She knew that he had major pull and that he could make things happen and suddenly she felt relief for Jarvis and their relationship. She knew her brother would be the difference maker.

After Jarvis and Damon were done tying up loose ends they turned themselves into the authorities back in Cleveland. After they were read their rights they were quickly ushered away, both to separate holding cells. Before they were able to get booked and processed in, they were taken out of their cells to meet with their lawyers who demanded to talk with their clients immediately. There were three lawyers seated when the two homies walked in. This three-man team were representing them both.

They sat down and quickly got enlightened about the charges they were facing. Both were being charged with a four-year-old murder of a Yg member named James Hall, a.k.a. Coupe, in retaliation for Marlo, when he got paralyzed. When they found out that a close friend delivered them into the hands of the police, they were shocked and hurt to say the least.

A month prior to Jarvis and Damon's arrest, KKBG member Eric had got knocked with a kilo and a half of heroin. Considering he had a record as long as his arm, he knew that he was about to lay it down for a long time so he did what was popular to do these days and became an informant.

He didn't incriminate himself or Wanisha although they conspired, however he gave the prosecutor most of the story in its verity, in exchange for a supreme time reduction. After they were enlightened of all of this, their lawyers also revealed that they were both under an investigation for the recent murders around the city that detectives believed they were linked to.

"We're going to do our job at the highest level regardless of an informant. What they think they might have now or what they might bring later, it doesn't matter," said Trevor the head Lawyer. "Also, Adewale told me to tell you guys to not worry about a thing."

Without bond, days dragged by far for the two homies as they went through court procedures. Jarvis worked out and stayed to himself as he continuously analyzed his future and what he was going to do once he was free again. He had millions of dollars to clean up and had the perfect woman in his life to help him complete the task. Kyla. She had rented a condo in Cleveland after he turned himself in and step by step she stayed by his side. Visits and love letters were a normality. One day after he read her letter he was surprised. Kyla had brought up marriage and wrote that she would love to marry him. He never considered marriage before and he also didn't realize how deep Kyla love was for him. Yet he appreciated her in his life. If it wasn't for her, his status wouldn't be nowhere near what it had become. In his heart, he felt entitled to be with her and he was cool with it. He had mad love for her and he appreciated her company. After he received that letter, she came to visit him the following day. He sat down and grabbed the phone.

"Hey baby," she greeted warmly with a loving smile.

"What's going on?"

"Needing you out here with me is what's going on. Can't you tell?"

"Yeah, after you proposed to me in ya letter," he smiled.

She giggled.

"Is that really what you want Ky, and if so can you give me some time to ponder?"

"Take all the time you need. I just wanted you to know where I'm at with all of this."

That night, Jarvis laid in his bunk, deep in thought. The loss of his mother created a deep void within him, that couldn't be fulfilled. He was guilty of her death and his heart was slowly bleeding with each passing day. How could I be a good husband in such condition," he wondered to himself as sleep closed in.

****

Omirah was crushed after she saw Jarvis face on Americas Most Wanted. When the news broadcasted his arrest, she had to restrain herself from running to his side. Marco scrutinized her behavior from Jarvis misfortune and he could tell she was deeply worried for him. She tried to disguise it but she couldn't and it angered him. They had become detrimentally distant to one another, until finally Omirah decided to follow her heart.

It was off season for Marco, but he wasn't enjoying it. Instead he was trying to re-create a spark between him and his wife, but out of the blue she decided to pour out her heart.

"Marco, we need to talk."

"Yes we do baby because." ------

"No Marco just listen to me okay! You're a good man, and a great husband as well. You're just married to a woman whose been in love with someone else for a long time now."

Marco slapped her viciously across her face. She didn't waver.

"I understand what you feel, so I accept that, yet I can't help or change what I feel Marco. So, hit me again if you choose, but I have to go."

Marco manhood was shattered, and he broke down in front of her.

"You're living your dream Marco....but it's not mine. Enjoy this and enjoy what life has to offer you. You deserve what's best for you. I wish I could've been, but unfortunately, I was unable to be."

She left without another word and was on the next flight to Cleveland. While on the plane, she wondered and worried about Wanisha who she hadn't spoken with in a long time, considering Wanisha was not reachable.

The more she thought about seeing Jarvis, the more nervous she became.

"What if he doesn't want to see me. What if he hates me for waiting all this time. What if he just simply doesn't care about me anymore," she wondered to herself.

The day after she arrived in Cleveland, she went to the county to visit Jarvis.

When they first saw one another, both of their worlds stood still. He couldn't believe that it was her and she didn't know what he was thinking. They both sat down and picked up their phones.

"Hi Jarvis. Is it okay that I came to see you?"

"Why wouldn't it be, and what took you so long?"

A feeling ran through him that he hadn't felt in a long time. She made him feel happy.

"I was coming. I just had to un-tie a few knots first. I'm getting divorced."

"What!" Jarvis contorted. "Why, what's going on?"

"If I tell you the truth, will you hold it against me?"

"Never!"

"Because I'm still in love with you and I never was able to disguise it. And it was hurting me that I was hurting him. It wasn't his fault it was mines."

Jarvis didn't know what to say. All he knew was that he still loved her, and her confession made him love her even more, although he tried not to show it.

"So, because of me you're getting a divorce?"

"It's not because of you, it's because I still love you, so it's because of me," she corrected him.

"I see," he replied. "Well I'm probably about to lose my life, so you gotta turn it off Meme. Go back home to your husband, and I can't allow you to do this."

"If you get life, I'll spend every day of your bid bidding with you. As long as I can come see you and touch you, I'll be okay. Is there a chance you can win?"

The tears in her eyes almost made him cry. She left everything behind to be in his corner. He didn't see this coming. He thought she was happily married.

"I can win it, but I'm preparing for the worst."

"Listen Jarvis, I'm not asking you to be with me or nothing like that but allow me to stand by your side okay."

"Truthfully Meme, I wouldn't want it no other way. In fact, I'm gone keep it a hunned. I feel like jumping through this window and hugging the shit out of you. I never stopped loving you either."

48

Considering Damon and Jarvis were on separate units, every Sunday they would meet up at church and discuss situations. Damon awaited him in the back like always and Jarvis sat down.

"I aint think you was gone make it," said Damon.

"I aint gone ever miss a chance to come holla at my bro," said Jarvis.

"Fa sho...Aye you heard about Eric's peoples getting killed."

"Yeah. His mama, sister, and her sister's boyfriend, right?"

"Yep. Triple homicide at his mama spot. And it aint no question that's Y-love's work."

"I wonder what unit that nigga on, and why he aint made bond," said Jarvis.

"Aint no tellin, but you ready to get this trial on the road?"

"Hold up nigga the preacher grilling you," Jarvis warned him. Damon and the preacher stared at each other.

"Sir, we are here in the name of the lord, what are you here for?" The white man asked.

"Since I'm at church, Imma tell the truth. I'm here to see my homie. This is like my brother from another mother, but um, I'll hold it down preacher man."

"Okay well try to pay attention because God definitely wants yours," said the preacher.

As the trial date neared, Jarvis and Omirah had become one. It was out of Jarvis control. He loved her and couldn't hold back. Although he loved Kyla as well, it wasn't as deep as the love he felt for Omirah.

When Kyla seen Omirah name on the visiting list, she asked him who the lady behind the name was.

"She's a friend of mine."

"Okay I would've believe that if you weren't sitting in front of me looking strange. Talk to me Jarvis. What's going on?"

"What do you mean?"

"What do you mean what I mean. I'm not stupid Jarvis. Don't act boyish with me, tell me what's real."

"My ex girl came back in my life aight. Damn. You HAPPY?"

"No, I'm not. I wanna cry because I can tell you love her. Don't you?"

He looked away.

"This is what I was afraid of. Wasting my time, Jarvis fuck you!" She got up and left without looking back, leaving him stunned by her words.

✳✳✳✳✳✳✳✳✳✳✳✳✳✳✳✳✳✳✳✳

Adewale was a strong supporter of Judge Rankins since the early stages of Rankins career. Adewale supported all of Rankins campaigns and charities for strategy purposes, but they were good friends as well. Therefore, a favor was never a problem.

Adewale wanted Jarvis and Damon set free so Judge Rankins strategized the case into his own hands and assured the lawyers that both Jarvis and Damon would win in a bench trial.

Omirah didn't miss a day, along with many of their friends, but Wanisha didn't show. She was instructed to stay in the shadows until they returned. Jarvis was surprised that Kyla remained absent through trial and never answered any of his calls. He at least wanted to have closure with her. He respected her too much to move on without it.

Jarvis and Damon were both found not guilty and acquitted by the courts. When the verdict was announced, the victim's relatives rushed Jarvis and Damon, and the KKBG members rushed their relatives. A brawl ensued, and enforcement was called upon. Nobody was seriously injured, but some people were arrested. Considering Jarvis couldn't be released until a worldwide check was ran on him, Omirah waited patiently in the parking lot, with Shonte who was also waiting on Damon.

Seven hours later they emerged from the building and a long celebrative moment took place in the parking lot.

Jarvis and Omirah went to her house that she was renting temporarily and made love like it was their first time creating magic. It was magic as their bodies became one, as if they longed for one another ever since they walked away from each other years ago. At one thirty in the morning, while Omirah was sleep, Jarvis called Kyla. He still felt they both needed closure. She answered on the fourth ring.

"Hello."

"Kyla, this is me Jarvis. I need to see you tonight. We need to talk."

"So.... who's coming to who?"

"I'm coming to you. Give me the address. He took Omirah car and drove across town to her place. He rang the doorbell and waited. She opened the door and stepped aside. He stepped into the house and noticed that she was packed up and ready to go.

"So, you're about to go back to Maryland?" He asked as he turned and faced her.

"Yes I am. Being here has been nothing but a total waste of time for me."

"So that's how you feel about us?"

"Us!" She retorted. "As in me you and her?"

"This aint about her. This about you and me......... Look, I knew her for a long time, and sometimes feelings never die. Mines for her never died. Is that a fault on my behalf?"

"Look Jarvis, we're not dealing with fault, right now it's about choice, and you have one to make. Don't tell me what you think, I wanna hear the complete truth. Are you done with her completely or can you not let go of her?"

"I can't let go of her Kyla, but I feel like I can't let go of you either," he honestly admitted. She was crushed by his words but tried her best to disguise it.

"Well let me make it easy for you. GET OUT! GET THE FUCK OUT OF HERE!" She shouted tearfully.

Without another word, Jarvis left. Nevertheless, he was hurt and torn between the two. The next day, Jarvis and his two lieutenants rounded up the remaining KKBG members and had a meeting in the projects. As Jarvis stood in the center of the circle, he observed undying love in everyone's eyes.

"First off, let me start by saying this, I appreciate the trial support that me and the homie needed. It's been real yall. A lot of people who started out with us aint here today.

Deceased from the representation of who we are, and in my heart, they'll always be remembered. We did what we set out to do by establishing a gold mine. We ate good, but now it's time for me to move on. The O.G. J.d. told me a long time ago that if I stayed in the game long enough, it will go from a blessing to a curse. Well when I lost my mother, I saw the truth in his words but, it was too late. Now I know it's going to be hard for yall to let go of this million-dollar establishment, therefore, my final advice to yall is to try not to stay in the game longer than you should. But while you're in it, only make moves with ya heart, and hold the hood down by all means. I won't be in this city too much longer, but yall will know where I'm at and I'll always be reachable."

That night Jarvis, Damon, and Wanisha were at her house discussing their future. Their lives had become one and his decision to move on had become theirs as well. They were leaving with him. They had plenty of money to clean up and invest, and that was the main discussion. They all decided that Minneapolis would be their new location, and they would be leaving within a months' time.

✷✷✷✷✷✷✷✷✷✷✷✷✷✷✷✷✷✷✷✷

Kyla showed up at her brother's mansion unexpected. Not that he was bothered by it, but when she took her sunglasses off he instantly became infuriated just like she knew he would.

"What happened sis. Who did this to you?"

She began crying as she prepared to tell a fatal lie.

"Jarvis thinks I'm cheating on him," she cried. Her eyes were black, swollen, and almost closed shut.

"Don't tell me no such thing!" Adewale spat. He lifted her chin with his finger and examined her face. She faked like she was ashamed to look him in the eyes.

"You sold that bastard into my good graces. I set his life straight and I set his life free and this is how he repays me!"

"I'm scared to go home. Do you mind if I,"---------he cut her off?

"Stay as long as you like, but you won't have to worry about that prick for long. I assure you of that."

Adewale had hit men all over America, and a lot of them wore badges. He got in touch with a few of his men in Cleveland, and immediately the hunt had begun. Kyla had self-inflicted pain on herself from the pain that Jarvis had caused her, and her intentions was to see him pay for it with his life.

It was close to midnight in Cleveland, Jarvis and Omirah were lounging on the sofa planning their future. He had spent most of the day with his son and was analyzing his departure from the city. He wondered if the move would affect he and his son's relationship.

"How about he come and stay the summers with us. Do you think his mother would have a problem with that?" Omirah asked.

"Once she sees I'm truly out of the game, I don't believe she would mind at all. Right now, I don't blame her for being cautious and over protective of him because of who his father is and what his father has been through."

Omirah nodded in understanding.

"Well we need to hurry up and leave this city, that way you can marry me," smiled Omirah as she was cuddled in his arms. They passionately kissed staring into each other's eyes.

"When you get done with your divorce, we gone definitely tie the knot."

Her heart smiled at the thought of being his wife. That was something that she's always wanted since she first met him.

****

He had been out for days now and haven't called Adewale to thank him for his assistance.

"I need to make an important call," said Jarvis. He grabbed the phone and called Adewale and he immediately answered.

"What's up my friend. How's everything going?" Jarvis greeted.

Adewale was stunned by his call.

"I'm fine. What took you so long to call me. Is everything okay?"

"Yeah everything is good. Just wanted to tell you thanks for everything, you've been a breath of fresh air in my life."

"Jarvis let me call you right back, I have to talk to you about a few things. Give me a number to reach you."

Jarvis gave him Omirah's home phone number. Jarvis waited for his call, but it never came. As soon as Adewale disconnected from Jarvis, he got in touch with his hit men and delivered Omirah's phone number. It didn't take long to locate the whereabouts of Jarvis. They now knew exactly where the call came from, and now Jarvis was living on borrowed time.

****

Lil Hurt and Cho-cho was parked a couple doors down from Wanisha's house. They didn't think she was home, but they believed that a huge stash of money was in there and they wanted it. Ever since Jarvis announced his retirement, Lil hurt and Cho-cho felt betrayed, especially after Wanisha and Damon decided to leave with him. These two homies were very avaricious, and their hearts were set on doing a two-eleven on Wanisha. They perceived her to be the weakest link out of the three.

It was two-thirty in the morning. Wanisha was in the bed next to her boyfriend Mel, who was asleep. She was restless, and sleep seemed far away as she analyzed her future in a new city. Excited about starting a new beginning with the two people she considered to be her brothers, she smiled at the fact that she didn't have to convince Mel to leave. Mel loved her to death. He was determined to follow her wherever she wanted to go. After everything that has happened in her life, he didn't think she would survive in Cleveland too much longer. He couldn't wait to put the city behind them.

After hours of contemplation and restlessness she decided to roll a blunt. She hopped out of bed and quickly rolled it then grabbed the remote-control flicking through channels. The porn channel grabbed her attention, so she tuned in. While inhaling the good smoke, something on the house camera caught her attention. She zoomed in and saw two figures in all black meticulously creeping by the side of the house. They were wearing masks and had pistols in their hands. Wanisha jumped up and ran to her drawer and grabbed a 40

Caliber and a 9mm Glock pistol. Mel groggily woke up from the sound of the steel click clacking.

"Baby what's going on?"

"Shhhh," she silenced him and turned off the television. The house was now completely dark. When she zoomed back in on the camera, the two figures were at the back door, preparing to kick it open.

"Stay right here!" she ordered Mel and left the room quickly. She quietly crept down the stairs and positioned herself on one knee as she waited for the intruders to make their move. After a few attempts, the door burst open and the intruders stormed inside. Before they could react, multiple gunshots chopped them down immediately and neither intruder stood a fighting chance.

"Hurry up Mel come here. I got these muthafuckas!"

Mel stormed down the stairs as Wanisha bent down and snatched the mask off one. She froze as dead eyed Lil hurt stared back. Mel snatched off the other mask and Cho-cho was revealed. Although they were dead, she snapped.

"YOU BITCH ASS NIGGAS WANTED TO DO ME! ROB ME!"

Pow pow pow pow, she fired numerous shots into their lifeless bodies until Mel restrained her and took the weapons from her.

"Go call nine one-one and tell them it's been a home invasion at this address and that your boyfriend shot and killed some intruders. Hurry up boo!"

"I can't let you,"------He cut her off.

"Boo I got this. Those guns are registered to me, and I have a clean record. Listen, I was defending my home. Now hurry Wanisha so won't nothing about this look funny."

Without another word, she followed his order.

Jarvis and Omirah were making passionate love in the bedroom when two hired assassins slowly crept into the condo. It didn't take no time at all to pick the lock and they figured it wouldn't take but a second to kill their mark and disappear. After quickly scoping out the downstairs area, they began a silent march up the stairs. The sound of love making lead them directly to the room. Jarvis was thrusting himself inside of her as joyous tears were bathing her face. "I love you so much baby, so, so much," she whispered into his ear as he released himself inside of her. Although the seed would never blossom, she was officially pregnant. A split second after Jarvis rolled over, the door kicked open as the assassins quickly sized up their targets. Caught off guard, Jarvis could only stare into the barrel unbelievingly as the first shot gun blasted. The second shot ended Omirah's life. Jarvis, who had a slug in his chest, helplessly laid back as he felt life diminishing from his body. As he struggled to breathe, flashes of his life clawed at his mind. An overwhelming desire to live enhanced his fear of death as he stared into the barrel of the shotgun that was pointed into his face. Then suddenly the shooters exited as if to leave him with his final thoughts. He knew that Omirah was dead, and he felt his life coming to an end. He knew he would be missed by many and remembered for decades. He also knew that his enemies hate towards him would soon transform into respect from the strength of his legacy. Tomorrow the streets would become enlightened to a great loss. A loss that could never be replaced......ONLY REMEMBERED.

ALL

OR

NOTHING

BESTREADPRODUCTIONSLLC

2018

In Memory of Jarvis Williams....

Rest in Peace to my father, grandparents, and all the other relatives that are no longer here on earth.

Shout out to my grandparents that are still breathing......

I LOVE YOU MR and MRS. THOMAS!!!!!!!!

Available now on Amazon and Kindle

2017, We lost A beautiful angel. A Spirit that cannot be duplicated nor replaced. A true woman of God who embraced me into her family without question.

GLADYS MARIE 'VELAND' MORRIS.
My Wife's grandmother.

AKA 'MAMMA'

She gave good solid advice and was always uplifting. One day she said to me, "Don't ever allow anyone to tell you you're not good enough. You're a child of God and we all make mistakes."

That has stuck with me ever since.

REST IN HEAVEN SWEET LADY!!!!!!

SHOUT OUT TO MY MOTHER TERESA THOMAS AND MY MOTHER IN LAW MYLA VELAND. I LOVE YOU BEAUTIFUL QUEENS!

MY CHILDREN: JAMYE MITCHELL, TIARA HARDNETT, TIANA HARDNETT, JOSEPH JONES JR. MYA MITCHELL, AND K. HENDERSON.

GRAND-DAUGHTER: SAMIYA HARDNETT

MY SIBLINGS: KENNETH & JANET THOMAS, ANHONY HARDNETT, JASMINE COOPER, ERICKA VELAND, TOBIAS & ANDRENIKA TEEL, JUWAN THOMAS, ANDRE & TAMIKA HALL, VALERIE THOMAS, HOWARD HARDNETT JR, JERRY RICHARDSON, CEDRIC WILLIAMS

TO MY WIFE TEA TEA!!

YOU'RE A CHAMPION BABY!

MY BESTFRIEND

MY QUEEN

MY REASONING EAR

MY SOULMATE

MY BUSINESS PARTNER

MY OTHER HALF!

THANKYOU FOR BEING WHO YOU ARE!

IMPECCABLE!

COMING SOON:

"A CURSED DESTINY"

BY C & T THOMAS

2019

www.ingramcontent.com/pod-product-compliance
Lightning Source LLC
Chambersburg PA
CBHW071258110426
42743CB00042B/1097